EXPATRIATE
GAMES

EXPATRIATE GAMES

MY SEASON OF MISADVENTURES
IN CZECH SEMI-PRO BASKETBALL

DAVE FROMM

SKYHORSE PUBLISHING

Skyhorse Publishing books may be purchased in bulk at special discounts for sales promotion, corporate gifts, fund-raising, or educational purposes. Special editions can also be created to specifications. For details, contact the Special Sales Department, Skyhorse Publishing, 307 W. 36th Street, 11th Floor, New York, NY 10018 or info@skyhorsepublishing.com.

Skyhorse® and Skyhorse Publishing® are registered trademarks of Skyhorse Publishing, Inc.®, a Delaware corporation.

Visit our website at www.skyhorsepublishing.com

Excerpts of this book first appeared, in different form, in *Opium Magazine* Issue 2.

Paperback ISBN: 978-1-62087-592-6

Library of Congress Cataloging-in-Publication Data

Fromm, Dave.
Expatriate games : my season of misadventures in czech semi-pro basketball / by Dave Fromm.
p. cm.

ISBN 978-1-60239-296-0 (alk. paper)
1. Basketball—Czech Republic. I. Title.
GV885.8.C94F76 2008
796.32309437′1—dc22
2008020276

Printed in the United States of America

For Leo

As I waded through the snow still sifting down onto the beautiful town of Kostelec, I wondered how to arrange things so the two girls wouldn't collide. For it was clear how Marie would decide: when a girl says she has to think something over, she's thought it over already.

I trudged back to town in the empty night, up to my knees in snow. A star that would not be blacked out hung over the castle tower, and I was blissfully happy. It looked like a swell season was about to begin.

—Josef Škvorecký, *The Swell Season*

Billy Hoyle: "Guy said I couldn't score. Called me a honky motherfucker."
Sidney Deane: "You *are* a honky motherfucker."
Billy Hoyle: "But I can score…"

—Ron Shelton, *White Men Can't Jump*

Table of Contents

CONTENTS

Author's Note

A COUPLE OF DISCLAIMERS are, inevitably, in order.

First, throughout the text, words and phrases appear in Czech, a language the author managed not to learn in his two years in Prague, despite the formal and informal efforts of many people. Czech is a tricky language, or so the author has been told, and he cut his losses after learning how to order beer. Accordingly, he apologizes in advance for anticipated errors of grammar and usage in the Czech phrases used herein. For that matter, he apologizes for such errors in the English phrases, too.

Second, this is a true story, in the sense that all of the people described in it are real and the events really happened in the order and manner portrayed—more or less. Some names have been changed. It is also, however, an account of the author's athletic and romantic adventures when he was substantially younger, and if you expect such an account to be free of some significant embellishment, you probably expect too much. Memories fade over a decade and things said and done compete with things one wishes were said and done. Nonetheless, the author tried to be as true as he could to the events as they happened, and nothing herein is made up. If it were, things might have ended differently. Certainly, he would have been taller.

Prologue: Chasing Something like the Dream

IN FEBRUARY OF 1994, when I was twenty-three, I decided to move to Prague, the capital of the still-in-transition Czech Republic, to try and join a Czech professional basketball team. I didn't have much of a clue what I was doing—I wasn't positive, for example, that there *were* any Czech professional basketball teams—and the endeavor seemed right on the border of audacious and dumb. It also promised to be more challenging than anything I'd yet tried in my nascent and resolutely unremarkable young adulthood. But it seemed important, in some transitional way, to not be afraid to attempt something hard, even if it was a little bit crazy, and I wanted to see how far hoop and I could go.

To prepare, I sought the advice of the toughest man I knew, and one who happened to be Czech: a formidable septuagenarian and Holocaust survivor named Jan Wiener. By the time he was my age, Jan had attended the death of his father, escaped an Italian concentration camp, and, after being recaptured in northern Italy, hanging by his forearms from the undercarriage of a train, had eaten one of the camp dogs. After his liberation, Jan joined the Czech resistance in London and flew bombers back over Prague.

Needless to say, these trials surpassed my own.

Jan was living in my small hometown in western Massachusetts, where he worked as a cross-country ski instructor and maintained local-legend status. He went back to Prague every October to teach classes at Charles University—I'd actually sat in on one the previous year—and as my new plan took shape, I'd begun charting his movements across town, hoping to receive his counsel. Jan had indulged my inquiries before, and when I'd settled on a plan, I sought his endorsement.

It was deep in the New England winter, and the narrow driveway that curved through the woods to Jan's home was banked with snow. I skidded up in my Ford Festiva and gathered my thoughts. A sizable white husky sat outside Jan's garage, staring at me with reserved indifference. It looked like the kind of dog that came with a military option, that you didn't want to be on the wrong side of, that if it were otherwise motivated, my Festiva would provide about as much protection as the helicopter had for the pilot in *Jaws II*.

But Jan had apparently put the word out, and the husky just blinked its blue eyes as I passed. Smoke rose steadily from the chimney into the gray sky, and Jan met me at the open garage door. Close up, he looked a lot like the husky: the same piercing blue eyes, the same close-cropped white hair, the same reserved strength. A heavy punching bag hung from a hook in the garage behind him. Jan looked like the kind of man who did not mess around. I suspected that he'd built his own house with wood he'd chopped out of the forest, probably with the dog's help, and knew each knot and plank in his walls. I had no doubt that, even in his seventies, he could beat the shit out of me.

We sat by the fire and he made tea. We talked generally about Prague—the alleys of the Old Town, the hidden courtyards near the Bethlehem Chapel, the small, wooded island in the Vltava where, after the war, Jan had open-air sex with an anonymous beauty. "She said, 'Pin me up like a butterfly,' " said Jan, smiling at the memory. "So I did."

I asked for—and he told again, a little wearily—his own stories of death, incarceration, escape, and eventual triumph; stories that were as dramatic as any Hollywood thriller, indeed even more so for being true. Jan had told them a thousand times, but still told them like a pro, and by the end I felt energized enough to broach the subject of my own adventure. I told him I was going back to Prague, to see if I could find a basketball team and join it for a year. I told him how I'd been struggling since graduation, not sure what to do with myself, not sure how to grow up. Now I'd settled on a mission, made a plan. Basketball in a foreign country. Character-building adversity. Ambassadorship-type stuff. A future that held hardships, border-crossings, and maybe, if I was lucky, girls who said "Pin me up."

Jan listened patiently and sipped his tea. I got the sense that this wasn't the first mission he'd heard about, and somewhere down low on the list of importance. His eyes took on the same reserved indifference as the dog outside. Eventually, I said what I felt like I could say, hearing as I outlined it what a childish, inconsequential plan it was. He's talking about life and death, and I'm talking about running off in my sneakers to play a game. I had visions of another summer of bartending, and my heart began to sink. Jan remained impassive. Having failed to secure an endorsement, it was time for me to leave.

I was at the door, keys in hand, when Jan took me by the shoulder and fixed his blue eyes on me. "David," he said, flexing his fingers on my arm and nodding toward some difficult future. "Don't back out."

I swallowed hard. Don't back out. Holy shit. There it was, I thought—a straight-up challenge from a Holocaust survivor. He got it. He got what I was talking about. Sure, it wasn't World War II, but there *were* trials to be endured. And he'd said, "Don't back out." That kind of challenge, from that kind of man, wasn't going to come along too often.

"I won't," I said, and meant it. We shook hands; Jan's grip was firm and controlled, the grip of a man at ease with himself. I thanked him and went out to the Festiva, nodding in solidarity at the husky. We were on the same page now. The Beastie Boys' *Licensed to Ill* was in the cassette deck, and I gunned the engine in time with the opening horns of "Brass Monkey," feeling like it was a soundtrack, like things were really, finally, beginning. I checked the rearview mirror, hit the gas, and immediately skidded the tail end of the car up over the low snowbank at the edge of Jan's garage and onto his small, pristine lawn.

When I got out to push on the fender, I saw Jan watching from his kitchen window. He looked concerned. I gave him the thumbs-up. Mission accepted.

It was months before I figured out that when Jan had said, "Don't back out," he had not meant "of this formative life challenge." He had meant "of my driveway."

EXPATRIATE GAMES

Part One:
The Walk-On

The New Central European Identity

THIS STORY ACTUALLY begins a year earlier, in the summer of 1993. I was twenty-two years old, newly possessed of a bachelor's degree in English, and a little lost when it came to what to do next. I hadn't graduated with much of a plan—certainly not one as methodical as my college roommate's, which was to return to his hometown, get a job as a high school history teacher, marry his girlfriend, and coach soccer. To me, that sounded pretty good—I'd seen his girlfriend—and I was jealous of his sense of purpose. My idea of "a sense of purpose" had been to fall in love with a pretty brown-haired girl from St. Louis just six weeks before graduation. After the ceremonies, she'd moved back home, rolling her eyes a little at my baroque overtures, and I found out how humid the Midwest got in June and, simultaneously, how fickle and regenerative a twenty-two-year-old heart could be.

Other options were unappealing. With growing postgraduate dread, I had taken the Law School Admission Test. The score that resulted seemed to reflect some kind of luck more than it did aptitude. I also took the Graduate Record Exam, and would probably have taken the civil service exam if I could have figured out where and when it was offered. (In 1993, figuring out the scheduling seemed like the first part of the civil service exam.) My LSAT results meant that the odds of acceptance to law school were pretty good, and I took that as a sign to wait a year or so before applying.

At the time, law school—or any other school—felt like some sort of surrender, and it seemed to me, vaguely, through an inflated sense of destiny, that the early twenties presented a window of opportunity, a window within which it was still possible to undertake tremendously questionable adolescent things, but this time as a putative adult.

The idea of this window became, of course, a means by which to delay thoughts of a more realistic future—a mental destination in its own right—and I thought about it often while not exactly leaping through it. While waiting for fall to arrive, I hung around the sweltering hills of western Massachusetts, serving daiquiris to tourists, and dreaming of audacious ways to delay becoming a lawyer. And then I got an idea: Why not move to Prague, the gilded capital of the Czech Republic, and try to play basketball professionally?

There. Talk about a sense of purpose. Was this how Louden Swain felt in *Vision Quest* when he decided to wrestle Brian Shute?

Czech basketball. I'd never heard of a Czech basketball player, either in college or the NBA. How good could they be? Maybe I'd even get paid.

As postgraduate ideas went, this one had some legs. There were at least four factors in the "plus" column: (1) I'd spent a weekend in Prague during a six-week junior year abroad backpacking trip, and had liked it then; it had a languid, timeworn beauty to its buildings, which contrasted with the energy and turbulence of its transitional population (plus, it was cheap); (2) I'd written my college thesis on "The New Central European Identity," an identity I'd conjured from the published essays of my senior thesis advisor, who rather compassionately gave the paper an A; (3) I'd been cut, two years in a row, from the Boston College men's basketball team during walk-on tryouts; and (4) I didn't have a better idea. Of the thesis, my advisor had said, in our last student/advisor meeting, "I hope you'll keep studying so that eventually you'll understand how naive this paper is." The equipment manager who gave the walk-ons our practice jerseys said, "You're too short."

In the "minus" column, there were some obvious, and significant, obstacles. I didn't speak Czech or know anybody, Czech or otherwise, living in Prague. For that matter, I didn't know anyone else who'd even visited Prague. I wasn't entirely sure if they had basketball leagues there, much less professional leagues. Assuming they did, I didn't know if foreigners were allowed to play. Bravado aside, I had no idea how good the teams in these professional leagues might be (if they existed), or if I was really good enough to make one (if that was allowed). And I didn't have much money. As obstacles went, these seemed noteworthy.

Most of my friends and classmates were off on more practical paths, moving to New York, or back to Boston, to be paralegals or stockbrokers. I'd dropped off an application at the New England Aquarium in Boston for a job that involved putting on a wet suit and cleaning the central shark tank. Even that seemed more practical than the idea of playing professional basketball in Europe. I needed to suck it up and do *something*. The time to get serious was coming, if it wasn't already here. There was a limit to how far you could get modeling your life choices on the plots of movies like *Oxford Blues*.

Still, I was looking for distractions, and as distractions went, being a European basketball vagabond sounded pretty good. The utter lack of a framework to make it work didn't stop me, day in and day out, from heading to the courts and working on my game. And then, almost threateningly, a framework started to appear. One day, in the local bookstore, my mother pointed to a small man with a white handlebar mustache and a straight back. "That's Jan Wiener," she said, half-mockingly, of the man who would become my unwitting inspiration. "He's Czech. You should talk to him about your future."

I approached him by the nonfiction section and introduced myself. "I'm thinking of going to Prague," I said, "to study Central Europe. I wrote my thesis on 'The New Central European Identity.'" I wanted Jan Wiener to think of me as a serious person (actually, I wanted *somebody* to think of me as a serious person), so I left out the more unlikely aspects of what I'd begun to refer to, vaguely, as "my plan." The educational benefits of "cultural exchange" seemed more respectable. And anyway, it was hard to imagine that there'd be repercussions.

Jan Wiener smiled benignly and said, "I teach a class at Charles University. If you're there in the fall, you can come by and sit in on my classes."

As that first postgraduate summer drew to an end, with little movement on other fronts, I gave that casual offer significant weight. August became September, the summer tourists turned into fall tourists, and my parents began to eye me warily. College friends were by then leasing cars, renting apartments, and going out to clubs where female bartenders poured shots of tequila down giant ice blocks into waiting mouths. I was passing the time parking cars, watching *The Commish*, and pining after a parade of circumscribed local girls. They wanted little to do with me, which made me pine for them even more.

I considered my situation: I'd doubled my savings over the summer. My game felt pretty tight. Jan Wiener was holding a place for me at Charles University. Real life could wait. The time had come to take the show, such as it was, on the road.

· · ·

FLASH FORWARD ONE year to September 1994. I was on a plane, in a middle seat, between a young woman with cheeks streaked by mascara and an older lady to whom I'd offered my peanuts. The young woman had been crying under the brim of her baseball hat since we'd left Boston. Beneath us, there was nothing but clouds and the flat gray Atlantic.

Between October 1993 and the following September, I'd been back and forth to Prague twice on reconnaissance missions, living in hostels, never staying longer than a few months, always about half an hour from jumping into a cab, going straight to the airport, and coming home. They were ridiculous trips. Sometimes I'd go for days without speaking to anyone. Other times I'd hear someone speaking English and follow them around. One March night during my second trip, unable to sleep, I'd left my echoing, rented apartment and gone in search of a telephone. I found one hidden in the locked-off foyer of what seemed like an abandoned megaplex. The dearth of telephones was one of Prague's eccentricities; in the early 1990s the waiting list for a private telephone line was allegedly a year long, and cell phones were still prohibitively expensive. The public phones ran on large octagonal coins or flimsy phone cards which seemed perpetually demagnetized. I'd fed a pocketful of coins into the phone, gotten a dial tone, and called my mother, waiting out an endless umbilical cord of numbers (the international phone number followed by a sixteen-digit calling-card code), and then, finally, hearing her faraway voice.

"Mom," I'd said, trying to keep the panic out of my voice, "I'm in Prague."

She'd known that, of course, but still sounded a little dubious, like she'd thought maybe I'd really just gone down the road to a friend's house. And it had sort of felt like that at times—a temporary and misguided sojourn, rather than an organized reconnaissance effort. Still, the trips had helped establish some things. Notably:

(1) The lack of language skills was an impediment, but not an insurmountable one. Turns out that there were, by some

estimates, about forty thousand young Americans making their way through Prague in 1993 and 1994. They taught English, started literary magazines and Tex-Mex restaurants, and crowded Prague's dark *hospodas* and grand, cobblestoned squares. You couldn't fall down without hitting one, something I learned by doing. They wore scarves and wool beanies and were often recognizable by their Adidas. They had even acquired their own acronym: YAPs, short for Young Americans in Prague.

(2) Prague had basketball teams. It had taken me about a month to even catch sight of a hoop, and even longer to find a pickup game. One night toward the end of my last trip, one of the Czech pickup players arranged a scrimmage between a group of expats and a local Prague club team. The expats met at a metro stop called Náměstí Míru and hiked to a huge gymnasium complex on a green hill in the Vinohrady neighborhood, about a half-mile behind the National Museum. I'd been on fire that night, drilling threes and breaking Czech ankles, and at the *pivnice* afterward, one of the club players said—it was a joke, really—"You should come play with us next season."

• • •

THE OLDER LADY hadn't pulled the plastic off of her little red blanket/ pillow combo pack but I'd opened mine. The pillow was soft and the blanket was warm but not so big; I had the sides tucked around my legs and had to crunch to get the upper edge even halfway up my chest. It was frustrating.

I focused instead on the larger challenge at hand. "You should come play with us next season," the guy had said. I hadn't gotten the details; his name, or the name of his team, likely contract terms, or a clear grasp of eligibility rules. Still, I felt confident that they would be there, and that when I asked, they would say yes.

Please be there. Please say yes.

. . .

I GUESS AN important question to address at this point is: Was I any good? All this talk about vision quests and trials of the self wouldn't mean much if I couldn't play ball. So how good a basketball player was I? Like most things, the answer varied, depending on who you asked. For example, I thought I was the best ballplayer I knew intimately—maybe even the best player I'd ever showered with, if I didn't count my dad. I was good enough to start for two years at point guard in high school, make some local All-Star teams, not embarrass myself too much at Division One walk-on tryouts, and lead the Oxford Blues seconds squad to an undefeated season as a JYA show-off in England. My dad, a small-college two guard, had bequeathed to me the traits found in gym rats everywhere: a respect for fundamentals, earnestness, and knee burns. A healthy amount of delusion. I was a decent shooter, a slasher who liked to pass. I hung twenty-four points on Wahconah Regional as a senior point guard for the Lenox High Millionaires, in a game where we scored only forty-four points total and lost by thirty, and won player-of-the-game honors over Wahconah's All-County forward, who went on to be a Division III star. At walk-on tryouts as a college freshman, after I got dunked on by the starting power forward, a six-foot-seven senior named Doug Able, my dad gave me a T-shirt that said LAST CUT—BIG EAST on it, even though there was only one cut.

. . .

THE OLDER LADY licked her index finger and poked it into the salty creases of the empty peanut packet.

It could get cold in Prague. The team I was going to find hadn't looked very well funded in our one scrimmage. Maybe I wouldn't be getting paid. I might be back in that mildewing hostel on Wenceslas Square, surrounded by snoring, beer-soaked Germans, or worse: I might be on the street. The older lady looked grandmotherly. I had a good track record with grandmothers. She had smiled and thanked me when I offered her my peanuts. A blanket was one of the many things I hadn't packed, and her blanket/pillow package looked just the right size to fit in my backpack. Maybe I should take it.

Wait.

Discipline would be paramount if this mission was going to succeed. In *Vision Quest*, Louden Swain threw away the buns for his burgers and wore that shiny tracksuit to keep his weight down, even though people made fun of him. He had a goal. I had a goal, too, and mine, which had seemed so far away before, was now almost within my grasp. I went over the plan again: hit the ground, find a room for the night, drop my bags, and start to scour Prague 3 for the gym where we'd played the Czech team months earlier. Prague 3 wasn't a big neighborhood and my pre-trip training had included a lot of running. I intended to run through the streets until I found a game. Discipline. Basketball was the thing I'd done longer than anything else. It had outlasted all of my romances (and occasionally been the cause of their collapse), and had provided the clearest moments of joy, and also of misery, of anything that I'd done in my twenty-three years.

On the plane, with the girl crying again and my own tiny airline blanket riding up my ankles, I remembered my father rolling around on our living-room floor on a Saturday morning in the mid-1970s as the Bullets beat the Sonics in the NBA finals. I remembered heating up during a tournament in England and scoring forty-three points, and then talking my dad through every shot from the pay phone across the street at some exorbitant cost, something like 50 pence a minute. And I remembered one Celtics–Sixers game at the Spectrum toward the end of Dr. J's career, the kind of game that those Celts teams always won in a condescending or unjust fashion. Doc was old and his legs were gone, and the Celts were up by two with three seconds left, poised to slide that blade in just a little deeper, and Barkley with his barrel thighs, playing like a young bull—he might have even been a rookie—tied up that chump McHale for a jump ball in the Boston end. Barkley won it (of course) and back-tipped it to Doc, who cranked up an awkward three at the buzzer, and Doc couldn't shoot threes to save his life, but this one hit nothing but net. And my dad and I jumped into each other's arms in our living room as the Sixers mobbed Doc on the Garden floor, and we screamed and laughed and raced out into the driveway for an early-spring one-on-one. And we weren't even Sixers fans.

I could think of plenty of times like that, when basketball had seemed to provide the medium, the context, for the only things that had ever really mattered.

I was trying to stuff the grandmother's blanket/pillow combo into my backpack when she reached for it. "That's mine," she said.

"Oh," I said.

What an idiot. You can't take your own airplane blanket off the plane, much less someone else's. We weren't even to Brussels yet.

"Uh, of course." I put the packet back on the floor by her feet and tried to project confused innocence. Damn it. Maybe she'd think I was Belgian.

I resumed watching the white-cheeked girl cry. She'd been weepy since she'd kissed her boyfriend good-bye at the gate—he'd turned his own baseball cap backwards for her. She was pretty, and pretty young. I felt old at twenty-three. She had a Walkman and a cassette case that said SPAIN in rainbow colors on her tray table. I stared at her until she stopped crying.

"So," I said, "Spain."

She was a junior at Wesleyan, going to Barcelona for a semester if she could bear it. Right then she was doubtful. "It's so long," she said, looking out of the plane window and drawing out the "so" like a beagle.

No shit. Ever since college, I felt like I'd been living in that temporal wormhole, where everything seemed like it would either never happen or was happening *right that moment*. Sometimes it was the same thing, both never and immediate. This girl would never get to Spain.

She started to cry again, quietly. I wanted to cheer us up. I considered telling her about my adventure, about how it was supposed to happen. Find the team, join the team, and set the world on fire. Nail down a purpose in life and never doubt again. I thought, too, about telling her how, if it all fell apart, we could each just go home, go back to Wesleyan or to the law school that was holding a place for me, return to the girl in the thick Midwest and the guy in the baseball hat, forget the whole thing.

That might make us both feel better.

When I was at walk-on tryouts as a sophomore, I almost got dunked on by a scholarship point guard named Howard Eisley, who went on to enjoy a solid NBA career as a backup. My walk-on squad was playing two-three zone defense while the scholarship players used us to run their offensive sets. Eisley had taken a skip pass on the wing, juked the block defender, and driven baseline, and I'd slid down from my elbow position to challenge him. I had a split second to decide what to do, and I thought, *Should I jump?*

If I jump, I'm going to get dunked on again, and probably get hurt, and it won't even matter if I get hurt, but Howard Eisley might get hurt and he's on scholarship. And at the last second, after I had committed to throwing myself in Eisley's path and getting poster-ized, he whipped a behind-the-back pass to a star freshman named Billy Curley, who was cutting down the lane, and I realized that my moment of truth was utterly irrelevant to Eisley's decision making—that he was playing a different game entirely, playing on a higher plane, about five steps ahead of me.

So, in the context of a continuum of basketball players, if Jordan was a ten, then Eisley was maybe a seven, and terrible guys like Greg Kite and Granville Waiters were probably fives or sixes, and they were still *NBA professionals.* Put Greg Kite on a court with the nine best players I knew and he'd score fifty. I played a lot, but I hadn't even made the Boston College team. On the real-world continuum, I was probably a two. A three, maybe, if it was a bell curve.

I told the white-cheeked girl about Eisley, and about how I wasn't sure, as a mere two or three on the basketball continuum, if it was really reasonable to even be on the plane, deferring admission to law school yet again, to move to Prague to try to keep playing a sport I was never going to be really great at. Was it? About how, no matter how many doubts I had, it was too late, and I should just tamp that shit down, see if I could get above a four and see what happened. She could survive a semester in Barcelona; try a winter in Prague with rudimentary language skills and a little man on your shoulder, alternately whispering *grow up* and *give it up* over and over again. Jesus. What if absolutely everything fell into place—which was never going to happen—and then I turned my ankle?

The white-cheeked girl didn't answer. She'd fallen asleep.

The Hotel Olšanka

O N MY LAST trip to Prague, I'd been staying with some Americans in a basement apartment in an area of Prague called Hradčanská. One of them had applied to a Western-style graduate school called Central European University, which had just opened a small campus in the Prague 3 neighborhood. Virtually all of the students in each CEU class came, through funding provided by George Soros's Open Society Institute, from former Soviet Bloc countries, but there was room in each class for a limited number of Westerners to enroll each year. My roommate was one of two Westerners admitted to the international relations program for the 1994–95 academic year.

It had sounded exotic. I was interested in international relations, generally. Who wasn't? And what better environment could there be than a class whose demographics might look like a conflict map? Tuition for the one-year program was only $8,000, and my roommate, apparently without much effort, had been offered a half scholarship. I had yet to hook up with a basketball team and needed a reason to stay in Prague that didn't feel like drifting, so I filled out my own CEU application and put it in the mail. It felt good to do something, and I figured there was no chance of it happening, but if it did, at least I'd have a friend in the program. Then my friend decided to withdraw his admission and left to move in with his girlfriend in San Francisco. I was accepted in his place. Classes started the first week of October. I went home to pack and fret.

· · ·

MY PLANE LANDED at Prague's Ruzyne Airport on September 5, 1994. Customs was intimidating but perfunctory—bored soldiers with guns standing in a hallway, in a place that had yet to transition from the era in which ordinary people didn't break the rules. Like much of Prague, the airport was slowly adjusting to the country's new open borders. In one central atrium, you could still get a ticket and leave your luggage on a shelf for a week.

I lugged my bags to a cab and gave the address for the CEU building, which I hoped to use as some sort of base. A half-hour later we pulled up next to a squat cement edifice in Prague 3. Huge tarps covered the western portion of the building; the architecture of the eastern portion resembled Boston's City Hall, a brutalist modern nightmare of square layers on top of columns. Men in dusty blue overalls carried plates of mortar and jackhammers around the outside of the ground floor. The words HOTEL OLŠANKA were visible on a tarp-covered wall. It was the same abandoned megaplex from which I'd called my mom six months earlier, now undergoing a facelift. I looked for the pay phone I'd used as the cab pulled up to the curb, but it was gone, ripped out of the wall.

It was midday and sunny, and I was running on adrenaline. I dropped my duffel bags and trudged to the front of the Hotel Olšanka to look up the street. I unfolded a wide map of the city and traced an outline of Prague 3. The Hotel Olšanka sat at the intersection of Ondřičkova and Táboritská avenues, on a tram line, next to a sprawling cemetery. Three blocks up Ondřičkova and six down Polská, my map showed what looked like the oblong bull's-eye of, perhaps, an outdoor track, marked SOKOL KRALOVSKE VINOHRADY.

Sokol was the Czech word for "falcon." It was also the name of a social health and self-improvement movement incorporating aspects of gymnastics and aerobic exercise and dating from the mid-1800s. Before World War II, the *sokol* organizers had provided a sort of Olympic quadrennial in Prague's Strahov Stadium—at the time, the largest stadium in Europe—where athletes from around the country would perform synchronized exercise routines in a national celebration. The gatherings were banned under Communist rule, but unofficial meetings continued in gymnasiums and parks. In the summer of 1994, Strahov had welcomed back the first post–Cold War *sokol* celebration, attended by tens of thousands of limber Czechs.

Most neighborhoods had their own *sokol* fitness centers, athletic fiefdoms spread throughout the city like YMCAs for health-conscious Czechs. Kralovske Vinohrady—the Royal Vineyards—was the historic name of half of Prague 3, the other being Žižkov. So, Sokol Kralovske Vinohrady—an athletic complex? I looked up Ondřičkova, past the enormous Žižkov Broadcasting Tower built by the Communists in the late 1980s, allegedly to jam revolutionary signals coming into Czechoslovakia from Radio Free Europe. The Tower looked like a cross between the Space Needle and a super soaker; it was so tall that you could see it from almost anywhere in Prague, a modern monstrosity in a city of spires. I'd heard Czechs call it "the finger of Communism." This finger pointed toward the future.

. . .

I DROPPED MY bags in a storage closet in one of CEU's administrative offices, where a disorganized staff was scrambling to comfort a

Balkan Noah's Ark of arrivees, and headed up Ondřičkova. It was getting late in the afternoon and I wasn't exactly sure where I would be sleeping that night, but I wanted to see if I was in the right general area. I hadn't changed clothes since Boston, and in the early September heat my underwear was beginning to chafe. I smelled not dissimilar to my surroundings. Beneath the Žižkov Tower, hundred-year-old graves stood in the shadows of elephant legs. I crossed onto Polská, a curving cobblestoned street lined with residential buildings turning gold in the afternoon sun. Like the rest of Prague 3, the area around Polská was shielded from the tourists and pickpockets on Václavské náměstí by the formidable edifice of the National Museum. At the top of Polská, the apartment buildings cleared and a large sprawling park came into sight. My guidebook said this was Riegrovy Sady, the Rieger's Garden Park, a favorite with dog-walkers and beer drinkers—demographics which covered most of the population of Prague. I followed along the park's edge, which rose and turned into a driveway and then terminated at the entrance to a massive complex—Sokol Kralovske Vinohrady, home of . . . what? Whom?

These would have been good questions to ask in April.

The building was enormous. The lights were off. The thick iron double doors were locked. I peered in through one of the small, reinforced windows, wire mesh embedded inside its heavy glass pane. In the fading light of the late afternoon, the inside of the building looked as silent and dusty as a tomb.

I walked back down Ondřičkova to the CEU campus, slightly dejected and more than slightly ripe. The Hotel Olšanka was across the city from the castle and hostels and friends I'd found the previous spring, and things felt a little disorienting. My expat bona fides were barely above tourist level, and Prague 3 was a total mystery, from the neo-gothic Church of St. Ludmila at náměstí Míru to the enormous cemeteries next to Hotel Olšanka. There were no expat pubs in Prague 3, at least none that I knew of, no law firms with their cascading lucre, no Derby, no Red Hot, no Globe. Nowhere, in short, to connect.

In 1994, Prague was a city with precious few working telephone lines, and if you didn't already have one, they were impossible to get. Cell phones and PDAs were unavailable, at least to the people I knew. Instead, the cafés and pubs and theaters and sprawling squares with their gilded landmarks provided a sort of social latticework that in other places was made redundant by the grid. Someone would say "Meet me at the Horse at four on Thursday" (meaning the statue of Prince Wenceslas on his horse that overlooked the long eponymous square in central Prague) or "Derby at nine?" And when they said it, they would mean it. Once made, plans couldn't really be changed. If you missed a rendezvous at Radost at 8:00 P.M., weeks could go by before you'd see that person again.

On my previous fact-finding mission, I'd made some friends among the thousands of expats floating through Prague. I'd roomed for several weeks with three guys from San Francisco who had moved to Prague with a glossy prospectus, financing from someone's older brother, and the aim of establishing a copy shop—the prospectus said "business center"—to service Prague's suddenly booming corporate needs. They called their company CHeK Group International, after the first letters of their surnames, and they lived in a basement apartment in the Hradčanská district of Prague 6.

By the end of that trip, the C and K had given up and gone home, frustrated by the cronyism and their own undercapitalization when compared to the sprawling Xerox business center then opening in Wenceslas Square. Only the H remained: Cameron Hewes, the de facto leader of the company. His girlfriend Lindsey was supposedly moving from Seattle to Prague to live with him. She'd been a year behind him in college, and a vegetarian, but it sounded like their love might survive Central Europe.

. . .

THE CEU ADMINISTRATIVE offices, such as they were, were still in disarray when I got back from the unsuccessful gymnasium trip, and the Student Affairs coordinator just shrugged her shoulders when I asked her what her recommendations were for residential accommodations. I had my tuition in traveler's checks in a pouch hanging from my neck. She shrugged again when I asked her to whom I should give it. Was there a bursar? A registrar? Not on-site, apparently. Should I give it to her? (I asked because I thought if I paid her, she might give me a room upstairs.) She declined, and suggested that I mail the money to an address in New York City. I decided to wait. I put my bags down and rubbed my shoulders. There was something Kafkaesque about the situation: We were standing in a hotel under construction. Every room on every floor above us had an empty bed in it. Indeed, most of the other students had already secured lodging right over my head. A Serb named Dragan started yelling at the Student Affairs coordinator, and pretty quickly she appeared near tears. After fifteen minutes she produced two keys and we each had a room.

"One night," she said. At least we were speaking English.

. . .

THE FIRST TIME I came to Prague looking for a basketball game, back in late 1993, I didn't have a full-fledged conversation with another person for two weeks, until I tracked down Jan Wiener at a Charles

University building located on a square called Ovocný trh, a name that seemed like it was short a few vowels. I'd gone there to cash in on Jan's "sit in on my classes" promise, which I'd come to believe really meant "I will take care of you." Jan was the only person I knew in Prague, to the extent I could even say I knew him. The administrators at the university offices couldn't locate him, but I walked around the interior hallways for hours, trying to blend in with the legitimate students, until I saw Jan's white mustache waving at me through a classroom-door window. I was so relieved I nearly waved back. After half an hour, his class ended, and when he came out into the hallway full of students, I stood up from a bench, smiled, and tried to project familiarity.

The New Central European Identity, my smile said. *I have come to sit in on your classes.*

Jan looked right at me, smiled back, and walked away down the hall to disappear into a faculty lounge. He had no idea who I was.

I'd chased Jan down in the faculty lounge and tapped on his shoulder. Eventually, he recognized me, and thereafter did, in fact, let me sit in his warm classroom and doze. He gave me a winter coat when mine was stolen at a midnight disco. He bought me lunches and brought me to important meetings with significant government officials I neither recognized nor appreciated. I became his attaché.

At one of these meetings, I spilled my demitasse of coffee on the official's desk. Afterward, Jan took me to a café and bought me soup and sweet Czech crepes called *palacinky*. I had been walking around the cobblestoned squares for about a month at that point and had seen nothing that suggested people in Prague played basketball, much less that there were organized leagues one could join. When it came time to pay, we walked to the counter and Jan spoke in Czech to the hostess. I shuffled my feet and tried not to drool on the glass display case full of strudel. Behind the counter a small pennant hung on the wall, pointing at the floor. In the fat end of the pennant was a blue basketball sailing through a red net.

I gestured to the pennant and grunted to the hostess in what I hoped was the universal *What is that?* grunt. She looked at it and said, in English, "A pennant."

I would need to know more. I took out the city map I kept folded in my pocket and spread it on the counter. I made hand gestures as Jan Wiener spoke with the waitress. We learned that the pennant belonged to her boyfriend, whose team had won the Prague city basketball championship the previous year. City basketball championship? There was a city basketball championship? Every year?

I pointed to my map. Where did they play?

"Here," she said, stabbing a neighborhood of shadowy blocks in the north-central quadrant of the city with her finger. "Sparta."

The next day, I sat in the expat café called the Globe Bookstore and studied the waitress's buttery fingerprint on my map, looking for large buildings that might house a basketball court. They all looked large. I'd been doing some English teaching, but the work was pathetic—I didn't know how to teach, and my only student was a middle-aged businessman named Marek whose English was fine, at least for the limited purposes of basic conversation. The "business English" he needed, I couldn't help him with. We sat in restaurants and had staggering conversations about the weather and the news, me asking him about Czech history and politics and him asking me about privatization and nondisclosure agreements.

At that point, things looked dire. It was mid-December and I'd been in Prague for a month, bouncing from hostel to hostel.

Marek and I held our next English class in a department store, talking about down and insulation. The students in Jan's classes were mainly visiting Americans, wrapped tightly in the comforting limitations of their semesters. They looked at me like I was a raccoon in their garage. I was beginning to suspect that I'd be headed home again, empty-handed, by Christmas, even further from a future than before.

I focused on the map. Sparta was a big neighborhood. Somewhere within it, at some point in the past, there had been a basketball game. I needed to find out where; I needed to make some headway toward a goal. If I didn't find a game soon, it would be time to throw in the towel.

I'd resolved that if I was going to get anywhere, I had to get better at being (1) positive, and (2) assertive. So as evening fell I took a tram to Sparta, my sneakers hanging from my backpack by their laces, and started walking around the dark, deserted winter streets. Mist haloed the streetlamps, and I listened for the sound of a ball bouncing behind stone walls. Basketball was good that way: You could hear it from blocks away, and if you listened closely, sometimes you could pick out details of the game just from the sounds. Were they running full-court? Were they just shooting around? What were the backboards like, and the rims? In Sparta, I was just hoping to hear a *thump*, repeated.

Once in a while, people would walk by me—men with fur hats, women in long coats and scarves. Sometimes they would stare. The fog, the coal dust in the air, the headlights and streetlamps glowing in the dark, the muted sounds—Sparta on a December night felt like every le Carré novel I'd ever read. I could imagine men with pistols in every shadowy stairwell, operatives moving in the fog. How long before the brass knuckles appeared? How soon before I got killed with a poison umbrella?

This went on for about two hours into the cold, bleak winter night, with no sign of a gym. Finally, I'd stopped an older woman. Our conversation had been brief:

Me: (*gesticulating*) Basket?
Older Woman: (Something in Czech.)
Me: (*motioning to the surrounding area*) Basket?
Older Woman: (Something in Czech.)
Me: Gymnasium?
Older Woman: (*pointing a pale finger up the block toward a vast stone building I'd thought was a factory*) (Something in Czech.)

She left.

I followed her finger, looking for a door, filled with a sort of clueless anxiety. I hadn't really thought much about what I was going to do if I found a team actually engaged in a practice, men in uniforms playing basketball. While it was the goal of this whole operation, that had seemed almost too far-fetched to even imagine. I'd have been happy with another pennant—maybe a team photo in a trophy case. What was I going to do? Walk onto the court and break out some Curly Neal?

We'd cross that bridge if we came to it, I guessed. It still seemed like the least of my worries. At the corner of the building, I pulled open a set of doors and stepped into a small blue-tiled municipal-looking lobby. Behind a thick glass window, a little man sat looking at his hands. I nodded at him like I'd been there before and crossed toward a quartet of windowed interior doors that looked like they led somewhere. Behind them, visible from the lobby, spread a glowing, glistening, empty hardwood court. Pristine nets hung from Plexiglas backboards, the whole thing silent as a church between masses.

The man behind the glass had called out to me.

"*Tso je?*"

I looked at him and shrugged. "*Nemluvim cesky*," I'd said, using up my supply of Czech words that didn't involve food.

"USA?" the man had asked.

I'd nodded, nonspecifically. "Basket?"

He'd pointed to a sheet of paper taped to his window. "*Sedm. Čtvrtek.*"

I'd looked at the sheet of paper. It was a weekly pickup schedule, and USA BASKET was penciled in on Thursdays at 7:00.

That pickup game—Thursdays at seven in Sparta with a group of expats and the occasional Czech—was the key that opened the door to a limited variation of Prague. It was only the expat variation—full of people drinking and not quite working and trying to stay in touch across the city—but until then, I hadn't even been able to access that group. Up until that first Thursday night, I'd been stuck in my role as the mute attaché to the kind but inscrutable Jan Wiener, or, worse, with the loud disconnected tourists at the Sport Bar Praha. The weekly pickup game changed everything, providing entry into the expat community—people with whom to get a beer, compare stories, and eventually, live. A month after finding the pickup game, I'd moved out of the hostels and in with CHeK Group International, into a small wine cellar room in the apartment they shared.

My entire Prague social life grew from that game: Cameron and his partners were regulars, as was Jack Levy, who was trying to set up an accounting company and refused to learn Czech; Big Mike, who oversaw an international shipping company from a height of six-foot-eight; two Israeli security guards who checked underneath their car for bombs every night before getting back into it; and Skee Graf, who seemed to embody the reinventive expat aesthetic better than anyone. In the brief time I'd known Skee, he'd moved in and out of sight, dating young and beautiful Czech girls, passing out old Russian passports and outdated currency, asking indecipherable questions like, "You know Ponyboy?" and, "Why do my hands always smell like chicken?" before vanishing again with such effortlessness that I sometimes wondered if he existed at all.

Other friends emerged: Fast Dave, the world-class distance runner and ladies' man; Shannon, the smart Russian scholar from Austin who made visiting Texas seem more appealing; Joel, the privatization specialist who'd come to a small office in the CEU from Manhattan to spearhead Columbia University's privatization project; and Julie, set on being a reporter and escaping the dailies of western Massachusetts. They'd all been there in the spring past, floating from flat to flat, from dinner to coffee to Czech-dubbed cinema. But that had been six months ago, a long time in expat terms.

We'd played basketball every Thursday for most of the winter and into the spring. Sometimes we'd meet up on a weekend and go find another gym someone had heard about. More often than not we got lost, or the doors were locked, or there was a handball tournament going on. But occasionally, a key would appear, or we'd get sent to another building, or we'd combine to speak enough Czech to sweet-talk a janitor. Our roving group of expat ballers began to enlarge. We picked up some Czech players who wanted to practice their English or hone their moves. We coalesced into a group. Eventually, one of the Czech regulars had set up an April scrimmage in Vinohrady with a uniformed local team. A real team! They ran plays and called timeouts and discussed things earnestly in huddles. There was, it seemed, a world of Czech basketball hidden away. Or maybe it wasn't hidden at all. I resolved to investigate.

Over a year later, here I was—back in Prague and dragging my bags up the stairs to a small room at the Hotel Olšanka. There were two flat, firm single beds, each covered with a thin duvet; a long flat desk; and a lamp. The electrical outlets had strange configurations of holes. I dropped my duffel bags on one of the mattresses and fell onto the other. It felt like plywood covered in a layer of Nerf. My sneakers were in a side compartment of the larger bag, while my socks, shorts, and spandex were rolled up and stuffed into under-privileged pockets along the periphery of the smaller one. This was only the first day of a long adventure, and it had felt like the longest day of my life. *Don't back out,* I thought to myself. *You are creating a New Central European Identity.* Would it be as naïve as the last one? I pulled the duvet up around me and tried to remember what I could about the team.

Honsa

ON DAY TWO at the Hotel Olšanka, I went back to the gymnasium at Riegrovy Sady with renewed hope and a mental phrasebook of limited use. The gym sat at the top of a slight rise, surrounded by quiet stone residential buildings and street-level neighborhood businesses with names like Dum U Cerveneho Lva and Pod Smetanou. One of the Thursday-night expats was a half-Czech businessman named Mark who'd been in Prague to oversee the opening of a chain of international grocery stores. Months ago, we'd gotten a team into an outdoor three-on-three tournament in one of the sprawling parks on Prague's northern outskirts, and after a day of dribbling on cobblestones and hoisting shots over angry Czech arms, I'd told him about my goal of joining a local basketball team. Mark said that if I went to a gym and said *Sokol trener-basket* enough times to enough people, I would eventually find the coach of the basketball team—that was, if one existed. Mark said that joining a team would be both easy and disappointing. He was confident of both, he said, although sure of neither.

Before leaving the hotel that day, I'd stuffed everything I might need into my backpack: my sneaks and socks, a towel, my passport, some money. I wore my jock beneath my shorts, my shorts beneath my sweatpants, and jogged up the long avenues to the gym, where the window to the reception booth was once again closed. This time, though, a tiny gray man in a blue smock with tufts of hair coming out of his ears sat behind the window. He wasn't moving. Indeed, it was possible he'd been there last night as well, sitting silently in the window like dust. I'd begun to recognize this as an archetype: the prerevolution municipal employee, not inclined to help.

I said *Dobry vecer* several times, before realizing that it was still only the afternoon. I knocked on the glass.

Minutes passed before he looked up. When he did, he pretended that he hadn't heard me, although I was barely four feet away, talking loudly.

"*Sokol trener-basket?*" I asked.

He looked at my feet and shook his head like I'd asked for money. "*Trener?*" he asked, sounding skeptical. His fingers were short and the index and middle ones were stained by filterless Russian cigarettes that bent as they burned. You could buy them individually for 2 crowns each at bars and kiosks.

"*No*," I said, nodding my head carefully. In Czech, the word for "yes" is *ano*, often shortened in conversations to *no* and accompanied by a nod of the head. It took some practice to be able to nod your head and say *No* at the same time, and I felt like I was joking while doing it.

"*Sokol trener?*"

"Yes." Damn it. "*No. Basket.*"

I tried pantomiming a foul shot, leaving my wrist cocked in follow-through. That seemed to energize him; a raised arm, a bent wrist, a strange foreigner at his window. I wondered momentarily what his politics had been, and if I'd evoked anything. Apparently so, as he launched into full-fledged monologue, complete with emphatic gestures to people I couldn't see and don't think existed. I stood there dumbly, staring at the doors behind him. Could I just run through them? Would they be open? This wasn't a police state anymore. What would happen? Who knew where they led in this huge building?

Finally, the gatekeeper stopped talking and stared wearily at me.

"*Sokol trener-basket*," I asked again. The doors were too far, at least metaphorically. I had nowhere to go and nothing else to say.

He shook his head slowly, looked around the empty room, and hooked a thick finger under his lower lip. Then he picked up the receiver on his rotary telephone and dialed.

I waited in the lobby, which was covered floor to ceiling in white- and pea-green tiles, intermingled in no obvious pattern. I tried to act nonchalant, stretching my hamstrings, as if this was reasonable, as if I spent many evenings in foreign countries, refusing to leave gyms, pretending to speak languages, asking for people who may not exist. I mean, *basket* sounded like it meant "basketball," and *trener* sounded like "trainer," which sounded in a roundabout way like "coach." But I'd been down this road before, and as I stood in the lobby I remembered that Mark once told me that the phrase *Ja mam kratkeho* meant "I am pleased to meet you," when in fact it was a colloquialism for "My penis is short." As the wait dragged on, I began to wonder what part of my anatomy I had described, and how I had described it.

Finally, the old man put down the telephone and returned to the door, this time holding a small slip of paper. "*Basket*," he said. "*No?*"

"*Basket*," I said. "*No.*"

He handed me a slip of paper, a secret note. He'd scribbled down two words with a stubby pencil: *Streda. Šest.*

I took the paper back to the Hotel Olšanka and cornered the Czech girl who gave out tickets to the cafeteria. She looked at it and pursed her lips. "Wednesday," she said. "Six."

• • •

EXPATRIATE GAMES

LATER ON, BACK in my room, I unpacked my duffel bags and considered my luggage. No winter hat, but six pairs of ankle-high athletic socks. No scarf, but a jockstrap. It was cold out, and fall was already giving way to a gray, unpredictable winter. Prague sat in a valley carved by the Vltava, the longest river in the Czech Republic, and many of the houses still burned coal. In the winter, the coal-choked hot air would occasionally get trapped in the valley by the colder layer above it. The old Czech grandmothers—*babickas*—swaddled in housecoats and notoriously bewildered, spent the winters with their scarves wrapped around their mouths and noses, looking like decrepit bandits. I could wear my jockstrap like a gas mask.

I'd brought the jockstrap because I didn't know if there'd be laundry facilities available, and in fact there weren't at the Hotel Olšanka—at least, not that I could find. A jockstrap seemed like the kind of thing one could wash by hand in a sink. Most of my packing had been done that way, with a sort of fundamental misperception of efficiency. When I was a kid, my dad used to come up to my room to say good night after his weekly pickup games wearing a T-shirt he would later wring out over the tub. After a game, he would smell like metal, like a battery, and when he'd hug me, I would squirm and scream and then try to fall asleep, my *Star Wars* pillowcase damp and alkaline. I had thought about that when packing for the adventure, and stocked my luggage with as many easy-to-wash items as possible—mesh over cotton, nylon over wool, and a new, elasticized jockstrap.

The jockstrap had been a staple of my high school athletic experience, with liability-conscious coaches reminding us frequently to "protect the family jewels." At twenty-three, I hoped that my family jewels were safe. In any event, I'd ceased believing that a jockstrap was going to make much of a difference, especially because it seems to share design elements with a slingshot. Wearing one was a bit like wearing one of those wraparound retainers that came with early-1980s braces, the kind where the orthodontist said, "Over time you'll forget you're wearing it," except that it's a bit hard to forget about something jutting out of both sides of your mouth, or snaking around your bare ass, for that matter. Still, I wore my jockstrap around a lot over the first few days in Prague, breaking it in, tenderizing the pocket, like you might do with a new baseball glove. Of course, with a jockstrap, you couldn't put your baseballs in it and stick it under the mattress for a couple of nights to break it in. Instead, I wore it around, day and night. It required occasional adjustment, a quick cup or a deep, realigning knee bend, and the other students I passed in the CEU hallways might have wondered why I needed to go into spontaneous half-squats. Or they might not have given it much thought. Clearly, I was an American, and there were cultural differences for which no explanations were possible.

Regardless, I wanted to be prepared, so I was wearing my jockstrap when I returned to the gymnasium at Vinohrady on Wednesday. I got through the main doors and entered a side annex. From behind a glass partition, a doughy old woman with hands like boiled potatoes pointed down a long hallway lined with numbered blue doors.

"*Osm*," she said in response to my "*Basket*," eyeing me like she thought I might steal something.

I was nervous. The team, to the extent it existed, could be behind door number eight, reviewing plays, taking showers, mocking foreigners, whatever Czech teams did in the locker room. They could say, "Sure, play with us." Or they could say, "Sorry, we're all set at the point for this season."

And what then?

The door was open. The room inside was lined with metal lockers. One tall, young man was pulling a pair of tight blue shorts up over threadbare briefs. He was about six-foot-three, with thin legs and a barrel chest. I didn't remember him from the April pickup game. Around him, three very young boys were changing into athletic gear. Was this the youth team?

Damn it.

The man squinted at me.

"*Basket-trener?*" I asked.

He nodded. "*No.*"

I started to turn around until I remembered that *No* meant yes.

"*Mluvite anglicky?*" I asked, running out of vocabulary I trusted.

"*No.* Yes." He smiled. He seemed happy the way people do when they get to answer a question in a foreign language, because it was okay to get it wrong.

I pulled my backpack around to my side, letting my sneakers— black, three-quarter-top Nikes, black laces—hang in the front. I hoped that they were conveying my court sense.

"I'm looking for the coach of the basketball team," I said, starting too fast and then slowing down.

"Yes," he said. "I am him."

Who? I looked at the younger boys.

"The men's coach?" I clarified.

"Yes," he said. He seemed a little frustrated, like he got that question a lot.

Behind his back, two boys put the third in a headlock.

"I am him."

I swallowed. *Don't back out. New Central European Identity.*

"I'd like to play with the team," I said, trying to sound assertive. I'd heard many Czechs use the word "possible" in conversations, to convey whether something was or was not likely to happen. It was not possible, for example, to rent a room at the Hotel Olšanka in any formal way. It could be possible to buy a gun, however, or to meet with almost anyone in the country provided you could pay for a reception.

With regard to joining the team, I asked the critical question: "Is it possible?"

There was a long pause while he looked me over. I hoped he understood that I hadn't worn my sneaks because you couldn't ever wear your good hoop sneaks outside, for both the obvious reasons involving traction and the less obvious ones involving the spirit of the shoe. I hoped that his review would note my tensile strength, my quickness, the blurry deception of my fakes. I hoped he would note my desperation.

He was quiet for a long time.

"Yes," he said. "It is possible. You come back at nine o'clock, tonight."

I smiled wide. We shook hands. He gave me an equally large, red-cheeked grin, but his eyes were noncommittal.

"My name is Honsa. John."

$$\bullet \quad \bullet \quad \bullet$$

I CELEBRATED THE discovery of the team by calling Cameron's old number from a pay phone in the lobby. He answered on the second ring. Another triumph!

His girlfriend had indeed moved from San Francisco to Prague, arriving only three weeks before I did. Her name was Lindsey, and I'd seen pictures; she was small and pretty, with short brown hair in a bob. Cameron said she was having something of a hard time adjusting to life in Prague. She'd made the mistake of getting a haircut shortly after her arrival, and wasn't happy about the resulting "Grace Jones meets Flock of Seagulls" look. To compound matters, she was a vegetarian, which meant that she was both unhappy and

35

hungry, as Czech menus were notoriously slim on their non-meat offerings. The most common one, and a staple of Czech menus, was *smazeny syr*, a patty of deep-fried cheese served on a bed of french fries with tartar sauce. It was delicious, in a sort of fatalistic way, but Lindsey didn't look like the kind of girl who was going to eat it very often.

We met for a beer at a pub called the Derby. Cameron was still trying to get his copy shop off the ground, among other things. I told him about the tryout, and the haphazard welcome committee at CEU, about autumn in the United States. He caught me up on the friends who were still floating around the city. Fast Dave was back from a summer spent working as a 'welcomer' at a hostel in Portugal. Shannon had gotten an apartment with Joel; she was working for a nonprofit, and he was lecturing at CEU in addition to his privatization project. Julie Jette and Jack Levy were still around, running into each other over brunch at Red, Hot & Blues or the Globe. There were no recent Skee sightings, but no major losses to the core group.

"It is possible," Honsa had said, and things were beginning to seem that way.

Practice

AT 8:30 P.M., in a light rain, Ondřičkova glistened, and what little traffic there was vanished. Honsa was changing clothes with two other players when I walked in. We nodded to each other silently, and Honsa made tentative, perfunctory introductions. The younger of the two was named Pavel Kratochvil, but went by Kratcha. He was pulling on late-model gray Converse sneakers and flowery Bermuda shorts. His hair was a brown mop, and he stood a slender six-foot-two.

The other player was a beefy older guy with thinning hair and a round face. He looked more like a janitor than a guard. He eyed me with disdain. His name was Slavek Honzik and he was, of course, the incumbent point guard. He wore a red, blue, and black track-suit top over a stained T-shirt.

As we dressed, Honsa and the other players chatted in Czech and didn't say much to me. I watched them dress and reminded myself that I was in a foreign country, and the sartorial clues were different. On courts in the United States, you could sometimes tell things about a baller from his outfit, and you could always tell someone who thought he was a baller but wasn't. The latter you could tell by the affectations, the wristbands across their biceps or multiple T-shirts or shorts that hung to their ankles, shorts that would catch the ball on crossovers and get as heavy as towels with sweat. And bicep wristbands were a tough sell for most pickup players.

I'd picked up most of my nonrequired hoop knowledge from a book called *The IN-YOUR-FACE BASKETBALL BOOK*, the definitive 1980s-era guide to pickup basketball. In it, eventual *Sports Illustrated* writer Alexander Wolff and his coauthor Chuck Wielgus reviewed the best pickup basketball courts across the country. They also devoted an entire chapter to deciphering such outfit hints as sneaker-lacing, visored caps, and the width of tank-top shoulder straps. Included in the chapter were photo illustrations of the various regional and social looks one might come across if one could, as they did, tour the country playing pickup ball. The "Inner-City Look" circa 1983 featured a knit wool cap, jaggedly cut-off sweats, and "serious" sneakers. The "Suburban Look" required a lawyers'-league T-shirt and a general air of entitlement. For the "Country Look," facial hair was a must but the cowlick was optional.

There was also a profile of "The Wrong Look," in which the study had a perm ("the white man's 'fro") and was wearing a watch and a buttoned-down shirt tucked into jogging shorts. Having "The Wrong Look" concerned me, since I spent the better part of middle school convinced that my mother had bought me women's jeans. Once, when I was in seventh grade, I'd had a nightmare in which my parents got divorced and then immediately remarried other people. My father remarried an artificial woman, more cyborg than bionic, with a stainless-steel right arm and a coffeemaker in a compartment between her shoulder blades. My mother remarried the guy who had "The Wrong Look."

On the courts where I'd been playing all summer long, the best clue to a baller's game lay in his footwear. Most serious players in the mid-1990s had moved toward the three-quarter tops, usually black, a trend begun by Nike and Jordan after they'd milked their original magnificent red-and-white high-top franchise for all it was worth. Three-quarter tops promised the support of the high-top without the weight and bulk that might impact a player's fervent pursuit of rise. Some players felt that the black shoes somehow made your feet look quicker, which seemed important to me. The black sneakers were quickly paired with black socks by Michigan's Fab Five, apparently on the theory that it made your whole lower leg look quicker. Hard to argue with the Fab Five, even though they never won anything.

Slava was lacing up a pair of gray, plastic-looking Adidas knock-offs that might have been white once, and pulling his socks high over his thick calves. He wore sweatpants cut off at the knees such that only about two inches of flesh showed between the tops of his socks and the hems of his shorts. His white T-shirt had greasy fingerprints on the front of it and stretched over his paunchy middle. He looked with suspicion and contempt at my flashy mesh shorts and ankle socks.

What to make of Slava? Did the rules apply? I finished dressing and followed the growing number of long, lanky players down a hallway and up two flights of stairs to the gym I remembered from that long-ago pickup game. It was cavernous. There were terraces on one side of the court—not the retractable sort of bleachers found in high school gyms, but actual rows of concrete stadium seats, maybe twenty rows high. At the far end of the court, past the baseline, there was another, smaller warm-up court set up sideways, covered with multicolored sets of lines from what must have been three different sports. All the lines made the courts look like a subway map of London. Beyond the smaller court, there was what appeared to be a retractable wall of wood paneling. Some of the lines ran under the wood wall, as if extending through it. Could there be even more beyond that?

Ten players eventually lined up for practice. I was the shortest. I stood off to the side, or, more accurately, the other players gathered together in a spot somewhere to my left. They threw sideways glances at me and chattered in Czech. It sounded mocking, to the extent it sounded like anything. I began to think I'd underestimated what a tough way to start this would be, appearing at practice as the new, short foreigner wearing relatively expensive sneakers and carrying a Walkman, unable to speak the language and yet to prove that he could play. But it was too late to change course now.

Honsa blew his whistle and I tried to follow the pack. We ran laps and did shooting drills for an hour. Players paired up during the drills, and Honsa sent me with Robert Javurek, an older player who, at six-foot-six, was also one of the tallest men on the floor. Robert Javurek also appeared to be something of a team diplomat, willing to reach out in the manner that a senior ape might reach out to a kitten introduced into the enclosure. His English was limited, but practical.

"You are. Are? Are here now," he said. "Yes?"

Motherfucker! This was the guy from last year, the one who'd extended the invitation.

I mentioned it while we shot fouls, but was unable to convey the full impact of what had been to him, apparently, an offhand and forgettable aside. His English was still much better than my Czech, and eventually we moved on to more immediate matters.

"Are you student?" he asked.

I nodded. "*Ano.*"

What else was I going to say? I tried to steer the conversation to him. What did he do? Was he a student?

He shook his head. Not a student, he said, apologizing for his English. He was a worker.

"What do you do?" I asked.

He looked in the gym air for a word.

"I . . . work?" he said. Bob had a massive head, sharp chin, and floppy hair atop a long, angular body. I felt like I knew him; then I realized he was a dead ringer for Shaggy from the Scooby-Doo cartoons.

We broke into position groups and I watched Bob scrimmage with some of the other big guys. His game seemed to be played on a horizontal axis rather than a vertical one. When he'd get the ball down low, he wouldn't go up with it so much as move sideways, wending his way through a thicket of arms and bodies to force up a shot.

We took turns shooting from various spots on the court, keeping count for Honsa, who revealed himself to be a rigorous statistician. Bob made 27 of 34 two-footers without using his left hand once. He made 5 of 12 foul shots. I shot threes from the international line, feeling eyes upon me, and hit only 6 of 14.

During a break, a smaller player named Radek joined us. Radek seemed to be both a player and an assistant coach of some sort. He smiled at me and extended his hand. We had guarded each other back in the spring pickup game, and Radek seemed to remember. I asked them questions about the team, the season, and the league. Bob said that the season would start in October. Radek explained that the team, called TJ Sokol Kralovske Vinohrady, was in a gap league between the national professional leagues and the local club leagues. As best as I could understand it, there were five national hoop fiefdoms—North, South, East, West, and Prague—and each had its own hierarchy of leagues. Three national leagues crossed all five fiefdoms. The top league was called the *Superliga*, and it was Sparta's *Superliga* pennant I'd seen in the café.

The previous spring, after finding Sparta's championship pennant, I'd seen a game between Sparta and a team from Turkey, and the style of play resembled a cross between Division II college basketball and some other, more lateral sport, like lacrosse. Guards delivered forearm shivers while checking their men at half-court. Enormous, plodding post players threw hips to the midsection and shoulders to the chin. The ball went down low on virtually every possession, and players literally threw one another into screens to shake loose. The big men—and they *were* big, bony and long-limbed—would occasionally send the ball whistling back out to one of the players spaced along the three-point line, who then chucked up long one-handed shots of which they made a stunning percentage. It looked like a classic two-one-two zone offense, inside-out, being deployed in Prague against a man-to-man defense. Individual moves were rare, players did not drive, and there were few dunks. Full-court passes were thrown underhand, and everyone seemed to take four steps per layup.

The second- and third-level national leagues were called, respectively, the First National League and the Second National League. Between the national and regional leagues was a bridge league called the *Přebor*, made up of the best ten or so teams in each region. At the end of the season, the top two finishers in the Prague *Přebor* would play in a tournament against the top finishers in the other four regional *Přebor* leagues. The winner of that *Přebor* tournament would be promoted to the national leagues for the following season. The worst teams in a league would be relegated to the league below it. Vinohrady, the team with which I was practicing, was one of the twelve teams in the Prague *Přebor*. Last year, Bob said, Vinohrady had finished fourth in the second Prague league.

I asked Bob how Vinohrady had moved up, if it had finished fourth the previous year.

"We bought . . . ?" Bob said, searching with his hands for a word.

Practice ended with a scrimmage, the first real opportunity to evaluate the talent levels of the team relative to my own. Honsa divided the team into squads. I stretched nervously and swelled up like a puffer fish.

The swelling proved unnecessary. Within five minutes it became clear that on any decent Division III court in America, the members of TJ Sokol Kralovske Vinohrady would be in trouble. Nobody could really leap, only one or two guys could shoot consistently, and ball-handling was an adventure. A couple of players showed flashes: a quick guard named Robert Vyklicky orbited between the left wing and the far baseline and put up arching threes, and a smooth six-foot-three outside shooter named Tomas Krysl knocked down a three in transition. Robert Vyklicky was the only player to drive the lane, and he looked headstrong but uneasy doing so. The big men were slow and flat. Kratcha, the youngster from the locker room, was fast and fluid but had trouble creating his own shot. A young blond horse named Tomas Polisensky had a power low-post game and a nice jump hook, but played small on the boards and smiled too much for a power forward.

The scrimmage seemed to reflect fundamental differences between the skill sets—and mind-sets—of U.S. and European players in the mid-1990s. The Czechs, at least the ones on this court, seemed relatively new to basketball, entranced by the geometry of it, the arcs and angles, the form and percentages. They focused on, and thereby excelled at, certain things—the three-point shot, the rolling hook, the multiple, inside-outside passes. They tended to be weak dribblers, their upper bodies churning like train pistons when they pushed the ball downcourt. They favored the pull-up pump-fake and the slide-step and eschewed going all the way to the hole. By contrast, the U.S. game I'd left behind seemed to have gotten bored of jump-shooting and was enamored with the idea of the dunk—not the dunk itself, which remained out of reach for many players, but the idea of it, which promoted patterns and spacing, encouraged individualism and explosions of energy. U.S. players, especially those in unstructured environments, overexposed to highlight shows and All-Star games, seemed to play with the idea of the dunk in the back of their minds. From the smallest point guard to the heaviest power forward, guys seemed to play to be part of the dunk, to dunk themselves, to facilitate the dunk. To drive the paint as if they were going to dunk, even if it just turned into a layup, going to the hole and planting, both feet square and the ball cocked back. Because maybe, just that once, they might then tomahawk the ball through the hoop, and hang for a second on the bent rim, and wouldn't that be just about the end of it?

I broke a sweat by my third trip upcourt. I hadn't spoken to more than three of the guys all practice, and it felt like they were watching me, waiting to see what I could do. Slava in particular had stayed within a knot of cronies and let me match up with Robert Vyklicky. I heard biting Czech words and chuckles. What were they saying? The limited Czech I knew enabled me to read a menu, slowly and with about 70 percent accuracy, but it did nothing to help process colloquial locker-room chatter and trash talk. If that's what it was. Maybe they were just talking about their summers.

I played it cool in the scrimmage, dishing off for a few assists and hitting on two jumpers and a baseline drive where I thought I'd get contact from Bob, but he stayed rooted to the ground. Was that a favor? Bob was earnest but unsuited to the game; he bounced shot after shot off of the bottom of the rim. His left hand seemed vestigial. Robert Vyklicky was quick and spotted up for three-pointers, but I stayed close enough to bother him.

After ten minutes, Honsa called off the scrimmage. Sweat dripped from my chin. Some of the players who'd been on my squad patted me on the shoulder. What was next? Were there cuts to be made? Would, as so often in the past, a list of names be hung on a door somewhere?

The other players filtered away toward the locker rooms. Honsa nodded at me and checked something off his clipboard. "Come back on Friday," he said, or something like that. "Seven-thirty."

. . .

My CEU program was a one-year master's degree in European Relations, accredited through an entity called the Open University—open, apparently, to anyone. Although classes weren't set to start for a week, most of CEU's students had arrived and begun to circle each other warily, gathering information. Who was from where? What had they done before? Where were they trying to go? They seemed like standard first-week questions, but they took on an added significance in Central Europe. Many of my classmates came from places that didn't exist, at least as political entities, years or even weeks earlier; there were Montenegrans, Slovaks, Slovenes, Bosnians, Croats, a Moldovan, one woman from Kazakhstan, and a mad-looking young man named Yevgeni who was from Siberia and said he was thrilled with the Hotel Olšanka because he'd lived for the past three years with his parents in a hotel room in Omsk.

Some of the students heard the names of oppressors in their hallmates' conversations. Others gravitated toward nationalist cliques. Many of them, however, seemed united in their curiosity and borderline disdain for Americans. (I liked to view myself as a facilitator both on and off the court.) There were several Kristinas, a couple of Helens or Heles, a stunning Pole named Beata, a stunning Bosnian named Una, and a girl from England named Jay who was the niece of the actor Tim Curry and bore an uncanny resemblance to him. Among the men, the program had several

Dmitris, a Dragan, a Janko, and a sweet, hulking young man from northern Poland named Dagmar. The only other American was a graduate student from Columbia University named Melissa, who appeared to be happy to be anywhere in Europe, where her boyfriend worked with the World Bank. We both wanted desperately to be accepted by our classmates, and as a result didn't speak to each other.

To fill the time and escape the hotel, I went to the American Cultural Center on Trziste Avenue. *Trziste* was a name that seemed like it ought to mean "sad," but meant "marketplace." The American Cultural Center was a clean stone and concrete building with a marine out front and a photo of Bill Clinton watching over the lobby. It was one of several expat hubs in 1994 Prague. Others included the Globe Bookstore, the nightclub Radost FX, the Tex-Mex brunch hangout Red, Hot & Blues, and an archipelago of bars. Most traded in a sort of bohemian cool; the Cultural Center traded in homesickness. There was a cafeteria that served hamburgers and fries, ice cream, and cans of American Coke rather than the sweeter Spanish version. Posters and fliers in English lined the walls, and the small library was full of newspapers, magazines, and books. The offices had computers and fax machines and thick doors. You had to walk through a metal detector to get upstairs.

An assistant cultural attaché named Bob Bailey came out to meet me. He was a young guy, probably not much older than me, and he seemed stunned by the good fortune of his assignment to Prague. He hadn't known where they would station him; Prague was like winning the lottery. His wife was as thrilled as a diplomat's wife could be with the assignment, which was to run for two years. Bob Bailey said he attended a lot of openings and cocktail parties, and wrote a lot of copy on U.S. foreign policy in the region for use by the cultural attaché himself. It was not a bad job, he said. I spent the afternoon in the library reading issues of *Sports Illustrated* and chatting with two girls from Seattle.

. . .

THAT EVENING, BEFORE it got dark, I walked diagonally from the Hotel Olšanka to one of the two huge cemeteries that sat just across the road, and spent an hour looking for Kafka's grave. It wasn't there—Kafka was buried somewhere else—but the cemetery, called the Olsanske Hrbitovy, was enormous, quiet, walled, and baroque, full of granite art deco mausoleums and creeping flora, and I quickly got lost.

Just before dusk, along the southern edge of the Hrbitovy, I stumbled across the grave of Jan Palach, the Czech student who lit himself on fire in January 1969 at the top of Wenceslas Square. Palach was protesting the Soviet tanks that crushed Dubcek's Prague Spring. His grave had no headstone—just a long bronze slab with the pockmarked, slightly raised outline of a man on it. There was also a black-and-white photo, wrapped in plastic, showing a serious-looking Palach in a wide-collared shirt and jacket. People said he'd been crazy.

A man walked by holding a small furry dog.

"*Neni tady*," he said, pointing at the grave.

I shrugged my shoulders. The man furrowed his brow.

"Not here," he said, swinging his arm up in a crescent to suggest the wide world.

. . .

THE NEXT EVENING, I headed up Ondřičkova to practice, past the red and gold facades of the old buildings. Old women perched like pigeons in their apartment windows, their arms folded and their chins wagging beneath their heads. Couples walked arm in arm in the park and a light breeze carried the scents of grass and brick and coal and lavender. A little girl sat on the stoop of the gym, sharing a mustardy hot dog with a similarly sized real dog.

I arrived early for practice and was eventually joined by fifteen other guys, including a new center named Tonda, who stood about six-foot-seven. On offense, Tonda seemed even less comfortable than Big Bob had in the pivot, but on the other end he swatted away shots with a pair of oar-like arms. Other new figures included Jena, a quiet small forward, and Martinu, a guard with the flat face of a skillet and long, curly hair was chewing tobacco during the drills and appeared to be swallowing the juice.

The better players began to assert themselves. Kratcha and Robert Vyklicky led the youth contingent—they were both students. Robert intended to go to law school after he graduated. After practice he gave me his business card with the name of his school and the title ADVOKAT beneath his name. Sweet-shooting Tomas Krysl was stronger and more bulky than Kratcha but inclined toward jump shots. He smiled easily and spoke fluent English. He also spoke French and a little German. He gave me a business card, too. His read, in English, TOM KRYSL, THE BULLDOZER OF GIRLS' HEARTS.

Michal Pietsch, yet another long-armed, small forward, was the team's most effective scorer. He had a sort of deceptive slowness to his game, like that of the erstwhile Lakers garbageman Ced Ceballos, and each time he scored, you kind of wondered how he was doing it. Ced Ceballos could do that for twenty-six points a game. Michal Pietsch looked good for a dozen. Center was still a no-man's-land, with Bob and Tonda vying for space, but there seemed to be room at the point for me. Slava and I were different types of point guard: He was a set shooter, running the offense; I'd become more of a slasher, good in transition, creating when the play broke down, taking guys off the dribble. Those skills hadn't gotten much work in high school, where such individual deviations got players showered with spittle during time-outs. I'd developed them later, on pickup courts where there were no set plays. I wasn't sure how they would fit in with Vinohrady.

We walked through the first of the team's plays. The players assembled by position and Honsa passed out a sheaf of papers with diagrams and words I didn't know on them, words like *dlouhy* and *kridlo*. Bob tried to explain them to me during time-outs. It didn't work. I tried to pick up the offensive sets by standing behind Slava, who was minimally helpful. Then we scrimmaged again, and I went off script a little but finished with fifteen points, my only three hitting nothing but net.

After practice, I went out to a cellar bar for beers with Bob, Radek, and Tomas. Radek had the season schedule, and we talked about the teams ahead, the results of the previous season's games, and expectations for the upcoming ones. Our opponents had funny names like Horni Pocernice and Kbely; funny to me, anyway. Radek pointed out the technical school on our schedule and I ridiculed it. We weren't going to lose to a technical school! I tried to ask some questions about how life had changed since the Velvet Revolution, but I asked them inartfully and got perfunctory responses. It did not seem as if life had changed a great deal—at least, not that my new teammates were inclined to discuss. Bob said he'd gone to Austria, but couldn't afford anything and came home.

I didn't want to fuel any more stereotypes than I had to, so I'd signed up for a crash course in Czech at CEU. The textbook for the course utilized common words in uncommon contexts; I could say things like "I would like four soups and six potatoes" or "Do you need a dog?" I knew the word for fish stew but not the words for history, or government, or the future. My teammates set about rectifying the disparity. Everyone always said that the best place to learn a language was in a bar, the beer lowering inhibitions and helping your tongue make adjustments to difficult sounds. Czech, for example, was thick with consonants and sibilants, some "r's" becoming "zh's," and "c's" becoming "ts's." A lot of the words seemed undecided until they got to the tip of your tongue.

Ti vole, Tomas said, was the default locker-room disparagement I was likely to hear most often. It meant, roughly, "You castrated ox." A missed shot, a bad joke, a spilled beer; you could say *Ti vole* for any of them. You could say it angrily or affectionately. It seemed to be an important phrase to know. *Bohuzel* meant "unfortunately." *Kureci prsa* was "chicken breast."

We got a third round. I told them I already knew some Czech phrases from my previous visits to Prague. Most I had picked up at the movies. They had limited application.

"*Ja jsem netopire*," I said, which, as I understood it, meant "I am Batman."

"*Ja jsem krasne a cerny.*" I am beautiful and dark.

They seemed to think those would come in handy, and we toasted to them, again and again.

The next morning, I didn't remember much of what they'd taught me. One phrase did resonate: "I will pay now." It was *Za-pla-ti-me*.

· · ·

By Monday's practice, the team had nineteen players, including a Nigerian named Claudio who could take off from the middle of the lane and throw down relatively impressive flickering one-handed dunks. Outside of the lane, he was harmless. Three other guys were dunking, including Tomas Polisensky—Poli—who did so with modest Caucasian flair.

I'd come to Prague to try to play professional basketball, but even in Prague (or perhaps because of Prague), that seemed like a real long shot. Because Vinohrady played in the *Přebor*, it seemed that it could accurately be called a "semiprofessional" team, provided one allowed for a fairly expansive interpretation of the modifier. Webster's Dictionary at the CEU's modest library defined "semipro" as "something done for profit or other gain but not as a full-time profession." That sounded expansive enough. I was profiting from my experience with Vinohrady—I got language lessons and access to the gym—and the possibility of additional profit seemed like profit in itself. I guess "club basketball" might have been just as accurate a description of the league; like a book club, except that people in a book club didn't call themselves semiprofessional readers.

As far as I could tell, the only truly "professional" players in the country—the ones who might be able to make a living by playing hoop—were the best of the *Superliga*. One guard named Hruby allegedly made 900,000 crowns (around $30,000) a year to play for Sparta, which was a lot of money by contemporary Prague standards, especially to play a sport that wasn't part of the national mainstream like soccer or tennis or hockey or Sokol aerobics. I'd seen Hruby play in the Sparta–Turkey match the last time I'd been in Prague. He was a bull of a player, big and strong, a wide-shouldered three-point-shooting Garde Thompson type with a neck like Brian Shute's in *Vision Quest*. Everyone else seemed to be working their way toward or away from that level, especially in the *Přebor*, where dreams of making a *Superliga* team were at least entertainable.

At Vinohrady's level, the players actually paid about $18 a season in club dues to indulge those dreams. The dues covered the cost of uniforms, the gym fees, and some travel. Honsa appeared to be coaching gratis. For some players, like Bob and Tomas Krysl and Slava and Michal Pietsch, the club meant a chance to continue playing hoop regularly with friends as they slalomed down the back hills of their youth. Others, like Tonda, Kratcha, Poli, and Robert Vyklicky, appeared to maintain hopes of success, and remuneration, at a higher level. I wasn't sure where I fit in the mix yet, but I felt reasonably confident that I could hang with Vinohrady. "Semipro" might have been a stretch, but it sounded better than "club." Shit, if I could live with "Last Cut—Big East," I could live with that.

· · ·

IN THE *IN-YOUR-FACE BASKETBALL BOOK*, Alexander Wolff wrote about playing one season after college with a team in Austria and doing his part for international relations by explaining the phrase "In your face!" to his Viennese hosts. In that tradition of détente, I arrived at the fourth practice and started saying, "*Tobe do oci.*"

My Czech language teacher told me that *Tobe do oci* meant, roughly, "Right in front of your eyes!" It was as close as she could get to "In your face!"

"*Tobe do oci!*" I said when I drove on Kratcha.

"*Tobe do oci, ti vole,*" I said when I drilled a three on Tomas.

"*Do prdele* (Go to my ass), *ti vole,*" I said to Poli, when I snuck up behind him and blocked his shot. "*Ja jsem netopire!*"

My teammates appeared entertained, as I'd hoped, and also a little nervous. They never knew when the *Tobe do oci* was coming. Or why. I spent the better part of practice trying, unsuccessfully, to explain what I meant, and why I said it. The concept seemed foreign to them; not to read too much into it, but the idea of trumpeting a momentary individual achievement in a collective endeavor seemed to amuse them. Maybe instead of, "I scored right in front of your eyes," the proper taunt for the environment would have been more like, "My team has successfully executed a play that has led to us scoring on your team." Or maybe there would be no taunts at all.

The first game—a preseason scrimmage—was scheduled for that coming Friday, September 16. Things were happening fast. Two weeks earlier, I'd been waiting tables at the Red Lion Inn, and now, there was Big Bob Javurek, three days' stubble on his lantern jaw, shocking everyone by dunking during a layup drill. He was wearing brand-new black Converse high-tops he'd cinched up with green and purple laces. Next time through the line, he tried to dunk again, caught the ball on the lip of the rim, and landed with a thud on his ass.

"You castrated ox!" we shouted.

Kratcha shouted, "*Tobe do oci!*"

We'd learned three plays, all variations on low-post screens for the pivot men. They were called "*Ctyri*," "*Sedm*," and something else that wasn't a number. (I'd only learned numbers, and could barely pronounce those. For example, "*Ctyri*"—"Four"—was pronounced by affixing the tip of your tongue to the bottom of your upper teeth and pretending to bite it off, all while saying "stodgy.") "*Ctyri*" had the point-guard screen for both the center and the power forward. "*Sedm*," or "Seven," featured a set of cross screens on the blocks. The other players stood around the outside of the three-point line, presumably hoping for a loose ball to bounce their way.

Honsa divided us into squads: I was on the A squad with Slava, Robert, Tomas, Tonda, and Bob. One of the other A-squad players was an undersized power forward named Petr Mondschein. Mondy had a shaggy head of dark hair which he corralled under a blue bandanna that made his ears flap out. With his deep eyes and pinched chin, he looked like a very large mouse. He spent half of the practice crashing the boards and the other half reciting a limited collection of Ice Cube lyrics he'd apparently committed to memory. Whenever Honsa would stop the practice to yell at someone, which was often, Mondy would twist into his version of the cabbage patch and shout out "You better check yourself before you wreck yourself." When practice ended, Mondy sat in the locker room with his headphones on, rapping along with a character called Ice MC, whose breakout hit (from the *Ice' n' Green* album) was entitled "You Gotta Feel the Feeling." I nodded along with his beat and we slapped palms. We were down.

· · ·

IN MY FIRST weeks at the Hotel Olšanka, my classmates had seemed suspicious of me. Now they seemed more curious. In the cafeteria, some of them were vying to see who knew more about American society and pop culture. Constantin, a young Muscovite with an Amish beard, approached me and said he had placed two bets with a Serb named Kristina Sug'ar.

"Is it *Witches of Eastwood*," he asked, "the movie with Dirty Harry?"

"No," I said. "*Witches of Eastwick*, with Jack Nicholson."

He frowned at this.

"And Billie Holliday," he asked. "A man?"

I shook my head. Constantin slapped his forehead and gave Kristina Sug'ar a purple twenty-crown bill, a Czech king hiding in the watermark.

· · ·

WE SCRIMMAGED THAT Friday against a team from an area of Prague 5 called Motol. The scrimmage was delayed by half an hour while a team handball practice finished on the court. The team handball coach had a beard and a wide, heavy stomach hanging out over his shorts. It seemed to be a point of pride.

Motol showed up with four or five players taller than Tonda, our starting center. Some of them were wearing thin black socks under new-looking black Nikes. I was the only other player on the court sporting a black shoe/black sock look. I looked at them. They looked at me. Their black socks looked like dress socks. Motol sucks!

At the end of the last practice, Honsa had passed out blank, numberless uniforms and then, separately, small fuzzy numbers. The home uniforms were white and felt like they were made of some plasticine polymer. We each got tank tops and tight John Stockton–length shorts with black slashes from the armpit to the hip. The away uniforms were plain blue cotton tops. There were no names on the uniforms, nothing to indicate who we were or what neighborhood we represented. I'd drawn the number five; Honsa handed me two large "fives" for the back of the tops and smaller ones for the hip of the shorts.

"Five" was not a number steeped in basketball glory. John Bagley had worn it, and Roy Marble, and probably some others, but nobody truly great. We were each in charge of affixing our numbers to our uniforms before the first game. I didn't know how to do that, and my teammates had scattered before I could ask for advice. Back in my dorm room, I'd tried to iron the numbers on with an iron I'd borrowed from a Polish girl down the hall, but they wouldn't stay on, and in no time I managed to burn a small hole in the back of the home top, the material curling and withering like hair. I also burned the rug, and then, with a loud spark and a puff of acrid smoke, shorted out the electricity on the entire hotel floor.

I returned the iron and got a needle and white thread from Dagmar, the effeminate Pole, whose offer to do the actual sewing

I declined. An hour and modest bloodletting later, the number fives were firmly affixed with ragged, uneven stitches. I'd put the home uniform on, careful not to make the hole bigger, and checked myself out in the bathroom mirror. It was not a good look. The outfit was tight and restrictive, like a wet suit or the unitard outfits Chris Corchiani and Rodney Monroe had suffered through briefly at NC State. The jersey clung to my waist like cellophane to a ham, see-through nearly to the point of transparency. As for the shorts, they were so short and tight that when I pulled them up, it felt like my balls were being tucked into my belt. They felt like the sort of shorts that were meant to be worn beneath other shorts, as a precautionary measure, by astronauts or people who worked in the extreme cold. As I posed in front of the bathroom mirror, dropping into a defensive stance, the shorts bunched like a diaper.

It didn't matter. *Gimme five*, Honsa might say in the huddle. Roy Marble! I'd memorized the sound of the Czech word for "five," so I'd understand when the crowd was chanting for me. *Pyet. Pyet. Pyet.*

Kratcha and Robert Vyklicky led us into our pre-scrimmage warm-ups. Motol looked downcourt anxiously. That's right, motherfuckers. Vinohrady in the house. I stretched my quads and calves; they felt spring-loaded. I got a ball in the shoot-around and couldn't miss, raining threes like Lamar Mundane, the ball floating out of my hands. As Honsa called us to the bench I hit a stop-and-pop three off the dribble that left the net whistling. UNLV had a shooter like that; his name was Freddie Banks.

Slava started at point guard with Robert Vyklicky, Bob, Kratcha, and Tonda. I watched and tried to pick up rule changes and patterns. The lane was trapezoidal, wider under the basket than at the foul line. When a ball went out of bounds, it could come back in play without a whistle, as soon as a referee had touched it. The game was divided into twenty-minute halves, with the clock counting up to twenty, rather than down to zero.

The team huddled, hands in the middle, and everyone shouted "Hey, ho!" Bob told me later it meant something like "Together, we jump!"

Slava began the game by hitting two long threes. He had the mechanics of a shot-putter. Then he hit a baseline jumper. He was the sort of player, like Knicks point guard Mark Jackson, who seemed to have the ability to exploit his own limitations. Tonda, similarly, was working a short arcing turnaround shot, his long arms letting him loft the ball toward the hoop at a nearly unblockable angle. We went up by a few, but Motol started racing down the court, firing threes and crashing the boards. Then, on a fast break, their power forward leveled Robert Vyklicky at mid-court with a lowered shoulder, and suddenly the game got serious.

"Daveed," Honsa said.

At the next dead ball, I went with Michal. I felt tight, wound up, surprised at how foreign the foreign court felt. All around me, people were speaking words I couldn't understand, warning of blind picks, setting defenses. For all the one-on-one stuff, basketball was indisputably about teams, not about individuals. Teams chewed individuals up. Teams funneled individuals into the lane and collapsed on them.

My teammates grabbed my arms and pushed me into position. I looked to the bench, at Honsa, for the plays. We were playing a zone defense, and I shifted around the top of the key, following the only familiar thing: the ball. A steal and Michal had the ball. I lit out on the break, and a Motol guard picked me up with a bug-eyed intensity I'd seen in plenty of high school sixth men. Michal hit me with a pass on the wing and I put the shot up almost before the ball got to me. It arched through the gym air, an unguided missile, and missed long.

First shot as a semipro. A miss.

My man was wearing wool socks pulled up high. He cut behind a screen and hit a ten-foot jumper. I came back at him fast, shook him at mid-court with a stutter-step, freed myself in the secondary, bearing down on the Motol big men. They were frozen, and I stopped at the foul line and pulled up. Bob was down low. I looked to him but he was tangled up with their forward. I shot again, but it caught the front of the rim and looped right back to me. I was closer by then, in the lane. Short jump hook. Money. I was in a vacuum, nobody else had moved since I crossed half-court, and I could see nothing but the front of the rim. Shot went up again, my third in the thirty seconds I'd been in the game. It squeaked around the rim and I started to fade back downcourt, but then it rolled up and off the flat back, where the cylinder met the glass. For a moment it sat there, dead, and then trickled off into the spatulate mitts of the Motol center.

I heard whistles and swooshing bird-like remarks from the Motol players. Motherfucker.

When the half ended, I sat and tried to remember whether I'd passed to anyone the entire time I was in. I didn't think so. That wasn't good. We were down, 36–31, and I finished the half two for eight, one of my misses a lunar probe of a three that hit nothing at all.

I calmed down in the second half, dishing to Bob for two layups that he missed and taking Bug-Eye to the hole for a lovely left-handed finger-roll that brought a whistle from Michal. At one point, Bob got hacked by a Motol forward and took offense. I shoved the other guy back while Bob cocked a ham-hock fist in his direction. The referee and other players jumped in before Bob could swing and everything calmed down quickly, but it felt like an important team-building moment; the first skirmish. Bob sort of nodded to me as we headed back up the court. We got momentum but the game unraveled when Martinu, manning the scorer's table, forgot to keep score and left us tied at forty for about eight minutes. By then, I was back on the bench, watching Honsa direct the offense as player-coach against Motol's B squad.

When the buzzer sounded, Bob slapped me on the knee.

"Daveed," he said, "*Pivo?*"

Beer, indeed.

Honsa called out to us as we left. "Training, *Pondeli*—Monday," he said, gesticulating in a way I didn't understand. Did hand gestures require translations, too? "Seven and half."

· · ·

SEPTEMBER 20 WAS a brisk, windy day, and I was heading to Petriny for a scrimmage. Petriny seemed to be as far from downtown as you could get without leaving Prague: eleven stops on the 26, change at Hradčanská, and seven or so more on the 1, out into the suburban fringe, where the team was to meet up, to travel out even further. The 26 went right through downtown Prague, and from the tram's back windows, I rattled by the city. Past Hlavní Nádraží, the main train station, where gypsies slept huddled together for warmth and waited for guards with dogs to roust them. Curving in a deferential arc past Obecni Dům, the art-nouveau municipal center. The government had shut the center down weeks earlier for renovations and to clean out the expat clubs that were taking root in the cavernous basements. One of them—Repre—had become a sort of twenty-four-hour rave.

Then north, across the wide and shiny Vltava. On the left, Prague Castle sat above the tiled roofs of Malá Strana. They'd built the castle around the cathedral, the spires of St. Vitus poking up into the sky from behind the castle walls, from within which the government was still run. The tram passed the floating Hotel Admiral and turned down Nábřeží Kapitána Jaroše, heading north again into Prague 6, past the Globe, whose nooks and corners seemed to be every expat's first stop. The bookstore sold tuna melts and brownies and offered a bulletin board so layered with notes from other travelers asking for help that people stopped and read at least in part to feel better about their own tribulations.

The tram turned left at Letná Park and back toward the castle, constantly on the horizon. A huge statue of Stalin used to look out over the city from Letná Park; now the expat business crowd played Ultimate Frisbee there on the weekends. The 26 kept going, up into the hills of Hradčanská, the castle neighborhood, and left downtown behind. I changed to the 1, which rattled further out of the city, until it ended at Petriny, where the bird-like Spravna Mira squad lurked. The court at Spravna Mira sat in a vaguely barnlike gym that looked like it was made of plywood. High above us, sparrows flew from rafter beam to rafter beam and shat in the corners.

My uniform chafed.

Slava started at point against a team of giants with long arms and big bellies. Bob, Kratcha, Mondy, and newcomer Ludek Pelikan, nicknamed "Peli," rounded out the starting five. Peli was about six-foot-seven and played, at times, both angry and out of control, as likely to dunk the ball as he was to buckle a knee. Kratcha started the game off by nailing long-jumpers and Mondy applied his repertoire of pump-fakes and pivots to the chins and midsections of the Spravna Mira post players. Mondy was the type of Oakleyesque player who seemed to need body contact to score, the type of player who could be held scoreless simply by backing away from him.

But Spravna Mira came back behind their two big men, who were camping in the lane and throwing in long sweeping hooks. They would only leave the lane long enough to set mobile, grappling picks for a couple of mediocre guards. One long-haired shooter was tossing up eighteen-footers with so much arc that they threatened to provoke the birds. Spravna Mira went up by five and I replaced Slava in the lineup.

This was our first game away from the friendly confines of Riegrovy Sady, a court whose whitewalled backgrounds and traction I'd spent the past weeks figuring out. This was a hostile environment! Spravna Mira's court was darker, more slippery. Their players were ugly and mean-looking; their ugly, mean-looking women packed the stands, chirping at us.

I took the ball and crossed up my man immediately, right to left through the legs. Past him, he's reaching . . . then a whistle.

What?

The referee made a punching gesture with his right arm and gave the ball to Spravna Mira.

Punching?

Next play, I pushed the ball upcourt, beat my man down the middle, and dished, hitting the referee in his knee with a perfect bounce-pass. Damn it. Two opportunities, two mistakes.

I sensed my teammates were getting anxious. They started to play frazzled. Tomas, on a couple of assists, short-armed layups. It was possible he hadn't expected the passes. Ludek Pelikan didn't know the plays yet, and camped silently in the pivot like a moa on Easter Island. Big Bob was called for three-second violations on two straight possessions.

Honsa sent Slava back in for me to finish the half, and at halftime took me aside and asked me to slow down, pass first, and generally focus more on running the offense. He was right—that was exactly what a point guard was supposed to do. I still had to quell a twitch of affront, an urge to tell Honsa how long I'd been playing basketball; how I'd once played in a pickup game with Kevin Duckworth, just two seasons removed from his best years with the Trailblazers, when he was staying at a health spa where I parked cars; how I knew who sang the National Anthem at the 1983 All-Star Game (Marvin Gaye, Detroit). None of it mattered if I couldn't play as part of a team.

In the halftime huddle, Honsa told me to start the second half and appeared to explain to my teammates that he had asked me to run plays and pass more. Everyone chuckled but seemed relieved. Kratcha, Michal, Bob, and Tomas's younger brother Lucas started with me. We ran *Sedm* and Bob scored. We ran *Ctyri* and Lucas got a jumper. Then, isolated on the left and after three passes, I took my man baseline and laid the ball high off the boards and over the long arms of the Spravna Mira big man.

They came back and a guard threw in an effeminate jumper, but Michal answered with a twisting layup and, seconds later, Bob picked up a loose ball and flicked up a two-footer. It dropped as he was fouled, and he let out a roar of challenge. It didn't matter that he bricked his free throw. I pressured their guard into a deflected pass and leapt out on the break. Ludek Pelikan sent a pass down the left wing and I hit a fissure in the lane hard, going up over their forwards with a relatively soaring finger-roll. It dropped. Vinohrady erupted in cheers and Spravna Mira called time-out.

We ended up winning by three. In the locker room afterward, Honsa said the second half was "super." It had felt super. *Vyborni.* I walked with Big Bob to the tram for the long ride back into town. Bob talked about his ankle problems, and why he couldn't get comfortable on the court. He said that he renovated apartments and was in danger of getting evicted from his own. He couldn't explain why in English.

Dunking

GROWING UP, WE would try to dunk all kinds of things, figuring out what we could hold onto and measuring our steps from the rim. We'd dunk tennis balls, crushed soda cans, softballs, cantaloupes. I dunked a slightly deflated volleyball once, but the basketball never went down for me.

I thought a lot about dunking. Once, my dad and I tried to develop criteria for ranking the dunks we had seen (he never dunked either), with the ultimate goal of identifying the greatest dunk ever. It was a pointless thing to do since all other dunks would pale in comparison to three we'd never see—our own, and Earl Manigault's circa 1965 jam over three forwards at the Rucker—but we did it anyway. There were three criteria for the greatest dunk ever; like a lot of criteria, they could have just as easily been applied to the wider world.

First, the greatest dunk ever had to be in a real live meaningful game, the more meaningful the better. The dunk had to *matter* to be great—jams that came out of Slam-Dunk contests and All-Star games seemed ersatz and accommodating by comparison. Of coure, there were exceptions: Ced Ceballos got creativity props for the blindfold dunk, and Julius's first foul-line jam had all sorts of sociocultural implications.

Second, and for similar reasons, there had to be a defender. Breakaways didn't count. A monster dunker had a victim, a Hektor to his Achilles. The bigger or better the defender, the more likely it was that the dunk would be special. As the NBA evolved into big-money entertainment, only a few players still seemed willing to try to block dunks (Mutombo, Mourning); most everyone else seemed reluctant to wind up on a poster. As a result, it was rare that Jordan or Barkley even had a chance to really exceed expectations. Although Barkley still did on occasion.

Finally, it was good if the dunk at least appeared to be an extension of the player's personal integrity. Speculating about the personal integrity of professional athletes is ridiculously dumb, but we tried to extrapolate from what we knew of the person's game, his home life, his childhood, so that the dunk might become a spiritual act, representative of the player's soul, his moral fabric. This was sometimes easier to figure out with guards.

These were the sorts of things I talked about with my dad. No doubt they meant other things. In any event, with those criteria, we sifted through the history of the game for dunks to rank. The list was bound to be incomplete—I'd never seen Gus Johnson gus-johnson a backboard, never saw Julius in the ABA, never saw David Thompson or Connie Hawkins at all. The Hawk at the Rucker, the Helicopter, the Goat—for a white kid from a tourist town in western Massachusetts who couldn't himself dunk, these were legends.

We had a subcategory for "college." There were three candidates for the greatest collegiate dunk I'd ever seen. The first was Houston Cougar Clyde Drexler walking over Memphis State's Andre Turner from the foul line during Houston's Phi Slamma Jamma NCAA run in the mid-eighties. On the replay, you could see Drexler sort of hurdling the six-foot-one Turner. Drexler had the ball hooked behind his head, seemingly oblivious to the man beneath him. Turner barely bothered to try to sell the charge.

Then there was Michael Jordan's first breakaway windmill cuff-dunk at the end of his junior year at UNC, the dunk that made him famous, where he stole the ball at mid-court in the waning seconds of the game, flew in parallel to the hoop, and sent the ball home with a sideways tomahawk. And, yeah, it's a breakaway, but it's an exception. The announcer's call was simply, "Jordan…look at that!" Jordan threw the same dunk down against the Milwaukee Bucks during his rookie year, when he was averaging twenty-seven points a game and still below the radar.

These two were pretty fabulous, but for the number-one collegiate dunk we went with an upset—Phil Henderson's emphatic throw-down on Georgetown's Alonzo Mourning in the 1989 NCAA tournament. Duke was playing scared, seemingly intimidated by Mourning's enormous wingspan and scowl. The Hoyas were in a zone, funneling everything toward their young big man. Suddenly, from the right wing, Henderson, Duke's enigmatic swingman, slashed into the lane with two left-handed dribbles, coiled himself, and rose up directly on Mourning, who appeared shocked that Henderson would dare. Before Mourning could react, Henderson tomahawked a dunk directly over him, Henderson's right arm splitting Mourning's two arms like they were goalposts. For a moment, nobody else moved—just Henderson, who came back down to earth and bounced a little, apparently stunned by what he had done. Then Ferry and Laettner screamed, and Duke took over.

In the NBA, there had been plenty of pretenders to the throne. John Starks's throw-down on Jordan and Ho Grant in the 1993 NBA Playoffs was up there, as were Kevin Johnson's dunks over Hakeem Olajuwon and others—what was Kevin Johnson thinking? Jordan had his own wing in the archives, but the dunk that did it for my dad and me belonged, almost inevitably, to Doc.

EXPATRIATE GAMES

Julius was on the break during a 1983 NBA regular season game against the Lakers, which the Sixers eventually won in four games. His 'fro was contained and regal. His socks were pulled high. His countenance was calm but severe. He was loping like a big cat down the left hash-mark, long strides chewing up the Forum pine, dribbling with his enormous right hand. Between him and the basket, the Lakers' Michael Cooper, defender extraordinaire and off-season high-jumper, left the gates of Troy and streaked into Julius's path. Cooper timed his steps with the Doc. The crowd murmured.

Still out beyond the three-point arc, Doc cut slightly toward the middle, cuffing the ball against his right wrist and swinging it like a sickle across his body, accelerating his natural momentum. He was too far out, we thought; he couldn't get to the rim without traveling. Doc took off. Coop went up as well, his arm extended. Without either slowing or acknowledging Cooper, Doc swung the ball back and around, smooth, smooooth. Cooper's shoulder blocked Doc's head. Their bodies crashed together, and above it all, Doc's long smooth arm with the ball still cuffed. The moon. The rock. Down it came—*Blam-lam*. When the teams met again in that year's Finals, it was over before it started.

Dejda

I 'D BEEN TALKING to Bob Bailey at the American Cultural Center about Jason Kidd when a girl with blond hair falling in ringlets over her scarf interrupted to ask whether we knew where to find a swimming pool. She smiled in a way that made her seem sort of like a wild animal, the sort of animal for whom showing teeth is both a sign of aggression and of vulnerability. Her name was Dejda Chandlerova, a name that sounded like a meteorological event. Di-E-da Supernova. She said she was half-Czech, working in a biochemistry lab at Charles University for some unspecified length of time, living in an apartment owned by her aunt, and eating dinners with her *babicka*. She had hips like the run of a luge course. I'd asked her if she could get a dinner on her own, which sounded in my head much suaver than it likely sounded out loud, where it came out as, "Could you help me order a pizza?"

She said yes.

We met under the statue of Jan Hus in Old Town Square and went to a subterranean pizza place called Kmotra, where I'd had a bad experience on a previous trip by confusing the meanings of the Czech words *cesnek* (garlic) and *zeli* (sauerkraut). Dejda took a while to start talking. I got a beer and she got orange soda, ordering in staggering Czech. Our pizza came and had green beans on it. She laughed through her nose and said she'd meant to get mushrooms. She switched to beer and we talked about where we were from and what we hoped to get out of the time abroad. I told her about Vinohrady and the CEU. She said she'd heard that there might be a pool at the Hotel Olšanka. I said I'd heard there might be a school there. A couple of times, she smiled so wide that I thought she might have multiple rows of teeth, like a shark. At the end of the evening, I said I'd ask about the pool. We made a plan to reconvene a few days later under the ornate awnings of the Obecní Dům, but when the time came she didn't show. I waited for half an hour before trudging back to the madhouse of the Hotel Olšanka, whose pool, I'd learned, was closed until spring, and would then be off-limits to students. Over the next couple of days, I checked the front desk, unsuccessfully, for messages.

We beat Sparta B by the score of 100–41 in our third scrimmage. Sparta B was the *Přebor* version of *Superliga* champs Sparta A, whose pennant had hung in Jan Wiener's café, and their players were tall but very young. Poli and Ludek Pelikan pushed them around, and even though Tomas struggled with his shot, Robert Vyklicky broke out of what he swore was just a preseason slump and dropped in several threes in the loose second half. Kratcha tried to go behind his back on a breakaway and threw the ball into the stands.

Afterward, Bob, Slava, Tomas, Radek, and I went out for *burcak*, a cloudy Czech wine that was available only during certain weeks in the fall. The Czechs showed *burcak* a healthy respect, as its sweet, fruit-juice taste masked the high alcohol content. Slava waved it off and switched to rum. The *burcak* was stronger still on an empty stomach after a basketball game. We were at a *hospoda* called U Sudu, and I was quickly too drunk to wonder what it meant, although it sounded a little like an indictment. The September evening was warm, and the crowd had spilled out across the sidewalk.

After two rounds of *burcak*, the pub ran out of its stock. Apparently, *burcak* was not mass-produced. The rarity added to its allure, patrons trying to drink as much of it as they could before it vanished again for another year. When the pub staff announced the end of the *burcak*, mini-revolts spread across the sidewalk. Bob suggested we head to "a real Czech pub" for a beer. I nodded and followed them down the cobblestones. Bob led the way, quickly and without much talk, to a bar called The Konvikt Klub, on Konviktska, behind the old Prague prison. There were bars on the window and the wait-staff wore striped shirts. Bob got a table in the corner and ordered three *tmave pivo*. The beers arrived quickly; they were dark and sweet and malty. Radek ordered himself *palacinky* and a dish described on the menu as "bloody headcheese with onions and vinegar."

Radek was the informal historian of Vinohrady. Over his plate of headcheese, he told me about our teammates. Slava, who we'd lost somewhere along the way, used to play in the *Superliga*. At twenty-one he had been one of the best guards in what was then Czechoslovakia, but that was seven years ago. According to Radek, Slava's descent from the heights of the *Superliga* began in 1987, when he started frequenting a student disco on the outskirts of Prague called Club 011.

That, Bob interjected, was "the start of the end of Slava."

Radek himself was one of those hustling players destined to be a coach. He finished his beer in three long sips, and his bald head glistened like a turtle egg. On Vinohrady, Radek didn't get to play much, as there were four guards ahead of him on the depth chart. Still, he was the last player to leave the gym after practice, having run a series of wind sprints and tapping the backboard twenty times consecutively.

Radek told me that he had a 65-centimeter vertical leap. I had no idea what that meant. Even if I'd been sober, the conversion would have been tricky. Radek said Charles Barkley had a 120-centimeter vertical leap, something he seemed to expect me to know.

Bob said that, because of his ankle problems, his vertical leap was only 60 centimeters. That still sounded quite high, I told him, but he frowned into his beer. Sometimes, he said, he wondered why he kept playing at all when Barkley could do such wondrous things. I reminded him that Barkley was not in the *Přebor*, and asked him about the play at Spravna Mira where I drove and dished to him for a layup that he shoveled in while being fouled. He shook his head, uncomprehendingly. After games, he said, he could never remember individual plays. That sounded weird, and a little wonderful. Sometimes I thought I could remember, in detail, nearly every significant play I'd made since middle school. They only got better.

· · ·

THE NEXT MORNING, October started, bright and unsympathetic. Summer was distinctly over, its legacy a slightly sickly tang of *burcak*. Autumn blazed in through the window at the Hotel Olšanka. Somehow, after the initial struggle to obtain a room, the school seemed to have forgotten I was there; it had let me stay where I was, and had not yet charged me any rent. Yellow and orange leaves drifted down from Národní Památnik na Žižkov, the national Žižkov monument. Atop it, an enormous statue of a warrior on horseback looked westward over the city.

According to my guidebook, the warrior overlooking the Hotel Olšanka was Jan Žižka, a Czech general who fought against the occupying armies of the Prussian King Sigmund in the fifteenth century. With Žižka at the helm, the Czech armies held their own against the Prussians; when he fell, the Czechs were routed. This seemed worth checking out. I got dressed and made my way through the narrow streets of Žižkov until I found a path that led up a green hill. The monument at the top was a lonely, quiet place with a museum and wide manicured boulevards. A small old groundskeeper urged me to be careful on the grounds. Beware of gypsies, he said.

Honors thesis topic notwithstanding, I'd been sort of blissfully, if embarrassingly, incurious about the little nation to which I'd moved. I'd read Kundera and Hrabal and Havel, but you could read those guys pretty easily without understanding them, and most of my available mind space felt devoted instead to a kind of pandering self-analysis. Maybe it was just a mid-twenties thing, or an expat thing, but I began to suspect that I was suffering from a sort of psychotic self-involvement. My college English lit professor liked to quote the writer Mary McCarthy as saying "We are each the heroes of our own stories." But my story was starting to seem a little myopic. I resolved to try and actually engage my surroundings, or at least appreciate them, and be able to say something insightful about Prague when the time came, inevitably, to leave it. The CEU's library might have been a work in progress, but it was strong in the "oppression of locals" department.

Accordingly, much of Czech history, and of Central Europe in general, seemed like it could be condensed to a struggle, initially literal, now more postmodern, against occupying forces. The first autonomous Czech kingdom, ruled by the Premyslid dynasty, appeared in 870 AD, when the early Premyslid Princess Libuse founded Prague in the crook of the Vltava. St. Wenceslas, for whom Prague's main "*Vaclavske Namesti*" was named, was a Premyslid. Czech autonomy continued in various forms until 1620, when the region fell under Prussian and Austro-Hungarian hegemony. From 1620 until 1918, the region had, according to Radek, "a German king." In 1918, Tomas Garrigue Masaryk became the first democratically elected Czech president, running on the Commandment-like platform slogan of "Do not lie and do not steal." Masaryk ruled until 1935, when, on the cusp of World War II, Edward Benes succeeded him. In the Benes election, the pro-Nazi Sudeten German Party, which held power in a wide swath of land along the Czech-German border, made significant gains. Benes fled the country in 1938, and a year later, German troops marched into Prague. The German-Soviet Nonaggression Pact ensured that no cavalry was coming for the Czechs. In Great Britain, Neville Chamberlain uttered his infamous apologia: Czechoslovakia was a far-off land, of which the wider world knew little.

In London, a Czech provisional government established itself despite a lukewarm welcome from the Allies, who, to the extent they cared about the Czechs at all, suspected them as collaborators. The provisional government deployed insurgents, dropping them into the countryside via parachutes to assassinate the tyrannical German *Reichsprotektor*, the Butcher of Prague, Reinhard Heydrich, then tried and failed to recall the order. When the assassination succeeded despite itself—a gun jammed, a grenade failed to detonate properly, and Heydrich died from septicemia caused when horsehair from the seat of his automobile was propelled by the grenade into his buttocks—Hitler responded by razing the suburban Czech towns of Lidice and Lezaky to the ground.

In 1945, Prague cheered the arrival of Soviet troops and Communism, a reception that quickly became less rapturous. Tomas Masaryk's son, Jan, was an early political resister of the Communists, until he was found dead in 1948 in the courtyard of his apartment building, several stories beneath his open window. His defenestration was called a suicide until a third investigation concluded differently during the Prague Spring of 1968.

After practices, Radek and Bob seemed reluctant to share anything more than their guarded, general impressions of the socioeconomic changes of the past five years. Both of them seemed to harbor a greater resentment toward the country's historic German oppressors than the more-recent Russian ones. Or maybe that was just how far they were willing to go with me. Three hundred years, they said, was too long to be under foreign rule. They felt that the 1945 eviction of three million Germans from the Sudetenland was a little justified payback, reclaiming the land for the Czechs. Bob said he was only a baby when Jan Palach set himself on fire at the top of Wenceslas Square as the Soviets crushed the Prague Spring, and that Palach must have been a madman.

I told Bob about a concert I went to on my second trip to Prague. A band called Laura I Jezi Tigri had played in a cavernous concert hall called the Belmondo Revival Club beneath the Palace of Culture in Prague 8. Bob said he went to graduation ceremonies there in 1987, before spending two years in the army and then one more as a policeman in downtown Prague. He worried about the Yugoslav mobs moving into the city. Watch out for the cabbies, he said.

Classes finally started at CEU, and the school's promise—and challenge—began to show. With students from so many different homelands, many of which were still in the thick of political transition or trying to survive the economic fallout, class discussions were intense. Two Serbs and one Bosnian hung on reports of fighting in the Balkans. A Hungarian named Csaba and Yevgeni, the Siberian madman, got into a shouting match over World War II capitulation. Janko, the Montenegran, smiled at everything but kept largely to himself. Irakli and Levan, two wiry Georgian soldiers with sunken eyes, smoked hand-rolled cigarettes and smiled when they said they'd never killed anyone.

. . .

EXPATRIATE GAMES

The FIRST HALF of the season was set to start on Monday, October 10, with a home game against a team called Praga. We had eleven games before Christmas, and Radek had given me a rundown of the top teams in our division. The USK B squad was the team to beat, he said. USK A had won the *Superliga* the previous year, and the B squad was made up of the players either just past their prime or not quite there yet. Kosire was the other *Přebor* powerhouse; we played Kosire at their place in our second game. Radek said they were great, but showed me a box score from a scrimmage they had with Motol in which Motol took them to four overtimes before losing. How good could they be, then? We had whipped Motol in a scrimmage. We didn't play Technicka Strojni, the third team of consequence in our division, until late November.

I bet Radek and Bob that we would finish either first or second in the *Přebor*. The bet was for a case of beer called "*Velkopopovicky Kozel.*" It had a picture of a goat on its brown bottles. They took the bet, shaking their heads, as if I had a lot to learn.

· · ·

To KICK OFF the semester, the International Relations department organized a trip to Cesky Krumlov, a small castle town and UNESCO World Heritage site in the southwest corner of the country, thirty kilometers from Austria and about twice that from Germany. On the bus ride down, my classmates discussed current politics in the region. Austria had just held its parliamentary elections, and the right-wing Freedom Party had captured 23 percent of the vote on a platform of xenophobic nationalism. The leader of the Freedom Party, Jorg Haider, was repeatedly described in the international press as "telegenic."

Lubica, a Slovak woman, hoped that the election results in Austria would take the focus off of her own country's second reelection of its president, Vladimir Mečiar. Mečiar was sort of the Central European version of Don King, an ex-boxer with a criminal record whose party's parliamentary strength was drawn largely from alliances with the local Communist sympathizers. Lubica said her name meant "beloved" in Slovak; Kristina Sug'ar said it meant "mistress" in Slovenian. Cesky Krumlov glittered in between bends of the river with the well-preserved lifelessness I remembered from home. It was stunning, with a rambling castle hanging above a picturesque town, but it seemed abandoned to the tourists. Perhaps it was the wrong time of day.

After we returned from Cesky Krumlov, I sat in my room preparing to read the assignments we'd been given for our first week of classes. The assignments were essays and news articles we photocopied and passed out among ourselves. We still hadn't really seen any of our teachers. I sat at the table in my room and ate Swiss wafer cookies, dozing off, and then the phone rang.

Prior to this, the in-room telephones had seemed largely decorative: They didn't let you dial out, and you could only take a call that had first come in to the reception desk, and then, if you were fortunate, had been accurately routed to your room. In the month I'd been in Prague, my phone had rung about three times, and each of those times had been after I'd gone downstairs, called my parents, asked them to call back, spoken at length to the Hotel's "administration" desk, and then run upstairs to take the return call.

I picked up the receiver. It was Dejda Chandlerova. She wanted to know if I was free to meet for a beer at an expat bar called Jama, on a small side street called V Jame off of Wenceslas Square. Was that possible?

It was possible. I'd gone there the week before with Cameron and Lindsey, and we'd spent the evening debating whether Cameron was nearsighted or shortsighted.

I said sure, and forgot all about my reading assignments. How had she gotten the number?

An hour later, I was still waiting for her at the bar, and she hadn't shown up again. I began to think about what Vitas Gerulaitis said after he finally beat John McEnroe after sixteen consecutive losses: "Nobody beats Vitas Gerulaitis seventeen times in a row."

Then she walked in. The bar was crowded, but men moved out of her way. Her hair was pulled back into a ponytail, and her long neck was wrapped in a blue scarf. She stood at the top step near the door, looked across the room, and broke into a smile when she saw me. She had a big smile, the kind that she could use as both sword and shield. She apologized for being late. I shrugged it off and ordered her a beer. We fidgeted. I heard about her week dyeing DNA strands. She seemed like a serious person. She heard about my week doing laundry in the sink. There was a long pause.

"We were supposed to have another meeting, you know," she said finally, smiling and reddening a little bit, like she was going to get candid. "After the last one. Did you just forget?"

What?

"What?"

"After the pizza," she said. "We made plans to meet again. You weren't there." She looked a little angry.

"I was there," I said. "Where were you?"

"At the Horse?"

The statue of Prince Wenceslas on horseback looking over Wenceslas Square? It was where we'd met the first time, and nowhere near the Obecní Dům, which was where we'd arranged to meet the second time. She hadn't stood me up—she'd thought I stood her up. And because I was such a badass, she'd called anyway.

We cleared it up, chuckling at the misunderstanding. I sipped my beer and tried to act cool. We spun in our stools and grinned.

Red-faced tourists pushed in around us, shouted for drinks, and counted out coins in their palms. One of them—a fat frat boy wearing a Gamecocks hat—grabbed me by the shoulders and shouted, "What are you doing here, man?"

Darryl Dawkins said he was from Lovetron, and that his name was Zandhokan, the Mad Dunker. I tilted my head toward Dejda and said, "We're newlyweds from Phoenix."

Dejda grinned. "We're honeymooning," she said.

"Woo-hoo!" said the frat boy, and ordered shots of Becherovka, a thick, sweet Czech digestif. Dejda rolled her eyes at me and smiled her big smile again. We had a secret. The liquor was cold and minerally. She put her hand on my knee to steady herself and left it there.

. . .

PRAGA CANCELED ON Monday, and at practice Honsa gave me a note reiterating the requests he had made at the Spravna Mira scrimmage: Shoot less and run the offense. It ended with, "I hope, you understand me." I nodded to him, and he grinned, relieved.

Marek, another power forward, came over and said he had brought me a woman named Eva who wanted to learn English. I wasn't sure how to react. *A woman named Eva* sounded like the sort of gift a man should want to get. Marek pointed to the stands and there she was, a pretty, teenaged girl wearing red lipstick and a frilly white blouse.

"You have some place for her?" Marek asked. "She can come to your place?"

Marek beckoned Eva down to the court and she shook my hand. She smiled a crooked smile and blushed. We arranged to meet on a Tuesday night at the Hotel Olšanka. She smiled at me again and said "Thank you."

EXPATRIATE GAMES

We scrimmaged all practice. Tonda was blocking Ludek Pelikan's shot and pushing him around on offense. Ludek got so mad after another Tonda jump hook went in that he whipped the ball against the basket stand and it ricocheted off and hit the trailing Radek squarely in the groin. Radek crumbled to the floor. Tonda and Ludek wrestled and while Poli was lining up a foul shot, Tomas snuck up behind him and pulled his shorts down. Practice ended. Mondy started rapping to Slava's Ice MC lyrics, and Bob told me that you could tell that Marek was stupid because he had a small dick.

The season was about to start.

Part Two:
No Sleep 'til Christmas

Game One

Radotin: October 17, 1994

Slava strained his groin in warm-ups, sliding into a defensive crouch too fast. Honsa huddled with him, assistant coach Radek hustling over to see if there was anything for an assistant coach to do. After a minute, Honsa put his hand to his forehead. Slava shrugged his sloping shoulders and limped to the scorer's bench, where he sat next to the woman manning the manual fliptop scoreboard. Ludek Pelikan didn't show up. Radotin had an older, slower team, made up of overweight ex–first division players and a couple of young hotshots, including one big guard with a modest blond afro and a goatee. They wore matching red tops and white shorts that hung to their knees. One of them was very big, six-nine or so; he hung out down low and threw up short hooks and dunks. The few fans in the stands watched him the way people watch bears at the zoo.

I started with Robert Vyklicky, Tonda, Bob, and Michal. Honsa paced the sidelines in a sweatsuit and a gray T-shirt. He had one of those magic-erase clipboards. Radotin's big man won the tip, but Michal elbowed in and snagged the ball. We were off.

Radotin started the game playing a zone, effectively negating the four plays I'd learned. We started fast nonetheless, zipping the ball around the perimeter, into the post, and back out. Tonda fed Bob for a pretty layup, and then another that Bob blew. Bob fed me for a three that whistled through; then, on a fast break, I kept the ball and cut into the lane for a floater. The bench cheered. Robert hit a three and a drive, but Radotin stayed with us behind the Giant and three other slightly smaller forwards who muscled in some ugly baskets.

Mondy came in and missed three consecutive threes but crashed the boards on each and blocked a shot to boot. I found Bob hanging out behind the zone and fed him for a two-footer, and then he got an eight-footer to drop as well. I faked a pass to Michal and drilled another three. They switched to a man-to-man to cool us off. The Goat picked me up at mid-court, but I shook him and got into the lane, froze someone with a fake, and put up a jumper over a tangle of arms. It went.

For a minute, it felt like we could be a formidable team and that my preseason confidence was well founded. But just as quickly, things began to sour. Robert Vyklicky started to complain because he hadn't touched the ball in two trips downcourt. On each trip, Michal had shot, and hit, but Robert started to gripe to me nonetheless.

"You have to pass the ball to me, Daveed," he said. "Pass to my side!"

The half ended with us up, 41–40. I had ten points on four-for-six shooting. I shouldn't have known what I had, but I did, and I could envision every shot individually, as well as several shots I didn't take but thought about. Robert told me again in the huddle that I needed to pass the ball quicker. Slava and Honsa, however, were complimentary as far as I could tell. Honsa, lost in a forest of translation, made erratic wide-eyed passing and shooting motions, before settling on, "Perfectni!"

Slava said, "Shoot more."

It occurred to me that maybe Slava was trying to get me in trouble with Robert Vyklicky, but he seemed genuine.

When the game started again, Radotin quickly went ahead on a layup, a low-post jumper, and three foul shots. The paint was clogged up with beefy Czech bodies and every shot drew a whistle. I drove and dished to Tonda, who shoveled in a layup. At the same moment, I heard a shout.

"Daveed!"

It was Robert, open at the three-point arc.

But what the hell? The big man got fed. We were scoring. What was the problem?

"You must pass me the ball!" he screamed as we headed downcourt. That, I thought, was a bit much. He'd gotten the ball plenty, and we were scoring. The game was tight. Stop bitching.

"Fucking relax, Robert," I screamed back, forgetting that *relax* might not be a word he knew. *Fuck* seemed pretty universal.

Mondy hit me for a three. Then Robert hit a three of his own. I stole the ball from the Goat, but he clobbered me on the break and the ref called a foul. Mondy powered in a rebound as he was fouled, and then powered in another. Our confidence was back through the roof. Tomas got one shot off before he was yanked for Michal; he avoided the customary low fives when he returned to the bench.

Radotin called time-out, and in the huddle Robert apologized to me. He seemed to mean it. It wasn't that he was a ball hog—he was just uncomfortable with derivation from the play, any play, but especially plays that called for him to get the ball.

After the time-out, Radotin climbed back into it at the foul line. Bob fouled out and their big men started killing Mondy and Michal down low. Robert began forcing up threes and missed four in a row. I hit a layup and a foul-line jumper. They kept feeding their giant for short hooks and jumpers and went up two. Then Robert was fouled on a drive, but he could only make one of two foul shots. We were down by one. We pressed the Goat and forced a turnover, and again Robert drove and got a whistle. Radotin called time to ice him. It worked, and he missed both.

We fouled the Radotin guard immediately. There were twenty-eight seconds left in the game and no shot clock. The Goat got one shot to fall, but we corralled the rebound on the second and called time-out, down by just a bucket.

Honsa was in full Doug Collins mode, slapping his clipboard in a proxy clap, and the team jumped off the bench to surround us. We gathered tightly together. In a hoarse voice, Honsa outlined a final play to tie the game. It seemed to be an original play—not one of the four we'd practiced. It sounded complicated. When he finished, everyone nodded. Then they looked at me, and it dawned on all of us that since I only spoke movie Czech, I had no idea what Honsa had just said. If he had said, "You can't handle the truth," I probably would have picked that up.

Honsa looked for Slava, hoping to sub him in for a possession, but Slava was across the court talking to Kratcha's pretty, redheaded girlfriend. The referee called us back out to the court.

Out of options, Honsa took me aside and pointed to Michal. "Daveed, you pass to him," he said, miming a chest-pass and pointing to the right side of the court. "Five seconds."

I nodded.

We inbounded the ball, and I dribbled at the top of the key for ten seconds or so as Michal wound his way along the baseline. The clock ticked down, and I considered taking my man to the hoop. He was back on his heels, off balance, but it was still a bad idea. If I missed, and even if I didn't, I'd probably be asked to leave. It wasn't the play Honsa called. Then Michal curled around a Tonda pick on the right side. His man was caught up behind Tonda, and I could see Michal's hands. I hit him with a chest-pass.

He slashed through the lane with long, slithering steps and looped a two-handed scoop shot over the Giant. It hung on the rim for a long second and dropped.

Michal leapt up in celebration, but Radotin came back fast. With two seconds left, the most assertive of their forwards put up a short jumper that bounced out, an awkward bounce along the baseline. I let the Goat get behind me and he grabbed the rebound; he was entirely behind the basket, nowhere to go. Michal had position on him, arms raised straight up, principle of verticality.

The Goat pumped twice and leapt sideways into him, shoveling a shot into Michal's chin. The whistle sounded an indictment. There was one second left. A tough call with a second left. The Vinohrady bench was furious. Bob had to be restrained by Tomas from confronting the referee. The Goat hit both foul shots, Robert missed from half-court at the buzzer, and we lost, 79–77.

I finished with seventeen on seven-for-ten shooting, but had gotten lost on that big bound. Bob got ten despite fouling out; Robert, for all his unhappiness, had sixteen, despite missing three free throws in the last minute. Tonda got a black eye from the Giant; Slava was nursing his groin. After each game, Honsa gave everyone a grade, from one to eight. I got a six. Robert got a six-plus. We were 0–1 and the two toughest games of the season, against Kosire away and USK B at home, were up next.

Slapy

WITH EVA ON my mind, I decided to revisit my brief and otherwise forgettable stint as an English teacher. Business Marek, my original (and only) student (as opposed to Basketball Marek, whose English was fine), had gotten me an occasional engagement teaching English to a group of Czech professionals at a monthly program run by a woman named Vera Palackova. I wasn't sure what possessed Business Marek to do that; it might have been that he thought it would help my teaching. Whatever the reason, seeking to heal the wounds left by the Radotin game, I left Prague to spend the weekend teaching English in Slapy, a small town thirty kilometers away, at a sprawling collective farm along the banks of the Vltava called the Hotel Ku-Ko.

I met a collection of other teachers at Hlavní Nádraží, the main station. To get to Slapy, we took a train south under the "Intelligentsia Bridge," a relic of the mid-'70s campaign to turn Prague's white collars blue. It was obvious that my qualifications to teach English were even thinner than my qualifications to play European basketball, but Marek said the money was good for a weekend's work. The *Přebor* was not a source of income, and I needed the cash.

There were sixty-five students in the program and nine lecturers. Over the course of three days we taught twenty lessons each, and at the end we were paid 4,000 crowns, or around $150. I was one of two American lecturers; the other was a fuzzy little guy from

North Carolina named Kelvin who spoke with a lisp. There were two dirty, charismatic Australians—Steve and Dominic—and a red-haired punk girl from Liverpool named Magdalena. It was an all-star lineup of accents.

One of the other tutors was an old bald Czech named Jerry, who was gregarious in inappropriate ways. He spoke like he'd learned his English in the locker room at a Soviet spy school. "Do you know the word 'poltroon,' Daveed?" he'd asked me when we met. Later: "What does it mean, 'a backwater'?" He made me nervous. Whenever he asked me anything, I would shrug.

Jerry would nod and smile. "Ahh," he'd say, like he'd found a rare coin or a shiny shell on the beach. "A colloquialism!"

I walked into a classroom on Sunday to find him shouting the word *tackle* over and over again. That was how you dealt with a problem in English, Jerry was telling his students. "Tackle! Tackle! Tackle!"

We ate lunch in a wood-paneled cafeteria. The Ku-Ko staff served us each a puck-shaped lump of translucent jelly, covered with onions. Someone said it was a sort of pork derivative that you spread on bread. Kelvin looked queasy. He leaned over to me and said, "My name isn't Kelvin. It's Kevin."

The weekend felt longer than it was. The students got fatigued and resorted to Czech more quickly, especially when they realized that some of the instructors couldn't understand it. The bar was open at both lunch and dinner, and the nights were long with gossip, songs, and the rumor of assignations. Come Sunday, everyone was ready to leave. For the last lesson, Vera supplied us with a terse lesson plan having to do with production processes, but told us that we were free to think of our own lessons instead. Magdalena and I played our class a tape of Elvis songs, and then discussed the lyrics. We killed twenty minutes explaining to Zdenek, a welder from České Budějovice, what it meant to be "Itching like a man on a fuzzy tree."

Our final meal was a *polevka* made from mushrooms and eggs. I resolved to go straight to Burger King when we got back to Prague and spend half my compensation on cheeseburgers and fries. As I got in the car for a ride back with Vera, Zdenek waved from the door of the hotel.

"Give you a nice trip," he called.

. . .

Kosire: October 26, 1994

Kosire played up in the hills outside of Prague near a pocket of housing developments. The developments all looked the same: thin, drab high-rise apartment buildings with yellowing grass in the squares between them. They were called *panelacs* and looked ready to collapse at any moment. I'd heard Skee lived in one of them, but nobody knew where.

Kosire had a bunch of older players, but they could shoot the lights out. The final score said we lost by five, but it felt like a hell of a lot more than that. I finished with thirteen points on six-for-ten shooting, not counting a forty-footer at the halftime buzzer that got waved off. Ludek Pelikan played like a monster, but Kosire hit everything they threw up.

Late in the game, I was pressuring their point guard, a barrel-chested thug with a weak handle, and he turned the ball over. I took it in for the layup. We'd been going back and forth all game, fouling each other, driving on each other, so he came right back and took a pass off a screen for a jumper. I'd seen that play already and got around the screen to swat his shot—*Tobe do oci!*—into Peli's hands, who shoveled the ball to Kratcha. On his follow-through, though, the point guard—Number Eight—swung his hand into my neck, on purpose, like a slap.

I didn't think much of it at the time—we had the ball, and I jumped out on the break. Number Eight had other ideas. When I leapt out, he lowered his shoulder into my chest, like a hockey cross-check. I hadn't seen it coming, and it was like running into a fire hydrant. I stumbled; Eight turned to run downcourt.

Motherfucker. My ribs ached. Plus, he had ruined my chance to get a layup, and points were how I was measuring my self-worth.

He had his back to me and I spent about a second considering my options—dialogue, appeal to the referees—before plowing my elbow and shoulder into his back. If I hadn't been so mad, I'd probably have thought better of it. He turned around as if to fight, but play was still progressing down the court, and I didn't really know what to say in Czech to convey the appropriate level of affront. After a second, he turned back around and kept running. So I cracked him again.

There was a break in the action, and we squared off. He said something in Czech that I didn't understand. I called him a motherfucker and then a punk. He appeared to understand me, and balled his fists. We began to shuffle toward each other, sort of fumbling into a fight. One of us pushed the other in the chest.

Big Bob appeared between us before I'd fully mentally committed to throwing a punch, and did it for me. Eight stumbled back and the other players jumped into a scrum of arms and jerseys. The referees rushed over and threw us out of the game. Bob stayed on the court. I walked to the bench, ejected and dejected, as my teammates shouted *Tobe do oci!* at Eight, who looked confused at what they were saying. It was probably a good thing, as I hadn't thrown a punch in anger in about twelve years, and I was pretty sure that the last one had been at my sister.

On the bench, Mondy cautioned me. "Daveed, don't fight him. He is—how you say?—crazy man. He has karate."

Shit. Just what I needed—to get my ass kicked in a foreign language. Still, some things could not be tolerated. With thirty seconds left, Kosire's other guard leveled Robert Vyklicky with a forearm to the throat. Benches cleared. There were more exchanges of epithets and more finger-pointing, but nobody fought. I came off the bench looking for Number Eight, but he was off to the side holding someone else. Slightly relieved, I helped Vykli up. Solidarity! I'd been in three shoving matches in the scrimmages and games so far, and I thought people were just picking on me because I was American, or because I was walking around with a giant chip on my shoulder, either of which might have been true. Still, the solidarity felt good, especially if it came with Robert. We still lost, 68–63.

. . .

I'D COME TO realize that I was an angry player—angry about not being better; angry as a defense to feeling inadequate. In a lot of ways, the anger had worked out pretty well for me, and I didn't feel too compelled to deal with it. But I found myself getting madder than usual during the games in Prague. I suspected that a lot of it was the same sort of defensiveness, magnified, and certainly everyone on the team was frustrated at the losses. The other aspect was the language: It was unbelievably hard not to be able to communicate fluently—with teammates, with referees, with the opposing team. It had occurred to me, early in the season, that the language barrier might give me *carte blanche* to talk trash without fear of embarrassment or retribution, as if I could say whatever I wanted to the guy guarding me and he wouldn't know what it was. I wasn't sure that that even counted as trash-talk, though. Was it talking trash to say things you fully intended not to be understood? And in any event, that might have worked if

I was Czech and the guy guarding me was American, but since things were the other way around, he understood most everything I said in English, and I understood none of his responses in Czech, which I suspected were far more witty and threatening than the tame "Can't guard me, chump" or "Fuck off, motherfucker" lines in my limited trash talk repertoire. Truth was, I was no good at talking trash in any language, and only considered doing it when I felt embarrassed or threatened, which, admittedly, was often. Maybe Jordan or Gary the Glove could talk trash as a way to gain a mental edge over an opponent, but doing it to get a mental edge over yourself seemed like a personal weakness. Say one thing right, I thought, and some of this anger might melt away. But get the pronunciation down ahead of time.

.   .   .

DEJDA AND I met up again, first at Jama and then to see the movie *Forrest Gump*, which had been dubbed and was showing at one of the many *kinos* downtown. The two beers at Jama to steady my nerves—So many teeth! Not to mention breasts!—seemed like a good idea at the time, but less so halfway through the film, when I was squeezed into the middle seat of the middle row of the theater, surrounded by sniffling Czechs. By the time Forrest started his shrimping business, the walls of my bladder felt stretched like a snare drum. There were about twenty people between me and any of the exits, so I screwed down in my seat and waited. I hoped Dejda might be mistaking my discomfort for sensitivity. Somebody may have died in the film, but it didn't feel like it was happening soon enough. By the time the credits finally rolled and people began to head for the exits, I was afraid to stand up, lest I upset the fragile hydraulics that were preventing me from wetting myself. Dejda, seeing me still in my seat, apparently moved, put her hand on my arm and tugged.

The *muzi* was crowded, and I had to fish in my pockets for the 2 crowns the attendant charged to use the urinal.

That turned out to be the easy pressure.

This was our second semiofficial date, and either I was going to kiss Dejda soon or we were going to become friends. Friends seemed more sensible but less interesting.

It was late. Dejda lived about two miles outside of the city center. We had to take a metro line to its distant end, and then she waited for a bus. There was no night tram back from Dejda's metro stop to the Hotel Olšanka, which meant that if I didn't get her to her bus by midnight I was stuck.

We rode the metro to Nádraži Holešovice, the smaller of Prague's two train stations, neither of which was generally inclined toward romance, even in daylight. I smelled soot and urine, and wasn't sure if it was the platform at Nádraži Holešovice or me. It had been a long movie.

A dozen or so people, normal, working-class Czechs by the looks of them, were milling around the terminal, waiting for the same late bus for which Dejda was waiting. I couldn't get the privacy I needed to make my move. We'd talked about the movie and everything else that I could think of, and finally waited in a painful, acute silence for the bus.

Fuck it. Time to bust out the new Central European self. I was going for it. She had sheathed her teeth and was blushing. I felt warm and congested. I started a little speech, which was going to end with some combination of a lean-in, hand-to-waist move. When I was younger—but not that much younger—I was so unclear on the whole kissing mechanics that on my first attempt, I leaned in toward my girl and, as our heads started to come together, put my hand right on her forehead, right there, like I was going to exorcise her. There had been no second attempt.

I'd barely started my little speech when Dejda interrupted.

"That's my bus," she said, as a creaking, leaning vehicle rolled up. Shit.

"Uh," I said, "is that your bus?"

"Yeah," she said.

Damn it! I looked at my shoes.

"Um, well . . ." I stammered, confirming the wisdom to put off law school.

I could feel Dejda waiting there in front of me. Strangers jostled around us. My balls seemed to retract into my abdomen. After a moment, Dejda shrugged.

"I better get on it."

The driver beeped the doors to let Dejda know he was about to close them, and she leapt up onto the steps. From the doorway, she yelled back to me. "Call me before the weekend," she said, and it sounded like an ultimatum.

The doors closed and the bus moved slowly away from the curb, like a big old animal. I checked my watch. It was 12:10. The metro had shut down. I picked up my ego and headed for the stairs.

·   ·   ·

OCTOBER 28 WAS a national holiday in the Czech Republic, commemorating the formation of an independent Czechoslovak state under the Masaryk (*père*) presidency in 1918. The holiday was not heavily observed in 1994, not in the formal style of the Communists or in any high national style, perhaps in part because the state it commemorated no longer existed, Czechoslovakia having split into the Czech Republic and Slovakia in 1993's Velvet Divorce. Shops were closed, but there were no large rallies and no long speeches.

October 28 was also my birthday, and I punctuated the first early evening of my twenty-fourth year by kissing Dejda—finally!—at the foot of Václavské Náměsti. No speeches there either. She was a soft, generous kisser, and I fell into it without obsessing ahead of time, but it still felt a little like wearing a tie near a gearbox, like things could get out of control very fast. Unlike the holiday itself, we were heavily observed by passing tourists.

The kiss set the tone for a good weekend. It felt like being in the zone, that state of hoop bliss where every shot was falling. On Friday, Cameron and Lindsey organized an expat surprise dinner at Red Hot, followed by a late-night Halloween dance party in the Hotel Olšanka's cafeteria. Dejda brought strudel laced with nuts and cinnamon. Strudel-making seemed like something of a lost art, like falconing, but Dejda made a mean strudel.

On Saturday, a group of expats played football in Letna Park and went to a costume party at a cellar bar called The Knights of Malta. We'd been told that it was a cross-dressing party, and Cameron and I went dressed as women. It turned out, of course, not to have been a cross-dressing party. A bit of translation humor, I guess. I ended that second day of my twenty-fourth year by kissing Dejda again, at the foot of the castle steps. It was dark then, but we were lit by the gaslamps and I was dressed as a woman. People honked horns.

The problem with being in the zone was that you couldn't acknowledge it when it was happening. When you were in the zone on the court, it felt like the ball just couldn't stay in your hands, like the minute it got there it had to launch itself at the rim. When Sleepy Floyd tied a record by scoring twenty-five points in one quarter of an NBA playoff game, he didn't stop to think about it, because *he couldn't*. Afterward, when reporters asked him what had been going on, he didn't seem sure himself.

"The basket," he said. "It just looked so big."

. . .

Praga: October 31, 1994

I started to fall out of the zone on Sunday afternoon. Somewhat inevitably, the burgeoning relationship had complications. Dejda had a sort-of-boyfriend back at home, and he was supposed to come visit her for Christmas. She showed me pictures; in one, they were sitting on the nose of a sailboat, holding hands. They looked tan and happy. He looked like he was about six-two.

We decided to wing it, see how things went, even though it was already obvious how things were going to go. A damp gray chill set in on Sunday and we went to a one-ring gypsy circus where a thin hippo ate heads of lettuce and ignored us. A dusky woman twirled twenty-six hula hoops around her body at once and ignored us.

Monday came and everything I did, I did poorly. I was unprepared for my presentation on Spanish post-Franco economics. I missed my only two shots in Monday night's game against Praga, a game we should have won. Three minutes into the second half, Honsa yanked me in favor of Slava, who was shooting well and finished with about fifteen points. Pele got into a fight with their power forward, and later Bob clocked the same guy in the jaw with his elbow and drew an ejection. Overall, everyone but Slava played miserably.

Afterward, Honsa asked me what was up.

"*Ti jsi neni tadi*," he said. You are not here.

I shrugged and nodded.

"*Zeny?*" he asked.

What was *zeny*? Sauerkraut?

"Women?"

I nodded again and said "*No*," which felt like saying "yes and no," and wondered how many times over the course of history a woman had taken the fall for a man's dissatisfaction with himself.

I wasn't sure why I'd started moping around. Basketball and the Prague excursion seemed—suddenly, embarrassingly—to be emblematic of the same weaknesses I'd been masking as strengths for years. Defensive. Easily discouraged. When I was younger, if basketball began to conflict with other, more real human relationships, it had seemed an easy decision—and the right one—to curtail those real human relationships, especially if they were complicated. I'd lost my first girlfriend in eighth grade because I'd gone to play pickup games at Pitt Park instead of going to her house to sit in the dark and watch MTV. Inevitably, someone else sat next to her, and that was that.

Years later, I would come to understand how young twenty-four was, and more acutely, how young *I* was, but that night, after the Praga game, Halloween had come and gone and twenty-four felt overwhelmingly old. I counted off my woes: enrolled in an academic program of dubious legitimacy that seemed like it might fold at any minute, repeatedly deferring any tangible shot at a real career, and making out with a girl who had both a boyfriend and an expiration date. My birthday was a holiday for a country that no longer existed, my all-volunteer team was zero and three, and I'd been benched. Maybe if I got lucky, I could lose my passport, pick up some gonorrhea, and stumble onto a uranium-smuggling operation. Those all seemed plausible. I went back to my dark little room at the Hotel Olšanka, did my stupid push-ups, and waited for my jockstrap to finish soaking so I could drain the sink and brush my teeth.

• • •

EXPATRIATE GAMES

BACK AT HOME, the NBA season had begun, and all eyes were on Glenn "Big Dog" Robinson, Milwaukee's rookie small forward out of Purdue and number-one pick in the NBA draft, who had signed a ten-year, $70 million contract. Big Dog was something of an anomaly: a legitimate bigger small forward, almost a four but more athletic, with a silky jumpshot. He was like Glenn Rice with another three inches, the biggest thing to happen to Milwaukee basketball since Sir Sid Moncrief, Terry Cummings, and Paul Pressey retired.

I forgot about my self-pity when Dejda invited me to come with her and her aunt and uncle to their cabin in the mountains along the Polish border. Dejda's aunt and uncle didn't speak any English, at least not to me, so the ride up was long and fairly quiet. And long. Several hours after we left Prague, we arrived in the Krkonose, the ridge of peaks that separated the Czech Republic from Poland. Czech legend said that giants roamed the range and threw boulders at anyone who tried to invade Bohemia.

The cabin was small and spare and sat on a wooded hillside near several mostly dormant ski resorts. There was snow on the ground, but not enough to draw crowds yet. The cabin seemed to be a place of fond childhood memories for Dejda, and we walked in the woods along paths she forgot and then remembered with delight. After her parents divorced, she'd become an All-American tennis player at UC San Diego. The Czech came from her mother. She had a photo of her father on her desk.

Dejda's aunt Vera made dinner: fish fried in butter and spaghetti with ketchup. Dejda and I ate what we could and then left to walk along the dark town road. It led to an empty ski resort. The night was unbelievably cold but Dejda didn't seem to feel it. I was worried about my fingers, and other appendages. The resort's bar was open and serving a handful of locals. We drank thimbles of Schnapps and *slivovice* until the cigarette smoke got too heavy.

We slid back to the cabin, where Dejda's aunt and uncle showed me to a tiny room at the end of a hall. Dejda was lodging somewhere closer to them. I had to take my shoes off and leave them downstairs; I had a hole in my sock. Each room had a woodstove, the only sources of heat in the cabin. Dejda's aunt and uncle left me to fall asleep and I tried to stoke my stove with small squares of wood from a bucket near the door. The stove would have been just the right size if I was toasting marshmallows for s'mores, but it was a little minimal as a survival aid. The bed was small and the duvet was stingy; when I pulled it up to my neck it came off my feet. The windows were single-paned, I hadn't brought long underwear. Outside the cone of heat provided by the fireplace, the air was so cold it seemed to shimmer. It was the kind of cold that made your lips thick and your loins ambivalent. I began to lose feeling in my unprotected toe. I tried to see my breath in the dark. It was there, for sure.

Then the door creaked and a set of teeth flashed in the room.

"Shhh," Dejda said, sliding under the duvet and pulling it toward her so that the far edge crept up over my backside. Her hands were cold, but everything else was soft and warm, almost threateningly so, and for a second as she pressed against me, I imagined how the rest of the s'more might view the marshmallow, and I wondered whether I was really ready for whatever was coming next. I entertained a moment's thought that maybe it wasn't her at all—maybe it was a ghost, or a stranger, or maybe I was just imagining it—a hypothermia-induced hallucination.

I started to speak, to say something dope, like a mack daddy, about how down with sex I might be. Anything, really, to make the whole thing feel artificial, and therefore less scary. But she cut me off. "Don't make any noise," she said, her wet voice somewhere near my shoulder blade. "You'll get us in trouble."

Her hands were icicles on my T-shirt, and then they were beneath it, and then our tops were off and I stopped worrying about macking, or hypothermia, or anything else.

. . .

USK B: November 3, 1994

Back in Prague and we lost again, and this time to USK B, the other really good team in our division. We played fairly well, though, and Lukas Krysl—Tomas's younger brother—scored a bundle, displaying an offensive assertiveness that bordered on gunning. I did some gunning of my own, and wound up with twelve points on about five-for-nineteen shooting.

Gunners had a negative connotation, in that it implied an excessive spraying of shots. But putting the ball in the basket was the name of the game, and there was plenty of room within the offensive pantheon for variations. Someone who shot frequently, and rashly, and with little success, was a *gunner*. Gunners ignored their teammates, and thus rarely lasted long in any organized context. But teams needed offensive firepower—can't score if you don't shoot, after all—so players inclined to gun had to refine their games and develop roles within which they could still indulge their need to let it rain. My high school coach had a formula he'd apply to determine if someone was gunning: If your point total was equal to or greater than the number of shots you attempted, you were okay. It was a formula weighted heavily in favor of the scorer, since if you took enough threes and got fouled on enough jump shots, you didn't have to shoot a very high percentage to remain in the black. In fact, it was hard to be considered a gunner under this formula, which was why we all loved it so much.

Shooters were not necessarily gunners because they could shoot well. Often, shooters occupied the role of specialists on organized teams; other players got the rebounds, delivered the passes, set things up. Shooters, everyone knew, saved their energy, floated around, and picked their spots like snipers. Scott Wedman was a shooter. So were Steve Alford and Dell Curry and John Paxson and Craig Hodges and Dale Ellis, although Dale Ellis was no stranger to the gun.

Scorers—who were not necessarily as gifted at shooting as shooters—occasionally had to resort to gunning. But scorers usually had their own advantages: They were able to create their own shots, something that shooters were neither inclined nor encouraged to do. John Starks was a scorer who'd been called a gunner; Danny Ainge—that chump—was a shooter. Reggie Miller was a shooter who, since he also had to be a scorer, was inclined to gun. Jordan, the classic scorer, had worked hard to become a shooter, and it showed in his 1992 Finals first-half barrage against a hapless Clyde the Glide Drexler and the Blazers.

Poor Clyde the Glide. He was a scorer who couldn't really score all that well, playing the wrong position in the wrong era. He had a small-forward's body and game—he had a B version of Julius's ABA power forward game, without the ferocity—but was stuck at off-guard. His production and his frequent-flyer mileage helped him maintain his fan base, but the rest of the league seemed to be asking him "What can you do?" He wasn't a shooter, but he could take and make the occasional three. He wasn't a ball-handler, and got exploited by the true dribblers like Isiah and Joe Dumars. He wasn't a jump-shooter, his flat trajectory finding the front of the rim more often than not. In the 1992 Finals, the media set it up as Jordan versus Drexler, and you just knew Clyde the Glide was in for it. You sensed that he knew it, too. Jordan was such a dominant and superior player, and such a megalomaniac, that he was going to use the Finals to show any doubters that there were no showdowns with him. Before Game One, the announcers had been talking about how evenly matched Jordan and Drexler were; that would have been enough for Jordan's blast-furnace competitiveness right there, but then they went on to talk about how Drexler might have been a slightly superior three-point shooter.

Jordan responded by hitting six threes in the first half of the first game, capping off the display with that backpedaling, smirking shrug. I worshipped Jordan, but he could be a prick sometimes.

Playing in front of people who'd been promised a showdown, Clyde kept his mouth shut, got schooled, and tried to do what he could, which was dunk on Stacey King three or four times a game. For his part, after the first twenty-four minutes, Jordan seemed to hold back a little. He'd already vanquished the old guard, Isiah and Magic, and there wasn't much point in getting worked up about Clyde. By then Jordan had begun his "killing them softly" campaign anyway, befriending his opponents off the court and cutting their hearts out on it. He repeated the trick against Barkley the next year, and later against the hapless Karl Malone, effectively taking on and out the five players who could occasionally suggest a challenge to his dominance.

Glide remained in limbo after those Finals, not to emerge until the Dream Team games in the Summer Olympics the following July. There, on a fast break, he got a pass—from Jordan, fittingly—and took off from about the three-point line, a la Julius, to throw down a monster cuff-dunk. As the team celebrated, Clyde jumped out of his crouch to celebrate, as if to say, "Oh yeah, that's what I can do." As if he could stop trying to be Jordan, and just be Clyde. Clyde could do things, too.

The Flat

FAST DAVE TOOK me to a vegetarian restaurant outside of downtown run by the Czech branch of the Hare Krishnas. It was a small branch. The food was good, if a little bland, and you only paid what you felt you could afford. The management didn't speak much English, which kept the proselytizing to a minimum. We got zucchini pizzas and thin soup. As Fast Dave was paying, I ran into Renee, one of the girls from Seattle I'd met at the American Cultural Center. Her roommate had bailed out of their adventure and gone home, leaving Renee with nobody to share her rent on a third-floor apartment in Prague 3. Did I know anyone looking to move?

I was still at the Hotel Olšanka despite the "one night" limitation I'd gotten on my first day there. I'd passed Dragan in the hallways and we'd smile; the administration seemed to have lost track of us among the other students staying there. The hotel still wasn't open to the public, and many of the rooms not occupied by CEU students were empty. Still, I suspected that my accommodations weren't sustainable. Tuition didn't cover any room or board, but the administration was so behind that nobody had asked me for rent yet. (Or, for that matter, tuition, either.) One Student Affairs coordinator had mentioned that at some point she'd give me a bill for the month and a half I'd been staying there, but then she'd quit and moved back to Scotland.

Renee's apartment had two large rooms, one of which was split in half by a partition that reached two-thirds of the way to the ceiling and two-thirds of the way to the far wall. Renee's idea was to use one room as a living room and the other as a bedroom, with beds on either side of the partition.

We tried that for one night. It was awkward. I could hear her breathing, and then snoring. I could imagine she could hear me, too. I bet she could smell all the smells I was making. I felt bad about reading in bed. She had to be able to see the light. Was it keeping her up? Was she wondering what I was reading? Did she want to borrow my Skvorecky novels?

I wondered, almost immediately, what would happen if I ever brought Dejda to the flat. I was still hoping for that, and fell into a fitful sleep, complete with its own awkwardness.

In the morning, we decided to convert the living room into a bedroom. It was slightly bigger than the other side of the apartment, but we each denied a preference. Renee won the flip for it.

It worked out fine for me. I converted one side of the partition into an office, with a desk for my laptop and a bookcase for the privatization reading I hadn't done, and pushed two flat single beds together on the other side to make a hard double bed. The bathroom was on my side, separated from the bedroom by a glass-paneled door. The small closet-kitchen was on Renee's side. Each of us had a bank of double-paned windows that looked down on a tree-lined street called Biskupcova.

Renee did something vague and businesslike for an accounting firm downtown. Her coworkers were mainly Czech men, and Renee's vulnerability, combined with the prevailing attitudes among her younger native coworkers, was battering her self-esteem. She seemed to be considering a dalliance with one of them, a kid who styled himself as a new-wave gangster and bragged about carrying a gun. He was rude and chauvinistic, but she was lonely and bored, so she put up with it. She'd initially resisted the apartment partitioning, but seemed glad to have some company. We went to a student bar across the street and shopped for dark bread and mandarins at a tiny neighborhood *potraviny* on the corner. The apartment didn't have a television or a phone, but there was a phone booth around the corner near the tram stop. Rent was about half of what they'd said rooms would cost at the Hotel Olšanka. I began to sleep well.

. . .

Kbely: November 10, 1994

Dopravný Podnik: November 18, 1994

We were now 0–6 and hoping for a win before Christmas.

We'd lost to Dopravný Podnik and Kbely, a team from the Prosek section of Prague, a housing estate north of downtown. In both games, we jumped out to fast starts and took leads, only to fall utterly apart. Fat men were getting fast-break layups on us four or five times a game. Ludek Pelikan was playing hard, but nobody else was helping, and nobody else was happy. Robert Vyklicky wanted to have a dialogue with me. He had asked, after loss six, "Daveed, can I have a dialogue with you?"

We were supposed to talk before practice on Friday. He'd promised to explain to me how to play within the team. I was thinking I might try to kick his ass.

I was still struggling to fit in with the team. Honsa asked me if I liked playing with Vinohrady. He thought my funk was a sign that I was unhappy with the team. I couldn't explain to him the truth—that I was still feeling a little lost and lame and was focusing those feelings on my inability to make a left-handed layup. The new Central European identity I'd imagined for myself now seemed incredibly naive. I was behind in my studies and first-term final exams were a week away. I couldn't seem to remember the things I needed to remember—like the history of the European Coal and Steel Community and the year Stalin died—because the available mind space was taken up by things like John Stockton's assists-to-turnover ratio and the best way to get Dejda to bring me back to that cottage in the mountains on the Polish border.

Perhaps not coincidentally, things with Dejda were going well. I had told myself that, despite the complications, this adventure needed a leading lady—that everything looked better with a romance. We were in Prague at the same time, for a limited time. We might as well hook up. It would be a shame to let common sense get in the way of a foreign affair, to let responsibility and foresight screw up the potential for short-term impulse gratification. Shit, if I was going to do that, I wouldn't have come to Prague in the first place.

As December rolled in, she began staying at my place more and more often. I got my stove to work and bought lemons and chocolate from the market across the street to ward off scurvy. We decorated a thin Christmas tree in a corner of the study. Dejda's grandmother had us over for dinner, and made pork and two kinds of dumplings. Dejda told me that, as part of a long-standing plan, her "former boyfriend" was coming to Prague on the 24th, and she wasn't looking forward to it—(then call him and tell him to stay home!)—but asked if I wanted to do an early holiday thing before then.

And because I'm a sucker, because she used the word *former*, I said sure.

Worse

Motol: November 23, 1994

Technika Strojni: December 2, 1994

We'd lost our first eight games, notwithstanding Slava going seven for eight from the international three-point line in the last game. To me, it was the international three-point line. To him, it was the only line. No surprise he was hitting. We lost anyway, to Technika A, the team of engineering students I'd felt so confident about beating at the beginning of the season. The league had banned Big Bob Javurek indefinitely for berating a referee after the USK B game. Tonda broke his ankle against Motol. Kratcha had broken a bone in his leg and was out for a month.

After practice I went out with Bob to U Vystrelenyho Oka—a pub whose name meant "At the Shot-Out Eye"—and drank *tmave pivo* and ate slices of dark Czech bread from a basket on the table. Dejda's old boyfriend was going to be the Grinch that stole Christmas, and even though they'd made their plans long before I met her, and even though she told me about him right at the beginning, it still sucked. I was sure, no matter how many side streets I took, no matter how hard I tried to avoid the bridge and the astronomical clock and the pink sunsets where the tourist battalions encamped, that I would run into them.

Bob was a bachelor. He drank half of his Radegast in one swallow. "After training," he said, pointing to his beer, "Is best, I think."

I nodded as he ordered two more.

"I think, your *holka*," he said, "your girl?"

"*No*," I nodded. "Girl" was the right word for *holka*. Bob was working hard on his English.

"She needs some kicking."

I nodded again. We drank more beer. Czech beer took some getting used to, at least in volume. Soon I was telling Bob about a scuba course I'd taken during my freshman year of college. Two hundred dollars and a midwinter dive in a frozen lake on Cape Cod that ended with a wet-suit rash that literally came between me and the first girl I'd worked up the nerve to try to sleep with. At the time I hadn't known it was a wet-suit rash and lost my mind, thinking it was some sort of preemptive sexual plague. I'd made an appointment to go to the infirmary but had to wait a week to get in. God and I got really tight that week.

When my appointment day finally arrived, the nurse was decidedly underwhelmed by my polka-dotted skin and said it was likely just something called rosacea. You could get it from laundry detergent. "Unless," she said, looking doubtful but also like someone who didn't want to miss an opportunity to turn the screws on a freshman, "it's syphilis."

Not only had I not had sex, but at that moment it seemed pretty definite that I never would. And I never used the scuba certification, either, which expired quietly, the most pristine laminated card in my wallet, with my clueless freshman face in the corner.

I told Bob all of that. There seemed to be parallels.

Bob didn't say anything. He just looked at me, deep in concentration. He either understood all too well, or didn't understand at all.

Later, we stumbled out of the pub and I walked Bob back toward his apartment. We walked along Vinohradská, dribbling Bob's practice ball on the uneven cobblestones. We passed the silent open square of Náměstí Míru and the Chapel of unlucky St. Ludmila, patron saint of Bohemia and converts, strangled by assassins hired by her daughter-in-law in 921. My pockets were full of slices of bread, and I offered one to Bob. He declined. When Christmas came, he said, he and Honsa and Radek would have a big carp dinner at his house and go to a disco.

"Which disco?" I asked.

He shrugged. "I am not a disco-boy."

We walked to the tram stop at Jiřího z Poděbrad, and Bob crossed the street and headed toward Marešová. Halfway across, he stopped and called out to me. "Daveed, bring your girl to Meteor," he said, raising his hand like we were in solidarity. Meteor was our next home opponent. "I will kick her for you."

Chvalkovicka

HONSA HAD SAID that the team would meet at the Českomoravská metro station at 7:00 P.M. I checked my watch. It was 7:08 P.M. I looked around the gritty concrete platform but didn't recognize anyone else. I'd missed them.

I didn't know where they'd gone. Českomoravská was both a metro station and a bus terminal, from which a dozen Soviet-era buses choked off into the city's outer rings of *panelacs*. My teammates had gotten on one of them, but I had no idea which one. Jesus. I'd even forgotten the name of the team we were supposed to play that night.

These sorts of things kept happening to me. How was I ever going to become an adult if I let them continue? Just last week, I'd nearly missed the game at Motol and had to sprint through a darkened *panelac*, listening for the sound of a ball on hardwood. It was clear that Honsa was growing tired of the schtick. If I had been throwing in twenty-five a game, he might not have cared. But I wasn't. I wasn't doing much of anything on the court, lately, other than throwing the ball away and taking ill-advised sorties down the lane.

I needed to make it to the game.

The bus schedule posted on a wall had the names of the stops on it. I studied one, hoping that some name would trigger a memory of the opponent. A bus had left for a place called Horní Počernice at 7:00 P.M., and another was due to leave at 7:20 P.M. Hadn't we already played them? Kbely was also on the list. Hadn't we just played them too? I'd chuckled at the name Kbely, safe in my apartment with Dejda. Kbely! Then they beat us.

I wondered what Dejda was doing now, and with whom.

Focus. Who was our opponent tonight? I had no idea. There were two different buses. And even if I got on the right bus, and made it to the right stop, I didn't know where the gym was. The gym could have been somewhere else entirely. Motol, for example, played its games in Petriny, not in the area called Motol on the map. I was sure it all made sense to the Czechs.

The bus to Horní Počernice rolled up to the platform and the doors shrugged open.

Shit shit shit.

I hopped on and immediately regretted it. The doors closed much faster than they opened, and with more conviction, and the bus lurched out of the station, onto a cobblestoned drive, and then onto a main road. At every stop, I stuck my head out of the open doors to read the name on the bus post. I put my glasses on and flipped my hood up. I held my sneakers by the laces like they were *nunchakas*.

The bus was nearly empty, and the few people on board appeared weak and sickly. In the overhead lights, their eyes shone yellow. We rolled past smokestacks and industrial parks. Through a crack in a window I caught a fleeting glimpse of a highway sign that appeared to say "Warsaw."

Warsaw? Fuck.

This was a mistake. It was 7:30 P.M. already, the Horní Počernice stop was still six stops away, and who knew how far the gym was from there? Miles? We seemed to have left Prague entirely and begun cruising some industrial netherworld on the way to Poland or Slovakia or somewhere. We passed desolate oil-stained bus stops with names like Hloubětín and Lehovec. They sounded like allergy medications. The other bus passengers were starting to look less weak and more rabid. They were starting to notice me.

I felt in my pocket for change and decided to get off the bus before we got too far away from the city. I had about 60 crowns for a cab; who knew how far that would get me? The bus chugged up to its next stop, a meager island on the side of a highway. It was dark out and the bus doors opened reluctantly. Nobody else got off. I hesitated for a second, and then just as the doors were closing, leapt out onto the highway, landing on the island next to Mondy, Honsa, Robert Vyklicky, Kratcha, and Ludek Pelikan.

"Daveed," they yelled in unison, raising their arms like goalposts.

The game wasn't at Horní Počernice after all, but at Chvalkovicka.

Who was our opponent? Horní Počernice.

We arrived at the gym at Chvalkovicka, which was at the end of a long road into the woods somewhere outside of Prague central and marked by a Christmas tree in front of a canteen-like side building. The tree was lit with red and blue lights and tasseled with stars. It sat in the quiet Czech woods, familiar and out of place.

Although we led 33–31 at the half, Horní outscored us by twenty-four in the second half behind a great young guard—the best player I'd yet seen in Prague, a slasher with the sort of innate anticipation that was hard, if not impossible, to teach someone— and an older, wider shooter who tossed in long, wobbling threes. I was still figuring out the structural differences of the Czech game: the way the sides of the trapezoidal foul lane angled away from the free-throw shooter, the math involved because the clocks counted up to twenty minutes rather than down to zero each half (how much time, for example, did we have when we had nineteen minutes and forty-six seconds on the clock)? But against Horní, I banged in a series of jumpers and a reverse for seventeen points, and Ludek Pelikan threw down a one-handed dunk on a fast break. It wasn't enough, though, as Slava and Vykli went cold early and stayed there. Toward the end of the first half, their center threw down a legitimate two-handed jam on Slava.

In the second half, we seemed to be going through the motions, and nobody got upset when we fell behind. Vykli and I had a silent rivalry that wasn't doing either of us any good, and I knew that I had to care more about defense and passing if I wanted to help the team. And I did. The novelty of the adventure had worn off, and it no longer felt like just making a team in Prague. The sheer oddity of it, meant anything. We were better than our record. I worried that I was becoming the Vinohrady equivalent of Vernon Maxwell.

Most of the guys had left the locker room when Honsa sat down next to me. Honsa's English was second only to Tomas's on the team.

"We are bad," he said.

Kratcha, one of the few players left, nodded. "It's sad."

Tomas Polisensky gave Kratcha and I a ride back to the Florenc metro stop. We went to the McDonald's and bought cheeseburgers and *hranolky* at 20 crowns a pop.

"We are so bad." Kratcha said, his mouth full. "It's sad." He laughed at his couplet, and then repeated it.

We walked along the sidewalk toward the metro. Christmas was only a couple of weeks away and carp, the staple of the Czech holiday meal, were churning in blue buckets on street corners. Shoppers would point to the carp they wanted, and the fishmongers would scoop the chosen fish up in a net, smack it on the head with a mallet, and wrap it in paper. I'd heard that you could also take the carp home alive and let it swim in your bathtub, if you had one, until Christmas. I didn't know how they managed that.

Prague hadn't seen more than a provisional dusting of snow. My parents were flying over for the holidays. They'd seemed skeptical about what I'd been telling them about the team, and the bread, and language lessons at the Shot-Out Eye. I hadn't even mentioned the spot on Charles Bridge that the Dalai Lama called the center of the universe, or how a man stood near it and sold chalky portraits of himself as the devil, complete with horns and forked tongue and spiked tail. He charged outrageous sums for his portraits, and it was hard to believe he sold any. Why so much? I asked him once, and he said he had a dolphin at home to care for.

Dejda and I decided to do our Christmas thing on the eleventh, when we both had some time to hang out. We met in the Old Town Square, watched the sun set early behind the astronomical clock tower, turning the sky around it pink and gold, and we grinned too much and kissed too much and generally acted young. Later, when we exchanged gifts beneath the tree, I got a coffee mug and she got a pair of red mittens. We drank weak Czech champagne called *sekt* out of the mug, and she wore the mittens when we hit the hard mattresses of my makeshift double.

She left early the next morning to get to work, and I fell back asleep and dreamed that I was on the old *Captain America* television show. The original Captain America had been a modest-sized white guy, but in the dream they had cast Magic Johnson in the title role. Magic jumped onto the back of a speeding train to save the woman within, and although he was wearing the Captain America costume, it hadn't been tailored to fit him, so his wrists were sticking out of the sleeves and the pant legs were high on his ankles, almost to the knee, and his head didn't quite fit into the hood with the little silver wings. And whenever he had a line to say he would just smile his Magic Johnson smile and say, "Man, I'm Captain America Man."

. . .

POLI AND KRATCHA were laughing when they came into the locker room for practice. Kratcha was still wearing a soft cast on the lower half of his leg and swinging on crutches. Outside the door, Mondy was French-kissing a short blond girl in fishnet stockings. Tomas's long-distance girlfriend, Martina, had dumped him, but he seemed to be taking it well, and had two dates later that week. Poli's cheeks were redder than usual and Kratcha's shoulders were dusted with the first real snow of the year.

Kratcha sat down across the locker room from me. "Daveed," he said, "do you like for rim-jobs?"

He was holding a small, thin book with a bright cover. It was called *Wang Dang American Slang*, and the subtitle promised that it was full of the hip words and phrases used by American youth. Kratcha handed it to me proudly. He'd been studying. *At last*, he seemed to be thinking, *we will be understanding of each other*.

I looked through *Wang Dang American Slang*, which seemed to be written by un-hip non-Americans whose primary source materials were Beach Boys lyrics and pornography. The chapter on sex was predictably the most extensive. Kratcha tilted his head in the direction of Mondy and his short girlfriend.

"She is a Bahama-mama, yes?" he asked, cupping his hands to a pair of imaginary breasts. "With knockers? Bazooms?"

It was hard to convince Poli and Kratcha that even un-hip American youths didn't call girls "Bahama-mamas" and nobody called breasts either "knockers" or "bazooms," unless they were sidekicks in plays about greasers. As for "rim-jobs," I felt like I was losing clout by disclosing that I wasn't even sure what they were, much less whether or not I liked them.

Vanoce

Pankrác: December 16, 1994

Pankrác came to Vinohrady for the last game of 1994 and the second-to-last game of the first half of the season. Demonstrating the recuperative powers of *Wang Dang American Slang* (or perhaps of rim-jobs), Kratcha had recovered from his broken leg. It must have been some sort of hairline fracture or bone spur, because he'd only been out of his cast a couple of days. Before the Pankrác game, the team unveiled a new pre-game slogan, replacing the relatively ineffective, "Together, We Jump!" The new one, which better embodied many of our feelings about the first half of the season, roughly translated as, "Go to my ass, ass, ass!"

Slava, Vykli, Poli, Michal, and Ludek Pelikan started. Pankrác's only threat was a rough small forward with a flowing blond mullet. We started out quickly as Peli dominated down low and Michal launched his slithery attacks at the basket, but the Mullet hit a three and jumped out for a couple of ball-pounding breakaway layups. He seemed like an angry man.

Honsa sent me in with Kratcha and Mondy to press. Pankrác's guards couldn't dribble, and we pressured them out of bounds. I got two quick layups off of turnovers and a three-point play. Mondy leapt out on the break and I hit him in stride for a power layup. Peli took a pass in the block, pivoted, faked, and drew the foul as his soft hook dropped through. We ended the half on an eight-zero run and led by four. I had eight and three assists.

During halftime, I looked up and saw Dejda at the top of the stands, near the exit. She was wearing her sheepskin coat and had her scarf tight around her neck. It was the first game she'd attended. As I watched she looked around the stands unhappily. She was sitting by herself. There were only about ten other people there. I caught her eye and she smiled and waved. Her ex-boyfriend came in three days.

I started the second half with Vykli and got a couple of quick buckets, but the fat older man I was guarding got by me and took a pass for a two-footer. I didn't feel distracted, but a minute later he did it again. I played eight minutes and then Slava came back in. I looked for Dejda, but she was gone.

Pankrác took a small lead. We were down five, poised for what was becoming a familiar collapse, but Slava and Peli were still playing hard, diving for loose balls. With two and a half minutes left, Pankrác's lead had grown to eight, Dejda was long gone, and we were looking at a winless Christmas. Honsa sat down between Jena and me and rested his head on my shoulder. He smiled like he was an expansion coach.

Honsa's youth team filtered into the gym and gathered behind our bench. They'd brought cowbells and small tin drums. They started to cheer, because they were little and didn't know any better.

Peli took a Vykli miss off the rim and put it back with a man hanging on his arm. The whistle blew; the bucket counted.

Honsa leapt up with a cheer so loud that it startled everyone. His youth team picked up on it and started to bang their drums. The sound of cowbells filled the gym. Peli hit the foul shot and the Pankrác lead was five. We pressed and Pankrác turned the ball over. Slava collected it and hit Vykli with a pass for a layup.

Honsa was stalking up and down the sideline now, shouting.

We kept the press on and Mondy tied up Mullet in the corner for a jump ball. Mullet was furious. He wanted a foul call but the referees wouldn't give it to him. We tried to goad the ref into tee-ing him up, but the ref ignored us. Off the jump ball, Slava stripped their guard and fed Peli for another two. The lead was down to one point, and on the sidelines we were all standing up.

Pankrác inbounded the ball and Vykli fouled their power forward immediately. The power forward was a heavy man with a swollen stomach. He was breathing heavily and missed the first foul shot when Jena, usually the quietest among us, screamed from the bench just as he let the ball go. He hit the second when Jena, employing reverse psychology, stayed silent.

There were six seconds left and we were down by two as Vykli raced down the left wing and got trapped. He had a bad habit of taking the ball into the corners when he was pressured and then picking up his dribble. Two Pankrác players were all over him and he looked for Slava, who was trailing the play as fast as he could. Vykli threw a weak pass as the seconds ticked away; Mullet raced in for the steal, but the referee blew his whistle.

A foul!

Pankrác was over the limit and Vykli went to the line for two shots.

They tried to ice him with a time-out. He looked a bit shaky in the huddle, and Honsa took him aside for a second. Nobody mentioned the Radotin game, when he missed those three big foul shots. The buzzer sounded. Vykli walked out alone.

He hit the first, despite the screams of the Pankrác bench. They looked down at us as if they were challenging us to a fight. Jena and I got on our knees and held hands. With his goatee, oval glasses, and close-cropped hair, Jena looked like a leftist, very antiestablishment, and it felt good to have him there on the floor, 100 percent vested.

Robert lined up the second shot and, in the quiet gym, hit it. He shook his fist and gave the Pánkrac bench a defiant look. We were tied with six seconds left.

We put on the press again, but this time the Mullet slipped behind it and the power forward, taking the ball out of bounds, threw a baseball pass in his direction.

Holy shit. Mullet was open. He was going to get a layup. On the bench, we all screamed and pointed. It was going to happen again. But at the last second, up stepped big Peli.

Ludek had been patrolling the back side of our press. He threw himself awkwardly skyward, like his namesake, and picked off the pass. In midair, he shoveled the ball to Slava, who was a step over half-court. Slava caught the ball, took a dribble, and launched a one-handed heave that arced up toward the rafters and hung there for a moment like a satellite before dropping resolutely down through the rim.

The buzzer sounded.

We'd won.

Everyone exploded, running onto the court, jumping on Slava. Peli picked up Vykli. Honsa gasped and panted, and Bob, still suspended, grabbed a loose ball and dunked. We stayed on the floor for five minutes, jumping and cheering, before heading down the tunnel stairs toward the locker room. Kratcha and Tonda raced to the pub, bypassing showers. Mondy cabbage-patched down the hallway. Honsa and Tomas and I hugged, even though Tomas and I had been on the bench for the decisive rally. I took that as a good sign. I wished that Dejda had stayed to see the personal growth.

There was an inch of snow on the ground outside. Christmas—*Vánoce*—was right around the corner, and under the holiday lights at the corner *potraviny*, the carp still churned, oblivious and content in their big plastic tubs.

Basketball was over until January 4.

· · ·

I HAD A week of no basketball and no school before my parents arrived. Dejda was off doing whatever she was doing, and I felt on the edge of a bout of dangerous self-reflection. That could be painful. My friend D.B. came over from England and we decided to split for an obligatory trip to Auschwitz. D.B. was the smartest person I knew. We'd met in college at Oxford, where he'd been slumming with American JYA students as a form of street cred. He had a mind seemingly unclouded by doubt and irrationality. He might not have always been right, but he always sounded right. Of course, the accent helped.

Auschwitz, as one might imagine, was not a fun trip. The best way to do it was to catch the night train to Krakow, get a nice room at one of the hotels, and wander the Rynek Glowny—the largest municipal square in Europe—then have potato pancakes at the Hungarian restaurant Balaton, go to Wawel Castle, and maybe stop by the Jagiellonian University, and then, when you're appropriately fortified and optimistic about the state of humanity, take a bus the extra two hours to the invisible town of Oswiecim, outside of which loom the haunted barracks and gas chambers and ovens of the sprawling Auschwitz-Birkenau complex.

Auschwitz presented something of a challenge for a twenty-four-year-old American Gentile. I understood the Holocaust as a sort of abstract historical atrocity. Standing under the ARBEIT MACHT FREI gate or walking under the gallows and into the ovens—I wasn't sure what to do with that. It seemed too much, so overwhelming as to be, in person, underwhelming. There were things my mind wouldn't really process: the long glass cases filled with hair; the luggage; the photos and pulled teeth and piles and piles and piles of things. Some people I'd seen on my first visit had just talked the whole way through, about the accommodations in Poland, and the bus trip, and the lack of an appropriate gift shop.

D.B. and I changed trains at the Polish border and got stuck in a smoky compartment with several Polish miners, including one named Christian who gave us brown bottles of Polish beer. D.B. wasn't much of a drinker. We tried to beg off by claiming we didn't have bottle openers, but Christian opened the bottles by linking their caps together and pulling them quickly apart. This caused beer to fly across the compartment and bubble out of the bottle-necks, each of which Christian immediately put to his lips.

Christian was pretty clearly the leader of the group, and he wanted badly to talk. We didn't want him or his friends to get frustrated. Every fifteen minutes he tried to engage us in German, even though we'd already used all our Czech and English words and hand gestures to explain that we didn't speak German. It seemed like a test, like Christian was inclined to kick German ass and wanted to smoke us out.

Christian was sitting very close to me, and his friends were smoking droopy hand-rolled cigarettes in the compartment doorway. There were about four of them. It wasn't exactly threatening, but it was the middle of the night and we were on a train somewhere in southern Poland; we were at a disadvantage. When Christian offered us another beer, it felt more like a command.

"We are good friends!" he said, repeatedly. "Everyone else, fucking off!"

He asked to see my passport and without thinking, I handed it to him. His friends started passing it around. It occurred to me that I would never get my passport back, and that I would instead be beaten senseless, and soon a heavy, bleary man with a thick accent would be using my passport to get through security in Newark. D.B. picked up on this possibility before I did. He was smarter.

Christian clapped me around the shoulders.

"Everyone else, fucking off!"

D.B. made a pretense of pointing out some secret aspect of my passport, and once he had it in hand, pocketed it boldly and gave me a disapproving look. We sat in silence with the Poles, hoping that our grins might suggest nonthreatening drunkenness, and then the conductor came through. We had pulled into Katowice. Time to change for Krakow.

We spent the next hour on the platform at Katowice, waiting for the connector. Katowice was a small southern Polish city that was apparently very nice in the daylight. The train platform was less nice at midnight. There was a soda vending machine at one end of the platform, and we partook of the spiritual powers of Coca-Cola, one of the more tangible reminders of home, even though the Coke sold in Central Europe was produced in Spain. Having a Coke on the train platform in the middle of the night in Poland felt like having a whiskey before a duel.

We arrived in Krakow the next morning and got a room in the massive Hotel Polonia, where we were apparently the only guests, and the barren lobbies and comatose staff made the place feel spooky. It had long, empty, red-carpeted hallways that looked like they might suddenly funnel a wave of blood toward us, like in *The Shining*. The heater in our room whistled and scalded.

Krakow itself was beautiful. The ring road around the Old City was lined with hotels of increasing civic convictions; they were massive edifices with names like the Warszawski, the Polonia, the Evropa. Inside the ring road, a tree-lined circle called the Planty Gardens had replaced the old city wall. Rynek Glowny, the main square, was full of flower vendors and the Sukiennice market at the square's center was lined with amber baubles and intricate chess-boards. Wawel Castle overlooked the dark, soft Wisla River and the outer, more-modern city. Every hour on the hour, speakers along the Rynek played a long unfurling trumpet call that stopped abruptly in the middle. It was the Trumpeter of Krakow, who'd been stationed on the city walls to warn of the advance of the armies of the Huns, and who'd taken an arrow through the throat halfway through his warning.

We ate pizza and drank cold Zywiec at a student hangout called New York Pie, and went to the castle, where in the lower passageways there was a shrine to the fifteen thousand Poles massacred in the Katyn forests by their Soviet counterparts. We walked around the Rynek, listened to a disco play Cranberries songs, and heard the Trumpeter of Krakow get cut short again. On the second day, we took the bus out to Auschwitz, with its haunted gates and gray pond. It was both overwhelming and underwhelming, again.

• • •

I RETURNED TO Prague feeling restless. D.B. headed home to England, where he was a lawyer. His departure, coupled with the weight of our Auschwitz visit, made me feel like I should perhaps return to the real world, go to law school, start a career. Get beyond this silly stuff and become an adult. I swung by school, but the Hotel Olšanka was empty, except for a handful of students who couldn't go back to their home countries for the holidays. Fresh from Poland, I briefly compared hardships with them: They faced dangers from war and ethnic cleansing, the potential for conscription, or crushing expense. I had ennui, and my parents were coming.

I got out of the Hotel Olšanka.

To distract myself, I wandered around the pre-Christmas city, wondering where Dejda was, if I should try to reach her. I wondered if she was still with her ex-boyfriend, still walking around the city. I wondered if the NBA All-Star voting was finished, and if so, where Latrell Sprewell finished. Before I knew it, I was in Staroměstské

Náměstí, the Old Town Square, where Dejda and I had grinned too much back on the eleventh. The Square was decorated with tinsel, fir trees, and a plywood-walled nativity scene on a bed of pine needles. People were drinking mulled wine and watching the afternoon sun fall in the sky, just like it did on the eleventh. It got dark around four P.M., and the Square was outlined by the glow of the snow on the cobblestones. Crowds gathered to watch the Clock Tower's hourly parade of saints and skeletons.

I headed back along one of the side alleys that led to the trams. Under an arch near the edge of the Square, I walked by a couple wrapped in an embrace. The man's back was to me. The woman's golden hair fell across his shoulder, and her hands curled around his waist. She was wearing a pair of bright red mittens. Hey, I thought for one wonderful second, what a coincidence.

D.B. said that he'd never really gone in for romance because his friends had suffered all their worst moments, and enjoyed only some of their best moments, because of it. He was a smart man.

· · ·

IN THE EARLY 1990s the Dalai Lama came to Prague for an official visit with Václav Havel, whose political star was then at its apex, and was walking along the Charles Bridge with his host. They stopped near the statue commemorating the martyrdom of St. John of Nepomuk. A plaque on the statue showed the scene: the priest in a burlap sack, tossed over the side, doomed for refusing to tell King Wenceslas what the queen said in confession. His watery death made him a hero, a patron against calumnies, and a protector from floods. A thousand hands had touched the falling priest's small bronze image for luck. It stood out from the rest of the plaque, which remained darkened with soot. According to the story, the Dalai Lama had announced that the spot was the center of the entire universe. Or maybe it was just one of them. I wasn't sure how Buddhism worked.

My mother, father, and sister arrived in Prague for the holidays. All week, downtown Prague had been preparing for the holiday festivities; in addition to the blue vats of carp on every corner, people had been lighting firecrackers and sparklers and singing holiday songs. In the alleyways, old men were selling impressive selections of fireworks made in China and Germany. Street kids and gypsies threw lit firecrackers at the feet of tourists. It seemed like a dangerous pastime given the number of private security guards stationed outside Himi's Jeans and the downtown banks, some of whom carried big guns and looked thin on both training and restraint.

I had booked my parents into a room at the Hotel Közel, which was located in the basement of my apartment building and run by the same family who managed our flat. I'd been down there once or twice to drop off the rent and it had looked clean and quiet. I thought that the proximity would maximize our time together.

My mother surveyed the place and announced, "I think they rent these rooms by the hour." She was turning fifty on New Year's Eve. It was a big deal that they'd come.

On Christmas Eve, we had dinner at a Yugoslavian restaurant called Dolly Bell. The decor was sort of "upside-down chic," which had to be some sort of metaphor for Yugoslavia itself. The ceiling had tables and chairs nailed to it; if you leaned back and looked up, you could imagine that you were floating above an empty restaurant beneath you.

We ordered a bottle of inexpensive *sekt* with our meals. It didn't have many bubbles, and we weren't sure if it was supposed to. My dad pointed this out to the waiter. "*Ne bublinki*," he said, making up what he thought might be the right Czech words for "no bubbles." We'd already had a few drinks at the historic Slavia bar on the way over, and my dad thought *Ne bublinki* was the funniest thing he'd ever said. The waiter brought us another bottle. It didn't have many bubbles either.

We went from Dolly Bell to midnight mass in St. Vitus, within the castle walls high in Stare Mesto. It was cold, colder even than it had been that night in the Krkonoše, and the hairs in my nose froze together as we waited to get inside the church. Inside, it was only marginally warmer, despite the thousands of candles. The mass was in Czech, and went on for an hour. A row of Asian tourists in the pews ahead of us fell asleep. My mother kept asking me what they were saying, but the only word I could recognize was *Buh*, the Czech word for "God." By communion, my sister couldn't feel her toes.

In the morning, my mother came out of her room at the Hotel Közel and saw a professional-looking blonde in a black leather bustier escorting two balding men in business suits to a room down the hall. My dad came upstairs holding a copy of *The Prague Post* with the week's theater and opera choices circled and underlined. He wanted to see *Rusalka* on January second. We ate toast and clementines and omelettes.

On New Year's Eve, we made reservations at a restaurant on the Vltava called Parnas. I got a message on the CEU bulletin board from Dejda; she'd gone to Austria to drop off her friend, and was returning to Prague on a 7:30 P.M. train from Vienna. Would I meet her at the station?

Parnas served game and fish, and before dinner the waiter brought over three special Drambuie and Scotch cocktails. My sister asked for a Diet Coke and settled for water. My mother had been sanguine about the Hotel Közel, but we thought she deserved something more dignified for her birthday, so we moved them into a fancy place called "At the Three Swans," which was tucked off of the castle end of the Charles Bridge. We stopped there after dinner to relax before heading to the bridge for midnight. Because I was a sucker, I left them at the hotel to go get Dejda.

I'd been trying to avoid thinking about her kissing her ex. At the time, I'd felt like the unlucky carp, smacked on the head with a mallet. I'd stood there for a second, not sure what to do, and then walked away as fast as I could. What should a real man have done? Maybe walk up on them, maybe do a little tae kwon do on the guy and express his displeasure to Dejda in no uncertain terms. I probably should have done that. Instead, I'd walked until I was across the bridge, safely on the castle side, and then sat down and felt sick. The truth was, I didn't mind her kissing her ex all that much—there was a reason she hadn't asked me to meet him—but I didn't want it to intrude on the fragile fantasy I'd constructed about myself, a fantasy about growth and maturity and, ironically, truth. I could barely sustain that fantasy on the best of days, and seeing Dejda with her ex just made it harder.

I forgot what a sucker I was when she got off the train and walked across the platform. Her face was cloudy until she saw me, and then she lit up like a farolito.

I took her back to the Three Swans and we all went out to the bridge and waited for the fireworks. We made our way to the center of the universe, through crowds of tourists and locals and enough mini explosives to blow a hole in the city. My sister had two bottle rockets under her jacket and I had something called a "Grand Piano" stuffed in my waistband.

The bridge was packed with people lighting fireworks and spraying bottles of *sekt*. My fifty-year-old mother, although fortified with Drambuie and caviar, was too worried about one of us catching fire to fully enjoy herself. My fifty-year-old father didn't seem to be worried at all.

Nobody trusted their watches, but around midnight a collective shout went up and the sky filled with projectiles; some flaming, some made of glass. I took out the Grand Piano and we lit it down the bridge from St. John. It went off like a cross between a flame-thrower and a pan-flute and sent sparks showering out across the dark Vltava and its ghosts.

The Washington Bullets had traded for Chris Webber, and Jimmy Jackson of Dallas was still, surprisingly, the NBA's second-leading scorer. I was at the center of the universe, surrounded by smoke and snowflakes and the people I loved most. Vinohrady had won only once, on a forty-footer at the buzzer, and I was kissing a girl who, hours earlier, had been in a different country kissing a different guy. All the joys and fears and frustrations of the past months— indeed, everything I'd felt since I'd turned eighteen—seemed present, acute, with me, on that bridge. St. John kept his secrets and protected the faithful from floods, but even he couldn't do much against what I was feeling there, then.

Back to Normal

Meteor: January 5, 1995

We lost the last game of the first half of the season to Meteor, a team out of Prague 6 led by a fat, pug-nosed guard who, according to Bob, had fought with Mondy last season and nearly fought with Slava this time. We all showed the effects of the two weeks off. Slava fired air-balls. Vykli dribbled off his foot. Tonda looked shaggy and swollen. Mondy had an exam the next morning in computer science, and he was trying to study on the bench.

When I went in for Slava—I was officially not starting now—I fell all over myself trying to play defense. Then I got called for traveling, stole the ball back, and drove the lane, but someone grabbed my arm and dragged me down as I prepared to leap. No whistle. Plain sight, referee right there. No whistle.

All the good cheer from the holidays vanished and I played out of control for the rest of the half. The referee waved me off when I tried to say in Czech what I felt in English—that he was missing calls—and I had to resist the urge to punt the ball into the stands at every stoppage of play. Late in the game I blew a wide-open layup and finished two for six from the line for a total of four points.

My teammates were no happier, and drew a record five technicals from the thin referee, who looked a little panicked by the end of the game. The bench earned two of them: one when, after a fairly clean no-call on Peli, Tonda loudly instructed the referee to "Go to my dick."

Honsa and I caught a bus back downtown together.

"I am very young to coach this team," he said, sounding both proud and defeated.

I had a black eye from where I'd tripped on myself and fell onto the court.

Honsa said he would spend the weekend watching his girlfriend play in the first division. I suggested we draft her for our squad. Honsa didn't know what to do to win games; he suggested we practice more.

I didn't think that was it. I thought we just didn't know how to win. We were as good as anyone we'd played yet, and we'd been in every game, albeit sometimes briefly. Maybe if things had gone differently in that first game against Radotin—maybe if I had boxed that dude out—we might have had some confidence. We might not be one and ten now.

I asked Honsa if he liked coaching. He said yes; he liked coaching us, and loved coaching his youth team. They played better than we did, he said.

• • •

VERA PALACKOVA CALLED to see if I'd come back to Slapy. Apparently, the mere act of wearing a tie last time had endeared me to her. I met my ride, a Czech named Frank, at the Smichov train station at 7:00 A.M. on Friday. He was a few minutes late, and I wrestled with whether or not to ditch him and go home to bed. I didn't know if I could take another weekend at the Hotel Ku-Ko, with its hard cots and flabby, viscous pork dishes. But I needed the money, and I was still a little wary of letting Dejda off the hook, although going to Slapy seemed like it would be harder on me than her.

Once in Slapy, I headed straight for the breakfast buffet and its *rohliks* and *maslo*. My co-instructors had gotten in the night before, and were already finishing their meals. Jerry the crazy bigot was talking to a guy named Brett, with whom I'd be sharing a room, and a twenty-seven-year-old from Vermont named Mary. She said she was an interior designer in Prague, but business was slow. I said I was a basketball player. She didn't look like she believed me.

The Hotel Ku-Ko was dusted with snow, and the collective farm's rolling hills and lake looked a little like my New England hometown. I started to suspect that some of the students at Vera's language school were having affairs with one another. They had a perfect cover: three days a month for six months in a riverside hotel with nothing to do but drink and pretend to learn English from Americans who pretended to teach it.

At dinner that first night, I began to consider having an affair with Mary; she had great calves, long and tapering and formidable. They looked like aubergine. Mary was funny and seemed bored in ways that made me wish I'd gone to prep school. She had big dimples and a bob cut and was three years older than me. It made her seem like a challenge. After dinner we sat on the lobby couch and shared stories: She had been planning to marry a Czech guy but it fell apart. I told her about Dejda and her ex-boyfriend making out in the Square, about *Vision Quest* and basketball. I told her that she had great calves, like aubergine. She said, "I know."

The next night the students put on a performance for the instructors. The show consisted of a few impenetrable skits and a painful Rockette-style song medley. An agronomist named Humpl ran around with a pair of women's underwear pulled up over his blue jeans and lipstick kisses on either cheek. Frank the driver bought Brett three shots of the local brandy, after which Brett passed out. Vera told us that the brandy had become hard to get because the government had determined that it contained "more than trace amounts of arsenic." She made it sound like a delicacy. The barman who sold it to Frank had gray skin and maybe half of his teeth.

We worried briefly that Brett might be dead, but then he vomited onto his arm.

Mary had a long neck. She bought us shots of the brandy and grinned. We drank them and she borrowed 20 crowns and went back for more. I wanted to tell her that she should put the coins under her tongue, like they do to pay the ferryman who takes dead people across the River Styx, but it didn't make any sense when I tried to say it. "More than trace amounts of arsenic" seemed like an irresponsibly vague conclusion for the government to reach. I could feel the brandy leeching straight into my bloodstream, and I wondered whether Mary might be trying to kill me. She seemed like she could have been the type.

Some of the younger Czech students cornered us and asked questions about American politics and social life. I didn't know most of the answers. Was medicine socialized? How did the electoral college work? Mary said things that I think she was making up. Finally there was a lull and Mary squinted murderously at me and whispered, "Let's get out of here."

Here we go, I thought, but I went anyway.

We walked around the waterfront and then I was freezing as well as poisoned. Mary talked about winter in Vermont and I wondered how this was going to turn out, if I was going to die from the arsenic, or the cold, or if Mary and I were going to have sex in a lean-to. All three of those things seemed possible when you were a semipro basketball player in Prague. I gave her my gloves and she threw snow at me.

She said, "I think we should cut to the chase."

Any normal guy would have kissed her at that point—she was a blinking neon sign saying, "Kiss me." I did not kiss her, even when she pretended to slip in the snowy parking lot and dragged me down on top of her. I did nothing. I was a chump. I rolled onto my back and looked up at the swirling stars. My teeth were chattering like they had a message for me. They wouldn't stop. Mary didn't say anything. We lay there through a confused silence. I decided to wait it out, and closed my eyes. After a few minutes, she huffed impatiently and said, "I'm going in."

I heard her get up, shrug the snow from her shoulders, and walk, on her beautiful calves, back toward the lodge. I waited a few seconds and then staggered off to my room. Brett sprawled, snoring, across my cot. Pieces of that night's dinner floated in our sink. I leaned unsteadily against the small window and wondered the things that people wonder when they're far from home: Where am I in relation to where I've been? Have I seen these stars before? And would Lenny Bias *really* have been better than Jordan? Was that even possible?

After lunch the next day, Humpl agreed to give the instructors a ride back to the metro station at the old Czech castle at Vysehrad, on a cliff just south of the city. Humpl still had lipstick on his face, and said he needed to wash it off with "soup and water." After forty-five minutes of driving, he pulled into the parking lot of the metro station.

Mary gave me her phone number and said, "Call me sometime," before walking away on her killer calves.

Brett and I waved to Humpl, who rolled down his window as he drove off.

"It was Humpl!" he shouted. "Hello!"

• • •

EXPATRIATE GAMES

HONSA PASSED OUT stats for the first half of the season. They were amazingly thorough. Poli was our leading scorer through eleven games with 97 points. I led in minutes-per-point, scoring one point every 2.24 minutes I played. Slava and I had each played 209 minutes in total, behind Ludek Pelikan, Mondy, and Robert Vyklicky. We were averaging about 65 points a game, and had led or been within six at the half in seven contests, including the one game we won.

I got an average grade of 3.93 out of 8. It was the third-lowest grade on the team. Only Big Bob and Poli were lower, and Big Bob had been suspended for most of the first half of the season.

Robert Vyklicky wanted to play one-on-one. He was upset about the stats, I guessed, upset that I had a higher minute-per-point average, even though he led in all the stats that mattered. We played to five, and I won, 5–1. He was frustrated; he'd missed a couple of layups that would have closed the gap, and he thought I'd held him on defense. When I hit a short jumper off the glass to win it, I had to hold back the urge to celebrate. He grinned bitterly, and asked to play again.

Part Three:
Downhill from Here, and then May Day

"The motherfucking saga continues . . ."

—NWA

Wins

Praga: January 17, 1995

We started the second half of the season at Praga. Praga's home court was a gym located right downtown, hidden on the upper floors of a big office building on the long Zitna Street that ran diagonally from the Museum to Karlovo Náměstí. I'd walked past it a dozen times on the way to the lab where Dejda did her biology experiments, never suspecting that there was a court so close. Gyms on upper floors always seemed mysterious and indulgent, like someone with money was hiding little oases for the tenants. A gym! On the fourth floor! What else might there be? A zoo?

Praga was the team against whom I'd pulled a virtual no-show in the first game, playing little and scoring nothing. From what I could remember, they hadn't been any good. We had just fallen apart.

Dejda's mother had come to Prague for two weeks. They planned to go skiing in France, which sounded unbelievably lavish to me. It was one of the things Europeans probably took for granted—going to a different country all the time. If you lived in New York City, you might go skiing in Vermont, which is nice, but it isn't a different country with different money and a different language. You hadn't fought wars against it. I wondered if it felt cool to live on a border, and go to a different country for lunch.

After I'd gotten back from Slapy and gone to Burger King, I'd told Dejda that I'd seen her making out with her ex-boyfriend in the Old Town Square. She'd frowned and asked, "Which day?" That wasn't the response I was hoping for, but I'd already made peace with the situation, and I still had Mary's phone number. I gave Dejda some distance anyway, which was hard because she could act like a puppy when she was enthusiastic. And she seemed enthusiastic about us.

Praga only suited up five players for our game. We had ten, although Peli, Mondy, and Tomas were absent. Tomas seemed to have a lot going on. I'd seen him giving tours of the castle grounds to French tourists. He kept trying to improve my Czech, and when that led nowhere, he started trying to improve my French.

I started with a new, gangly center named Martin, along with Tonda, Michal, and Tomas's younger brother Lukas. Praga had one decent player, a lithe young forward who had nobody to run with or to get him the ball. Praga's other players were older and out of shape. We jumped on them quickly and I got an early foul-line jumper to fall, but they came back on some improbable threes and the forward's arching jump hooks over Tonda. They led 12 to 10 when we suddenly went on a run. I got six quick points in transition, and Tonda began to assert himself in the lane. I faked a pass to the wing, penetrated to the foul line, and pulled up for the jumper, but instead dropped a pass down to Martin, who scored. Slava came in for the last couple of minutes but did little. Vykli did less.

The second half was more of the same. We inaugurated a new 1-2-2 press that wore down Praga's only ball-handler. Kratcha came in and stole some passes. Slava heated up and hit three threes. Jena scored off a no-look pass and got fouled. I hit Martin with a behind-the-back pass for a layup, which he missed. Late in the half, I drove the right side, rose up over their forward, and dropped in a layup while getting hacked. We won going away, and I finished with fifteen and a bunch of assists, the team playing really well for the first time in weeks. We might have enough time to save the season, which continued in a week against Radotin at Vysehrad, the high castle on the cliffs south of downtown.

The second half of the academic year began as well. All of the students had made it back to the Hotel Olšanka from their respective holiday havens. They held a party in the conference room, lining a table with exotic bottles with Cyrillic and Magyar lettering, the liquors inside pink and green, syrupy or scarily clear. The only real clique that had seemed to develop during the first half of the year was among the Serbs. Bad things had happened and were continuing to happen throughout the Balkans, and the Serbs seemed to be connected, in one way or another, to many of them. At the party, they gathered together and sulked in a corner until someone put on a Yugo-rock cassette, and then they jumped up and danced.

· · ·

IT SNOWED AGAIN on Wednesday night, and in the park next to my apartment, nervous parents watched kids on sleds being chased by dogs. The dogs barked at me when I jogged past them. One chased after me, snapping at my legs. I kicked at him, just a little, to keep him from biting me, but he seemed to think that was a game and chased me all the way back to my apartment. At practice, Kratcha, Jena, Honsa, Bob, and I whipped the others in a scrimmage.

Afterward, we went to the Pod Smetanou. Slava was drinking rum and saying, "Fuck! Shit! Bitch!" over and over again, slinging the words together so that they were just one. "Fuckshitbitch!"

"*Ti vole*," I said to him.

"Fuckshitbitch," he said back. There was something on his mind.

Michal, Vinohrady's resident Slavologist, spoke to Slava in Czech. After a minute, he told us that through Slava's connections, the team had been invited to play in a tournament in the southeast of France after the regular season ended. We were supposed to play two games in Grenoble before arriving in some mountain town twenty kilometers from Albertville.

May in the Alps with Tonda. International semiprofessional basketball player. Representing Vinohrady on the European stage. Shit. Slava said it would cost everyone who wanted to go 2,000 crowns—or about $70—to cover transportation, lodging, entry fees, and food. I'd been to the American Express office earlier that day to change my monthly $100 traveler's check, and gave Slava the money on the spot.

"Fuckshitbitch," said Slava, pocketing the money, but now he was smiling.

• • •

DURING THAT FIRST summer after college, as I'd watched my friends move on toward futures that seemed infinitely more promising than my own, I developed this very specific fantasy of what it would look like when my life got going. In the fantasy, it was late at night, and I was up, sitting at a desk, holding my glasses in my hand like I'd just taken them off to make a point. The desk was covered with meaningful work—some virtually unsolvable problem that I could unravel only if I applied myself fully. A beautiful, uncomplicated woman slept in a nearby bed. The bedside alarm was set for 7:00 A.M. It was a detailed fantasy, and I was impressed that I'd managed to fit it in between shifts as a parking lot attendant at Tanglewood.

Late in the evening after the Pod Smetanou, I was back in my apartment struggling through a statistics assignment. It was almost midnight. I took my glasses off and held them as if making a point. Dejda, about to leave for France, was snoring slightly behind the partition. Or maybe that was Renee, in the next room. The alarm was even set for 7:00 A.M., which was when Dejda had to get up to make it to her lab.

Was this my fantasy realized? I'd just paid $70 to play in an international basketball tournament to a man with a forty-inch waist, and CEU's accreditation hadn't come through yet from the Open University. Was this it? Our statistics professor was some sort of apparatchik from Romania whom nobody could understand. And Dejda was far from uncomplicated. Even her hair products, which she'd begun storing on my bathroom shelf, were far from uncomplicated.

Still, it felt good, like some things had fallen into place. They were all temporary things, but they had fallen into place nonetheless. Was that good? I knew that I was happier focusing on what was going on in the present—the team, the girl, the degree requirements—than I had been fretting and imagining some indefinite future. Maybe that was the trick, simple like all tricks when you saw how it was done, nothing more than misdirection.

. . .

Radotin Two: January 25, 1995

On the way out to Radotin, I met up with Honsa on the metro platform at Karlovo Náměstí. We slapped hands and nodded like we were members of a secret society. The court was a ten-minute walk away along the southeastern banks of the Vltava, in a dark and unassuming building called Sokol Vyšehrad. We arrived and sat in the bleachers just as the Radotin Under 17 squad finished a practice with two line dunk drills. I'd never seen an Under 17 squad run dunk drills, but nearly all of those kids were throwing down serious dunks. Better dunks than I'd seen in some college warm-up lines, much better than anything I'd seen in my high school career. The ones who weren't dunking compensated by sticking long threes while their teammates tried to goal-tend.

This was a revelation. The Radotin players were strong and flexible and tall; they looked like they'd been specially engineered for basketball. It was stunning. Here in Prague there were players who would whip a substantial majority of their peers in the States. It was as if, for a ton of socioeconomic reasons, they didn't know they shouldn't be that good.

Sports were sometimes presented as the last great meritocracies in American society, places where you succeeded based on merit, on physical performance, rather than on connections, or money, or other skewing variants. With basketball in particular, this notion sometimes begged questions of athletic ability. I was no social scientist, but a lot of people in the States still seemed to subscribe, either outright or implicitly, to the myth of an athletic disparity— the idea that there were athletic characteristics more common in certain racial or ethnic groups. In football, for a while, the discussion had been about the cerebral aspects of playing quarterback— "cerebral" being code for "white." Basketball, where 80 percent of the players in the NBA were black, seemed to some to be a prime example of an athletic disparity. Players and commentators talked about it pretty openly. A *Sports Illustrated* article quoted Dennis Rodman (not exactly a reliable social scientist, but still) as saying that it was simple. On the court, the black guys just knew they could take the white guys. Christian Laettner, in the same article, observed that at certain levels in his summer camps, the black kids seemed to excel where the white kids fell away.

Watching the NBA did nothing to detract from this belief: You just didn't see a lot of superathletic white guys setting the NBA on fire. Larry Bird, the great white superstar, was famously unathletic; it was part of his allure. His occasional dunks—usually reversing the ball one-handed after an arms-out baseline drive—were the ultimate "fuck you" to the leapers and speedsters—the Michael Coopers and Robert Reeds—trying to guard him. Other than Tom Chambers and Rex Chapman, who seemed to come from other planets, there were few white "athletes" in the game. And, sure, you could define *athlete* all kinds of ways—one being as anyone good and tough enough to make a living playing a sport—but you still didn't see any white guys taking quarters off the top of the backboard or catching shots in midair, as Derrick Coleman did against Indiana in the NCAAs.

I wasn't sure about any consistent athletic disparity between any racial or ethnic group. It seemed to me that where the meritocracy broke down was in the applicant pool. Whatever skews took place in the elite margins of athletics could be traced to a disparity in the group of people applying for the positions. Among any group of people, some would be stronger and smarter and faster and more willing to work hard, have better hand-eye coordination or stamina. But the disparities were, by and large, individualized. It wasn't that black guys could jump higher than I could; it was that *that* black guy (and *that* white guy) could jump higher than I could. And as an athlete moved into progressively better and better circles of competition, the individual disparities became more acute. If you weren't a leaper, didn't work at it, and spend days thinking about it, then there'd be plenty of guys who could sky higher than you. Professional sports were at the highest, thinnest margin; only the best, luckiest, and most dedicated of the applicants would get there. If more minority kids had access to, and pressure to succeed at, certain athletics, and thought of athletics as a viable option for the future, that skew would reflect at the margins.

The converse was of course more devious; that the nonminority kids chose other avenues, like grad school or jobs in management, and didn't linger in sports where their chances of long-term career success were infinitesimal. Nonminority kids might look at sports, subscribe to the perception that they were less physically gifted, and choose the other avenues available to them. Minority kids might look at the riches of the athletes, compare it to more limited (or not as visible) opportunities in front of them, and reach for the stars. The skews were reinforcing, and if you looked too long at professional sports, they could begin to seem like a carrot, dangled by the majority, to maintain the status quo.

What was interesting was that of the 20 percent or so of NBA players who weren't African American, a growing number of them were foreign-born. Indeed, there were nearly as many foreign-born "white guys" in the NBA as domestic "white guys." It suggested that in other environments—Prague, maybe—the populations were free from the social weight sports, or at least basketball, had in America. Nobody was making any money playing basketball in Prague, so the applicant pool was largely composed of people who sought out the sport. And since there wasn't much of a minority population in Prague, the majority kids had no perception of athletic inferiority to either slow them down or break their fall. Thus, the dunk lines at Radotin. Why not?

We watched in awe as the Under 17s finished. Mondy said that they were the second-best team in the country in their age group, behind Brno. If they were the second-best team in the country, I couldn't imagine how good Brno must have been.

Our game began, and I started with Martin, Lukas, Vykli, and Michal. It was a strange lineup. Vykli got a quick steal and we broke away two on one. I was on the left, he fed me early, and my steps weren't right. The ref whistled me for traveling. A minute later,

I drove the lane, a Radotin guard grabbed my wrist, and I lost the ball. No call. Another player lowered his shoulder into me and the ref called me for a charge. I missed a three and got whistled for a reach on defense. Finally, their guard got a breakaway, I was back, he tried to shake me at the foul line with a basic stop-and-go, but I knew he was going left all the way. He started to go up and threw his right arm out into my chest. He thought he was in the clear, but I went up and spanked that shit into the Radotin bench. He grunted and came down awkwardly, looking at the referee, who dutifully blew his whistle to scald me with an unspecified foul. The substitution buzzer went off and Slava came in.

We were close for three quarters and then Honsa pulled Slava and Vykli, both of whom were having good games, and put in Jena and Kratcha at the guards. The Radotin guards ate Jena and Kratcha up with a press and they won by about twenty-five. Vykli had seventeen, but the absence of both Peli and Tonda, coupled with Bob's continued suspension, left us unable to stop their big men. I kicked in ten minutes, one point, four fouls and about fifteen turnovers.

I searched for reasons for my poor play, my worst game in months. The night before, at a new pizza place called Rugantino, Fast Dave and I got into a pizza-eating contest. The pizzas were hot and cheap—about $2 each—and when it was over we'd put away seven between us. They'd been grumbling inside me all day. Maybe that was it.

Or maybe it was the referees, or, more specifically, my inability to handle them. It was tempting to think that in pickup play the games are rougher and, with the lack of referees, harder to police. But pickup was sort of self-policing. You called your own fouls. You knew when something was affecting your shot, or when someone was holding you. Nobody fouled too hard because they had to play offense too. On some courts, where calling fouls was frowned upon, you could figure out the code and play within it. That was what made playing with referees so much harder than playing pickup: When players called the game, a system of checks and balances existed; you couldn't expect to make an unjust call on one end and have it not affect a later play at the other end. With referees, the players surrendered that control, and everything could seem—as it did at Radotin—totally arbitrary.

Or maybe it was lingering guilt about flirting with Mary, or lingering dismay at not sealing the deal there, or the weather, or the moon, or just one of those nights. Danny Smiricky, the hero of Skvorecky's *The Miracle Game*, suffered through gonorrhea and Communists without losing his head. Radotin had been beatable. I needed to level out.

.   .   .

WE WERE IN the middle of the second term at CEU, and the Hotel Olšanka was a hive of activity. At only eight weeks long, this was the shortest of the three terms. It felt like it was dragging nonetheless. I was taking classes in comparative politics, international relations, and privatization, the latter taught by Joel Turkewitz, Shannon's roommate and an occasional baller in our old expat pickup games. His class, about the interaction of local owners, foreign investors, and the state was the kind of class I would have found really interesting if I'd been doing the reading regularly and not spending so much time at the Shot-Out Eye, learning Czech with Bob and Radek, or trying to get Dejda to skip work, or, for that matter, if I'd had my eyes up when walking around Prague. Privatization—the process by which the state ostensibly melted away into the hands of private investors (with all the competing incentives attendant to such a process)—was going on all around the city, every day, in ways that seemed both idealistic and brazenly corrupt. The daily newspapers—both Czech and English—were full of stories about the bidding for state-owned utilities, telephone lines, railroads, and banks.

The classes at CEU were like that: fairly straightforward subjects taught within an environment in which the subjects were still themselves evolving, to students whose own home environments were evolving as well. And over each class hung the weight of recent history in the region, and the sense that its history was never really in the past. Our security systems professor, Otto Pick, would occasionally make comments intended for the microphones he was convinced were still in the walls.

The campus was going to move at the end of the year. It had been confirmed. The economics department would be split between Essex and Budapest. Sociology would get shipped to Warsaw. My program would be lengthened to two years and meet, rumor had it, in a wing of Prague Castle. The hotel had apparently finished its renovations and was eager to begin operating as a conference center. Some of my classmates had found a rather fantastic day spa operating on the top floor of the hotel. The hotel management didn't want the students using any of the renovated facilities, but a few of them had snuck up and come back with reports of steam rooms and naked lumpy men they'd seen lying on the massage tables. Melissa, the only other American in the program, approached the chaos calmly; her grades wouldn't transfer, and she'd already locked up a postgrad job in a Washington, D.C. think tank.

Cameron had decided to relocate as well. He'd gotten a job directing an online publishing company in Budapest called Word Up. He said that he and Lindsey planned to move down to Hungary in the spring, although Lindsey didn't look so sure. Fast Dave was talking about heading to Greece when his Dutch girlfriend Femka arrived in May. There was no news on Skee.

As usual, when faced with uncertainty, I spent my energy evaluating the state of the NBA. Orlando had Nick Anderson and an ascendant Penny Hardaway complementing Shaq, but the Jazz and the Suns were close on their heels. Dallas had built a three-headed scoring machine out of Jimmy Jackson, Jamal Mashburn, and Jason Kidd. They were each bruising perimeter players, solid guards with little transcendence to their games (Mash, occasionally), the antithesis of Denver's Mahmoud Abdul-Rauf. I loved Mahmoud, loved him even more as Chris Jackson when he was at Louisiana State and scoring twenty-eight a game as a freshman in the SEC.

Was there a better college scoring guard than Chris Jackson? (No.) He came into LSU and joined a Dale Brown team led by the grinding Cajun forward Ricky Blanton. Jackson stood maybe six feet in his hoop sneakers, and he had this compact, almost chunky-looking body—big butt, low center of gravity—and Tourette's syndrome, and just *lit people up*. Everyone in the gymnasium knew he was shooting, and he would come downcourt, throw a crossover, and go up from twenty-five feet with one of the quickest releases ever, and drill shot after shot. I'd heard that he spent his summers jogging backward down the beach in Mississippi wearing military boots. I had no idea what that would do for you, but I felt like I should start doing it as soon as I moved to a place with a beach. My dad and I had a grainy videotape of an LSU game against Vanderbilt, and Vandy, playing out of their heads, might have even won the game, but Jackson came through there like a force of nature. Vandy did not know what to do with him. Nobody did. Guys were just getting left flat-footed, the ball already in the net, or Jackson already heading the other direction, spin-dribbling out of a trap, double-pumping a three, hanging in the lane until the defender had gone up and come back down. The differences between Jackson's game and everyone else's didn't seem attributable to practice or talent. They seemed physiological. They weren't the same games.

It was almost a shame to see that team change so dramatically the following season, when the role-playing Blanton, Wayne Sims, and Vernel Singleton yielded to freshmen Shaquille O'Neal and Maurice Williamson and a resurgent Stanley Roberts. Talk about an embarrassment of riches. That LSU team had more talent than more than a few NBA teams, but couldn't really figure out how to put it together. After the season, Jackson left for the pros, and had a solid NBA career with Denver, Sacramento, and Vancouver, a career fifteen-point-per-game performer, with a couple playoff series wins, a fifty-point game under his belt, and a game where he got hot and put up something like thirty in the fourth quarter and overtime. He lost a lot of weight in the pros, and was undersized at off-guard, matched up against Jordan and Reggie Miller. And then he got in trouble for refusing to stand during the National Anthem, and eventually went overseas. But that first season at LSU, maybe the best season of any college player since Pistol Pete, Jackson was just off the hook.

· · ·

AT THE NEXT practice, Vinohrady took a vote to see if we wanted Peli to keep playing with us. Peli also played for a team in the second national division, but got less time there. To him, Honsa explained, "We are nothing," except a chance to get some exercise. Peli proposed to keep playing in the games with us, but to stop showing up for the practices. He wasn't there when the voting took place, and it went against him, 9–5. I'd voted to keep him since he was a nice guy and our leading scorer, and the only big man we had who had dunked in a game.

. . .

WE PLAYED KOSIRE on Friday, at home. I asked Honsa to let me match up with their point guard, Number Eight, the crazy little karate man I'd almost fought with the last time we played.

Honsa shrugged and asked why.

What I really wanted to say was how important the team had become to me, and how badly I wanted to demonstrate that I could, and would, contribute, even if it meant sacrificing my own game to shut down Number Eight. But my efforts went awry, as they usually did when I forayed into Czech.

"*Bohuzel, zavreno*," I said, clapping my hands shut.

Honsa looked at me uncertainly, but then clapped me on the shoulder and nodded. Unfortunately, Number Eight, if you own a retail store, or a restaurant, I am going to close it.

Madness

Košíře 2: February 2, 1995

Mondy and Robert had finished their exams, Robert getting two Firsts and a Second in his three tests. Like the metric system, it sounded impressive. Mondy's results were less clear. He was studying politics. He borrowed my Public Enemy tape at practice and returned armed with new lyrics.

We faced Košíře without our exiled Pelikan. Košíře had become one of the two most formidable teams in the league, with either USK B or Horní Počernice, depending on whether I asked Honsa or Radek. Tomas had hurt his elbow and couldn't play. He manned the scorer's table with Big Bob, still on suspension.

Honsa went with a new lineup to begin the game. Slava started at point, Vykli and I started at the wings, Michal—who was a small forward on a good day—started at the power forward spot and jumped center, and Martin played center. It was a small, fast, guard-heavy lineup, not unlike Don Nelson's Run-TMC teams at Golden State who never won anything but put on a good show. Of course, Golden State had gym rat and shifty lefty Chris Mullin, who was still throwing down the occasional non-white-man dunk; Mitch Richmond, a hybrid guard with a power game; and Timmy Hardaway, the toughest cover in the league, who bounced and bashed through the lane like he was a giant walnut. We had Slava, Vykli, and me.

And the weird thing was that we whipped Košíře. Absolutely killed them.

Point guard is the hardest position to play in basketball. Point guards start all the plays, push the ball upcourt, and settle the team down. Their roles are nuanced; they might try to score, but not too much, but also not pass too much. They need to identify how their individual teammates are playing, see who has a hot hand, who is off. They need to channel their coach, call the defenses, set everything up. And they do all this all game long. By their passes and play-calling, they can authorize a player to shoot, and when a player feels authorized to shoot, he's more likely to shoot well. The point guard was almost always in the middle on the break, making decisions about who should get the ball, and where and when. They needed to be unselfish, but still retain their own scoring threat, lest defenders sag off.

Off-guard was a more lenient position. I'd played off-guard one year in college, in England, when the point guard was the junior-varsity starter for Holy Cross. He was as solid as a cue ball and zipped around the court, threading passes that hit his teammates in stride, but he just couldn't shoot. My role had been to float around the three-point line, or cut through the lane, and put the ball up whenever he fed me. It was like being Byron Scott circa 1985, the best job in the NBA.

With Slava at the point, Vykli and I got to roam and trap. I picked up Number Eight full court while the rest of my team fell back on defense, denying him the inbounds pass, and when he got it, shadowing him up the court. If he gave the ball up, I tried to make sure he had to work to get it back. In *Hoosiers*, Gene Hackman sends Buddy in to stick with Forty-One, who was killing Hickory, and says "if he's chewing gum, I want to know what flavor it is." Eight wasn't chewing gum, but he smelled like the *mineralku* tonic the Czech barbers would offer you after a haircut. It made your scalp tingle.

Before we knew it, we were up, 18–2. Slava fed me with a pass and I hit a three. Vykli pulled up on a breakout for another three. Eight kept trying to go right but I wasn't letting him get there. He cut back to the middle of the lane. I gave him some space and reached around to tap the ball out from under him—not a textbook defensive play but one that worked on occasion. Out we sprung on the break, with Košíře's best player back. Martin hit me with the outlet and I stuttered down the left side of the lane before swinging the ball back to a trailing Poli for a two-footer. The Košíře player took a swipe at Poli, a high swipe, around neck-level, and Poli went down. Players gathered around and it looked like we were going to rumble.

The referee blew his whistle repeatedly and ejected the Košíře player. His teammates grabbed him and pushed him toward the locker rooms. Poli, whose girlfriend was in the stands, got up and looked for something to do with his energy; after a moment, he turned and punted the ball up to the high ceiling. It rattled around among the girders like a pinball before dropping back down. The referee seemed almost grateful for the distraction. Slava missed the ensuing technical free throws, but we were up 34–18, and at the half it was 40–24. On the bench, Honsa looked quietly amazed. Eight hadn't scored and the four little kids behind our bench, the members of Honsa's youth team who had become our cheering section, were exhausted already.

We were all pretty quiet at the half, smiling, like we knew that we were putting our best selves, not our regular selves, on display. A team in the zone. How long would it last? Nobody knew, and we didn't want to jinx anything by talking about it.

We started the same five in the second half. I picked up Eight full court again, and soon he wasn't even bringing the ball up anymore. I got a breakaway, and Vykli got another. Slava lined up a three, and then I was leading a break, paused slightly at the foul line, and dropped a pass to Michal who was trailing down the center of the court. He hit the layup with the foul.

Košíře was frazzled, trying to get an offense in gear without their best player or their point guard. They forced passes and turned the ball over. Slava tipped away a pass and I broke out on the left side with only Eight back.

Okay, chump, I thought, remembering the slap and cross-check from up at his place, the push-fight. Let's see your karate. At the three-point circle, I juked left and crossed over to the right. He bought the fake and I was by him, by his little pug face and barrel chest and furtive hands. I had the ball in my right hand, almost cuffed there. Karate! Could I pull a Doc and windmill that sucker up for a dunk? The thought crossed my mind. Then Eight grabbed my left wrist with both his little dwarfish paws and pulled me down.

I landed with a thud on my hip bone. The benches jumped up, shrill Czech filling the air. Honsa called out to the referee, his arms forward, pleading for a response. Two shots and the ball, the worried ref said. Or so it seemed.

I looked at Eight to see if he wanted to fight me. I couldn't tell. He sort of shrugged and smiled, and I wasn't sure if it was the basketball shrug that said, "You had me; what did you want me to do?" Or maybe it was the hockey-sort of shrug that said, "Yeah, let's fight—why not?" with a tack-on about the martial arts.

Step to the back, Flavor Flav said on one of the Public Enemy tracks on heavy rotation in my Walkman. *I'll show you some of my techniques and stomp a mudhole in your ass.*

I looked to Honsa. He was standing on the sidelines, staring at me. I remembered our talk, about focus and sacrifice, about team goals over individual ones. Team goals demanded maturity. I breathed deeply, went to the foul line, and sank the foul shots. We inbounded the ball and I walked it up to Eight's side of the Košíře zone and drilled a three in his pug karate face.

Five-point trip. Maturity. *Tobe do oci*, motherfucker!

The rest of the game was out of control. We scored nearly at will. Slava hit two more threes and then stole an inbounds pass for a layup. Slava got steals the way crocodiles got tourists: by staying very still, in plain sight, until you forgot he was there. Jena got off the bench to drive on the Košíře center and lay the ball up high over him. Mondy played only about ten minutes but managed to foul out anyway. The final score was 94–60, meaning that we'd scored fifty-four points in the second half and gotten a glimpse of what we could have been, or what we were, down deep, when we played right.

At the Pod Smetanou afterward, we celebrated Vykli's twentieth birthday. Bob ate the floating sausages and Radek ate headcheese. Slava ate chicken and drank Moravian wine. Kratcha told me that, regarding the trip to France, there was a decision to be made about whether to take cars or share a bus with the women's team going to the same tournament. Slava swore the women's team was the *second-best-looking* women's team in the city. The players were overwhelmingly in favor of the bus.

Kratcha said that next year he wanted to come to the States. He thought Seattle might be the place for him. I asked him why and he said, "Shawn Kemp." Everyone was laughing and smiling, hunched forward over the wooden table, over their food and drink. Basketball Marek showed up wearing a suit and tie. Tomas was buried under a pile of coats. Honsa sat with his arms around his girlfriend Mischa, his red cheeks red again.

Kratcha turned to me and said, "The season was bad, but tonight, it was good."

. . .

I LEFT AFTER two beers to meet Cameron downtown. It was already 11:15 P.M. I was worried that I'd broken my wrist falling to the floor in the second half. I also wasn't sure if I was still covered on my dad's health insurance. That was something I'd vowed to figure out the last time I was in Prague and Skee took a bunch of us up to the Krkonose for a ski trip. On top of a Czech mountain on rented skis was not where you wanted to wonder about insurance, especially if you didn't ski.

My classmates had organized a bus to the small southeastern Czech city of Znojmo. We were supposed to leave early the next morning and spend the weekend in a wine cellar. My wrist was swelling up and Znojmo seemed like a long way to go for wine. Dejda was still in France with her mom. She was going to be there for a week, and I didn't want to feel like I was just sitting around waiting for her. I'd had bad luck in the past with girlfriends who went to France. It would be better to be in Znojmo, doing my own thing, than waiting for Dejda to come back and tell me about some waiter she'd met who also played guitar. Znojmo, then. 7:00 A.M.

I found Cameron in a smoky Irish bar called Molly Malone's, a bar hidden off of a crumbling terraced sidewalk in a quiet neighborhood over near the Anezsky Klaster. Cameron was sitting in the back room, near a wood-burning stove, with the Bagel King of Budapest. The Bagel King had been a corporate attorney at a big New York law firm until he decided to leave it behind and seek his fortune in Central Europe. He'd opened up New York Bagels franchises in Budapest and was looking to expand to Prague. He was a little drunk on a combination of Becherovka and his own mythology; his opening line to the stunning blond women moving among the Molly Malone's crowd was "How's your English?"

Molly Malone's, like most of the new bars springing up in Prague (especially the Irish-themed ones), was full of foreigners.

Not so much expats, who were more inclined to find a small Czech *hospoda*, build a rapport with the proprietors, and then feel superior. These were out-of-towners: the film students on winter break; the advertising guys; the horse-training investment banker from Virginia who, upon overhearing us, asked "Are you American?" and then "What are you doing in Prague?" which were the two questions that virtually the entire long-term expat community had agreed not to ask each other.

Cameron told the horse-training investment banker that he was writing a novel, which is what the horse-training investment banker wanted to hear. The American novel died with F. Scott Fitzgerald, he said, and moreover, American women were no good. They were only after your money. He had a wife and kids back in Virginia and a beautiful Czech girl on his arm. He described her as his girlfriend. She shook our hands limply.

I knew her. She was a friend of Skee's. Her name was Yanna, and if he thought she was his girlfriend, he deserved what was coming.

We left and went to a place that sold ice cream and a thick red liquor called Vat 69, and then to a last-stop place called Pizza Taxi. The Israeli embassy guys were there, sharing a doughy square of pizza. They checked their car for bombs and then drove us to a cabstand down the block. It was nearly 2:00 A.M. and Cameron and I hailed separate cabs. He was headed back to Hradcanska, to the basement flat where Lindsey was sleeping. I had to get back to Prague 3. I asked the cabbie how much, and he said "*Sto.*"

A hundred.

I said "*Padesat*"—fifty—which was still more than the meter would have come to.

The cabbie said, "Meter." The cabbies would rig their meters to charge the higher out-of-city rates.

"*Padesat.*"

He shrugged and I got in. *The Prague Post* had reported that some cabbies had wired their passenger seats so that they could administer an incapacitating shock at the touch of a button if there was a fare dispute—that is, if the passenger objected to being ripped off. According to one of the expats quoted in the story, the experience was "like being struck with an electric truncheon."

I eyed my cabbie suspiciously and tensed my buttocks against the truncheon. It seemed like weeks ago that we'd whipped Košíře. I focused on the dashboard, where lurid postcards of women's breasts were lined up, each with a telephone number beneath them.

Renee was snoring in her half of the apartment when I snuck through to mine. It was nearly three in the morning. It was tomorrow, and Dejda was due back soon. Znojmo could wait, I decided. I sat in a chair by the window, watched the moon, and thought about the game until the room stopped spinning. In Skvorecky's short story, "A View from the Tower," Danny Smiricky and his putative girlfriend survive a rock-climbing mishap outside of their town and are admonished by their rescuers. Skvorecky wrote:

> As Krsak was carrying on, I recalled how Irena had blown her soul away and I mine. A green halo hung around the moon and a fine cotton dust descended on Kostelec deep in the valley below us, dust expelled from the cotton mill's exhaust tower during the day. Now, in the moonlight, the dust cloud twinkled like a gigantic swarm of locusts with mica wings. Lenecek began sermonizing about how mountain climbing led to life-and-death friendships, although it was absolutely safe, and I wondered what the souls were up to in the tops of the pine trees. Would they seek each other out? Would they find each other?

· · ·

USK B 2: February 7, 1995

USK B played in a modern gymnasium complex called Polimanka where the national team played its home games. Some of USK A's players were in the stands. The rims were tight and unforgiving, but the floor had traction and there were no birds flitting around in the rafters.

USK B was the best team in our division, and they immediately showed why, jumping out to a sixteen-point lead in the first ten minutes. They had a young small forward who was being groomed for the *Superliga*. His teammates ran crisp, efficient plays for him, and he knocked down several modest baseline jumpers in a row. His father was apparently a *Superliga* star, USK A's leading scorer for years. I wondered if his son was suffering under the weight of that legacy, and whether he got grief at school for not playing a real Czech sport like hockey or soccer or handball.

Halfway through the first half, we were already trailing by a lot, but it freed us up to play more loosely. Mondy hit a couple of three-pointers, a rare occurrence for him, and powered in a layup while getting fouled. Vykli and I trapped and ran at their guards, confusing them with our lack of organization. We were the Minutemen to their Redcoats. I began to break down guys off the dribble, getting into the lane for layups or short jumpers or dishes to our bigs. USK B began to switch guys on me, each one slapping the court like a sea lion, each one reaching, inevitably, and getting left behind. I hit Vykli on the break for a layup, and on the way back he offered a palm and said, "Daveed!"

It was never really close, but we made it a game, and even swung some of the USK A players to our cause. We lost by seven and I got twenty-one, finally playing the sort of hoop I'd been expecting of myself the whole season.

· · ·

EXPATRIATE GAMES

I CALLED MARY from the cold pay phone on the corner of Strašni and Biskupcova. Dejda was still in France. It felt big, like a transgression. I should have gone to Znojmo.

It turned out that Mary was in the process of moving back to the States. We talked for a few minutes, but whatever magic we'd shared in Slapy seemed to get dissipated over the staticky telephone line. She may have lost interest after I didn't pull the trigger in the snow that night. Or maybe she just lost feeling. For my part, it felt like calling her was enough and I didn't push to get together.

Instead, when Dejda got back from France, I took her to Slapy.

The food was as bad as ever, but Dejda was a hit with the students and with Vera, and we walked along the river as winter began to slalom toward a wet spring. Vera gave us our own cabin in the woods behind the main building. It had a fireplace.

I had spent so much time worrying about the beginning of the adventure that I hadn't given much thought to the end. It was only mid-February, but it was hard not to look ahead to the end of the season, and the big emptiness of whatever was next.

Humpl gave us a ride back to Prague. Fast Dave, who'd come out to teach, sat in the front and Dejda and I sat in the back. She fell asleep on my shoulder, and I looked out over the coming four months, the arriving spring, the thawing, the eventual departures, and felt the first tremors of the ache that, come summer, would roar through like a train.

• • •

BISKUPCOVA, THE STREET where I lived, was a cobblestoned avenue lined with three-story apartment buildings. Most, like ours, were gray and unassuming, but had tall slender trees in the front and small plots of green in the back. The building three doors down had a bronze plaque on the wall commemorating a Communist journalist who'd been shot. I couldn't make out who shot her, or why, and kept forgetting to ask Dejda. Across the street there was a pharmacy, and around the corner a small deli sold smoked fish and gelatinous things in tins. Next door, a huge blue pub catered to students of the nearby economics school. It was a ten-minute walk to a small movie theater, whose neon KINO sign stood out against the accumulated soot of the building itself. A long park stretched out just across the street, and as the nights got warmer it was full of children, lovers, old ladies, and small dogs.

Biskupcova ran parallel to Koněvova, the main thoroughfare through Prague 3. Along it, there was the economics university and student dorms, and an outdoor hoop court I'd been eying since November. There was even a medical center I'd vowed never to go to, even when I thought I'd broken my wrist. (It felt fine the next day, and in any event was my non-shooting hand.)

People said that Prague 6 was the neighborhood of choice for expats, with its embassies and villas and wide parks, its metro access and proximity to the airport. But I was happy to be where we were, with the brothels and the bars and the *kino*. We didn't have a metro stop, but three trams and one night-tram stopped right outside, across from the fruit stand and a plumber. The recorded voice that announced the stops was hypnotic.

"*Pristi zastavka,*" the voice would say as we approached our stop, "*Vapenka.*"

"*Pristi zastavka,*" when we were there, "*Strasni.*"

I started watching the bushes along our sidewalk, waiting for their buds to open.

Kbely and Skins

Kbely 2: February 17, 1995

Honsa announced that we had to beat Kbely if we wanted to stay in our current division the following season. Both Praga and Kbely, the other two division doormats, had more wins than we did. If we didn't beat Kbely, we couldn't hope to avoid the cellar, and relegation.

Slava, Vykli, Martin, Michal, and I started in what was becoming a regular lineup. Kbely took the court in yellow shirts and blue shorts. They had some height, but it was the usual heavy older height. Their guards were bearded and spindly-legged.

Honsa assigned me to Kbely's off-guard. He urged me not to fall for the beard.

"Daveed, he is . . . tricky," Honsa said.

The game was brutal. I got undercut on a drive through the lane and hit the floor hard, but the layup dropped. One of Kbely's big men put Mondy in a bear hug on an out-of-bounds play. Mondy shoved him off and they drew double technicals. Vykli got tripped by the last man back on a breakaway, and jumped up into his face. Still, we carved out a lead one possession at a time, as Slava and I got hot and big Tonda came in to power up a few two-footers. At the half we were up by eleven.

Honsa's youth team had come to our game again, and this time they'd brought additional noisemakers. One boy had a tin bugle, another had a drum, and a third had a pair of shiny cymbals. They were merciless in their abuse of Kbely foul scorers.

We applied the press to start the second half, and I kept waiting for my man to show me some of his tricks. Kbely was ill equipped to deal with our press and turned the ball over immediately. I got a layup and a jumper to drop. Vykli found his range and hit a three. Then he got fouled on a breakaway and buried the foul shots. On defense he shuffled his man toward the left corner of the half-court line, into the triangle where no guard ever wants to be, and I ran up behind and stripped the ball. Vykli jumped out on the break and I led him for the layup. It was all going great, until Kbely suddenly got red-hot. They began playing like we had against USK B, loosely, firing away, relaxed. Their small forward started throwing in ridiculous threes and my man—who'd kept his tricks to himself since I nearly took his head off with a sweeping block attempt in the first half—hit two threes of his own.

We were up by one when Honsa called time-out. The referees huddled and concluded that it was our third time-out of the half; the rules only allowed us two. They assessed a technical. That was just flat-out wrong, but nobody could prove it. Honsa went temporarily insane—he was usually pretty stoic about on-court mistakes, but this was an affront to his stewardship. Radek, who was shooting fouls with the B team on the side court, had to come over and calm him. After five minutes of vicious Czech, the referees stormed back onto the court and awarded Kbely two shots and the ball.

Maybe it was karma, or the loonlike song of the bugle, but Kbely's forward missed both foul shots and their center came up short on a jump hook on the ensuing possession. We rebounded and Michal gave me the ball. I fed Slava on the right as Vykli circled the back side of Kbely's zone. As he swung out to the left wing, Slava passed back to me at the top of the key. I turned as if to hit Vykli, and as I did the entire Kbely defense shifted toward him. They'd seen this play before—it seemed to be Czech Basketball 101, the man running baseline to baseline for a three. Suddenly, there was a lane down the right side. I hit the crease on the dribble—Kbely's guards caught flat-footed by the derivation—and went up over their big man, who stayed earthbound. The layup kissed off the backboard and dropped through the net.

Kbely got a short jumper to fall, but we worked the ball around with under a minute left, up by one and content to hold it. Kbely was trying to press, but with Slava, Vykli, and me on the court, they couldn't corral us to trap. Finally, Vykli drove and pulled up for a slightly off-balance foul-line jumper. It wasn't really the shot you'd want someone to settle for in a one-point game with no shot clock. Conventional wisdom was to hold the ball and make them foul you, but maybe Vykli didn't want to get fouled. Whatever his thinking, the shot went up and I joined the crowd of yellow shirts going to the boards. But the ball rattled around in the cylinder and dropped. Vykli pumped his fist and his white cheeks flushed red. We were back up by three. Kbely raced downcourt and rushed a three of its own. It missed, I corralled the bound, and they had to foul me. I hit the free throws and we won by five. I finished with twenty.

Kbely was our fourth win overall, but our third in the five games we'd played since the second half began. We were gelling. The whole season, we hadn't played a team we couldn't beat when we put things together. If only we could figure out how to do it consistently.

After the game I met Dejda, Cameron, and Lindsey at Rugantino. It was Dejda's birthday and I'd found an expat woman who made and decorated birthday cakes for 300 crowns, or ten dollars, apiece. She was expensive for Prague, but it was so hard to get things that had the power to make you feel like you weren't missing things from home. The woman dropped one off with the Rugantino owners and we shared it with the people at the adjoining tables.

Afterward we walked the lamplit avenues and shadowy back alleys around the Old Town Square. Prague was full of passageways, doors that would let you cut into a building, through a courtyard, down a stairwell, and emerge from a different building across town. I'd found a tunnel that connected the street by Kmotra with the top of Václavské Náměstí, near the Radost FX nightclub. Someone said that before the Velvet Revolution, when the Communists were still in charge, Havel used to take the tunnels through downtown with the other Charta 77 members to avoid the police. And now we used them to get pizza.

The night was incredibly mild for mid-February, and the main downtown thoroughfares were filled with people. The four of us rounded a corner off of the Old Town Square and walked into the path of a group of skinheads. There were maybe a dozen of them, young, wearing the uniform I'd seen in documentaries—bomber jackets and camouflage pants tucked into boots. One of the stragglers was urinating as he walked, leaving behind a slick-looking slalom of piss on the cobblestones. They didn't look particularly threatening; they looked like kids, like the generic self-conscious toughs you could always find on the periphery of the locker room. They were laughing and passing green bottles of beer among them. They walked by us and vanished into the dark pedestrian zone.

I hadn't had a lot of firsthand experience with overt racism growing up in western Massachusetts, an area that was relatively rural, middle-class, and monochromatic. The little racism I'd seen was more of the low-intensity kind—just as bad, maybe, but certainly easier to ignore (for me). It was sort of pathetic to acknowledge, but I'd never felt like I'd seen any act of racism that might have required me to do something in response; certainly not skinhead-style racism, which was unheard-of in my part of New England. Where I was from, nobody did racist things, and if someone said racist things, well, they didn't get invited the next time everyone went to Pizza Hut.

Skinheads in Prague were a rare sighting, at least for expats like us. Every once in a while you'd see one or two in a tram, or in some area outside of the center, usually an area prominently marked with racist graffiti. Out in the *panelacs*, maybe, or riding a metro home from some sporting event late at night. Semicosmopolitan, tourist-friendly downtown Prague was not typical skinhead stomping grounds.

Cameron and Lindsey and Dejda and I kept walking toward Václavské Náměstí, our path leading down a passageway behind the Gothic, twin-towered Týn Church. The Týn Church had survived fires and mid-construction wars and was the most recognized landmark in the Old Town Square. Beneath its two towers, a row of smaller palaces had been constructed around the base, like rococo barnacles on a gothic ship's hull, obscuring the small tunnel that led to the church's entrance. The Communist leadership of Czechoslovakia had been headquartered in some of those palaces, and from their balconies would oversee the orchestrated celebrations of the regime. Kundera had written about one such celebration, during which snow had begun to fall and the Czech Communist leader Gottwald had offered his fur hat to his Soviet superiors. Years later, Gottwald was eliminated in a purge and his likeness erased from the regime's records, including its official pictures. As far as the Party was concerned, all that remained of Gottwald was his hat on another man's head.

I'd found the path we were on during a sprint to the metro I'd forgotten why I was running; it could have been anything. The path came out at Mustek, the commercial area at the foot of Vaclavske Namesti where vendors sold sausages, prostitutes opened their robes, and old women promised to pray for you if you gave them 5 crowns. Cameron and Lindsey had gotten ahead of us, and were walking hand in hand. They might have been talking about their own future. Lindsey wasn't sure what there was for her in Budapest. She had roots in the Pacific Northwest, and didn't seem inclined to forget them. The expectation seemed to be that Cameron would eventually join her there.

I bent to tie my shoe. Dejda and I were arguing about something, maybe one of the many trips she wanted to take before the summer, maybe money (those topics were related). Then Dejda said, "Can you hurry?" She sounded urgent, and I couldn't figure out why. One of the vestiges of a totalitarian regime was a low violent-crime rate, and downtown Prague was usually safe, even late at night.

I looked up. The skinheads were coming up the path behind us, apparently having found nothing to hold their interest in the Old Town Square. They were grunting and shuffling, frustrated, occasionally shattering their empty beer bottles on the cobblestones, leaving the glass to glitter. We moved a little off to the side and walked on slowly, stopping to look into windows, acting inconspicuous, waiting for them to pass. We reached the edge of Vaclavske Namesti's well-lit pedestrian zone and they were still behind us. Ahead, Cameron and Lindsey had stopped and were looking back behind us. They looked concerned, and it wasn't for us.

A lone small black man was walking down the street, past them, toward us, right into the skinheads' path.

As far as I could tell, Prague's only significant minority population was the dark-eyed Roma, who were blamed for all sorts of social ills and stuck closely together in brightly clothed groups, generally at the train stations or in flats along the outskirts of the city. It wasn't uncommon for anybody with darker skin, like Fast Dave, to be stopped by burly Czech police on the sidewalks, who would ask to see his visa and if he had a job. On the court, the only black guys I'd met were Claudio and a couple of his friends. They were Africans, in the city on some kind of educational visa, finishing engineering degrees and watching each other's backs. As far as I knew, there was only one black guy playing professional hoop in the Czech Republic that year, and that was an American named Tracey who'd arrived in Prague from some small college in the Southwest after other possibilities had failed to pan out. Tracey was a crowd favorite for his big dunks, but otherwise had struggled to fit in with his team, at least in the one game I'd watched him play. Tracey wasn't wandering downtown Prague alone at night, and in any event, at 6'6" he would probably have been fine if he had.

Dejda and I fell silent as the black man walked toward the skinhead pack. He was slight, middle-aged, wearing a thin, shiny jacket and a wool hat pulled down over his ears. He looked African and could have been anything—maybe a cook, maybe a professor. He, too, was watching the street behind us, and where before we'd heard grunts and shuffling, we now heard an almost regimental silence. The man was already past Cameron and Lindsey and was heading toward us. He didn't break stride as he approached, didn't speed up or slow down, didn't look up. As he passed, we turned slightly to follow him, still stopped before a window, but able to see what was going to happen.

The skinheads had tightened up, and as the man passed, one of them put a forearm into his chest, popping him quickly and almost casually. We tensed for more as the man stumbled, but he stayed on his feet and kept moving. The pack snarled, but didn't pursue him. They seemed tired and disappointed by what they probably expected to be a big night out downtown. They passed Dejda and me and headed into the open air of the Square, toward the *parek* vendors and the sex shows and the metro.

The four of us stayed quiet until we'd reached the welcoming lights on V Jame. It didn't take much imagination to envision a different encounter, one in which the skinheads hadn't let the guy off with a simple punch. For that matter, it was just chance that Fast Dave hadn't been with us in the street. We'd asked him to come out, but he'd been meeting other friends. What if he'd been able to come? For that matter, where was he?

We all sat in silence at a table in Jama—four relatively privileged white people talking about how they felt after less-privileged white people assaulted a black person seemed a little too much. Lindsey started to cry quietly, I guess out of frustration. Dejda and I let our mild argument descend into a fight. I wondered what the man we'd seen had said when he got home, if there was someone there to say it to. He hadn't been beaten up; he'd just been degraded. Certainly there were a lot of variables, but we'd watched it happen, and we didn't get to make it about us.

· · ·

Dopravný Podnik 2: February 22, 1995

Vinohrady regressed against Dopravny Podnik, losing so badly that I couldn't remember the score afterward. I had another up-and-down game, throwing the ball through Michal's hands in the lane and missing Lukas on a break, and finished with twelve. We stayed close for most of the first half, but they went on a thirty-to-six run in the second and we couldn't recover.

The buds on the bushes outside my apartment still hadn't blossomed, but spring was starting to show up. The kids who, back in the fall, used to walk beneath my windows on their way to the courts down the street were back, dribbling down the sidewalks. Spring fever seemed to be contagious. *The Prague Post* was running stories about the Czech police confiscating suitcases and car trunks full of enriched plutonium. It didn't fill one with confidence. I found a recruiting advertisement for the CIA in an issue of *The Economist*, filled it out, and dropped it in the mailbox by the Romanian Embassy. The CIA sounded interesting, or at least more interesting than law school. After Czech semipro basketball, how hard could it be? The NBA All-Star Weekend in Phoenix was a bust, except for Mitch Richmond's MVP award, which seemed scant consolation for breaking up Run TMC.

Dejda talked me into going to Budapest for the weekend. I'd been once before, during my Junior Year Abroad rail trip through Europe, and remembered the Hungarian capital as distinctly larger and, surprisingly, more westernized than its Czech counterpart. We'd seen Dunkin' Donuts and 31 Flavors placards in the subways.

Budapest was a nine-hour overnight train ride from Prague. Cameron's vague job with the Hungarian media enterprise apparently required him to go there frequently. He asked me to meet him on the way to the train station. We bought *pareks* near Obecni Dům, the small wieners peeking out of the tops of mustard-lined crescent rolls, and Cameron gave me a small data tape.

"I need this tape to get to Budapest this weekend," he said. "And I can't go. Will you drop it off for me?"

Cameron could be a little intimidating—he'd gotten the good apartment in Hradčanská, was going to Yale someday, and introduced himself as "an entrepreneur" at parties. I felt a little pressure to demonstrate my competence to him, so I said sure, no problem, happy to be of assistance. He gave me the address of the *Budapest Sun*, an English-language newspaper. He said an editor would be waiting for the tape.

Cameron was gone and I was walking toward the train station when I started to wonder what was on the tape—I hadn't asked—and how well I knew Cameron. Where'd he gotten the initial funding for CHeK Group International again? And why weren't any of his partners still "around?" How was he supporting himself now that the business had gone under? An "editor" was expecting the tape? What gives?

Then it hit me. Cameron was a tall white guy, a man of relatively few words, apparently competent, somewhat mysterious, from a small town in the Pacific Northwest. That had "CIA" written all over it. And now I was his courier. My application must have arrived in Langley. This was a screening interview.

Dejda and I picked up second-class round-trip tickets for 2,100 crowns, or about $35 dollars each, at Hlavní Nádraží on Friday night and huddled into a train compartment with a sweat-stained businessman who propped an open brown bottle of *Velkopopovicky Kozel* in his crotch and fell asleep. Dejda whined a little because we hadn't gotten the private sleeper compartment—it cost about four times as much, and was less private than it sounded—and put her head on my shoulder. The compartment was heated, the windows didn't open, and the businessman's open beer sat there, in his crotch, tempting me. The data tape was in my neck-pouch. Was this part of the interview?

The border passed without incident during the early hours of Saturday morning, and at the Budapest train station, we negotiated with a wizened Hungarian woman for a room downtown, within walking distance of the lovely Café Gerbaud. I'd become acquainted with the process of showing up in Budapest and haggling for a room with the people who held small PENSIONE signs on the platforms. It had felt pretty weird the first time, during my JYA trip from Athens to Paris, when a guy in the same Budapest train station followed my friend Mike and I across the platform, telling us how cheap and safe and clean his flat was until we finally agreed to drive with him across the city to check it out. On the ride, in the back of the stranger's car, I was sure we were going to wind up in an abattoir and have our limbs sold one at a time, but instead we wound up in a big house with a bunch of Australians. When our host was showing Mike the back yard, I asked one of the Australians if the place was legitimate, and he sort of shrugged and said yes. Of course, everyone knew that Australians could survive anything as long as they were allowed to sing about it, so his endorsement hadn't meant a whole lot.

There were no Australians in the room Dejda and I arrived at, although it did take half an hour waiting on the sidewalk before a small man in a tracksuit came by with a key to the front door. Once in the foyer, he led us up a long, sweeping circular staircase to a high-ceilinged apartment with a small balcony. Central European capitals were still good that way; these tremendous grandiose downtowns were full of apartment buildings that the locals had been holding on to forever, and now that tourism was infiltrating the post–Soviet East Bloc, they could rent them out for rates that seemed exorbitant to the locals but reasonable to the tourists.

We dropped our bags and headed out into the city. Budapest was dotted with cafés the way that Prague featured *hospoda*, and the Gerbaud, with its floor-to-ceiling windows framing a sunlit triangle called Vörösmarty Square, was the most famous of them. A small parade was passing through the Square, and we sat in the café, sore and sleepy, watching dancers in what looked like aluminum-foil dresses sashay across the windowpanes. Ribbons of cigarette smoke curled up from silver ashtrays on the small marble-topped tables. Our waitress brought thick Turkish coffee with the grounds still floating across the surface, along with water and creamy, chocolate-filled cakes wrapped like presents in waxed paper. I got a second piece of cake and Dejda said, "I just think you really like food," like I was supposed to feel bad about it.

We walked across the Chain Bridge and watched the slow Danube, the longest river in Europe, slide past beneath us. We hiked up the hills on the Buda side of the river where they rose to the reconstructed castle walls and the unpronounceable Hálászbastya. It was a long walk to the top, but once there we could look back over the dusty city. Budapest stretched out as far as we could see, the city fading into the grainy air, the castle walls reflected in the mirrored windows of a modern office building appended to the courtyard. Prague might have escaped significant destruction during (and after) World War II, but Budapest had not been so lucky, either during the war itself, or again in 1956, when its indefatigable citizens staged the first large-scale revolt in Central Europe against Communism. Soviet troops had bombarded the city, targeting the castle and its bridges. Whereas Prague could take your breath away, when you rounded out of curving Celetna Street at dusk into Staroměstské Náměstí, or when you looked from the center of Charles Bridge back onto the cartoon silhouettes of the gold-tipped Old Town towers, looking at Budapest from the Buda castle walls inspired a struggle more than a dream. The revolts of 1956, the rise of "spontaneous privatizations" in the mid-1980s, the Latinate spice of its political turmoil—all of it suggested a city inclined toward headlong pursuits, for better or worse.

Cameron's tape was still under my shirt. It seemed to be getting heavier, and I wanted to complete the mission. We found the drop point on a four-foot Fodor's foldout map we laid out on the hood of a parked Skoda. It did not seem discreet. Could this be how the real CIA does it? The newspaper office was on the ground floor of an old stone office building on one of Budapest's wide avenues.

Through the glass doors in the foyer, the interior offices looked authentically cluttered, with stacks of newspapers and translation dictionaries on the shelves. What a good cover, I thought. Nobody answered the door when I knocked.

Hmmm . . . a complication. Where was the "editor" I was supposed to meet? A man across the hall with a broom said, in thick-tongued English, "Newspaper?"

I nodded. I wasn't sure what to do next. This guy looked like a janitor, but it was already late on Saturday and we were staying across the city and leaving the next day.

"We're from Prague," I said. I didn't have a code word in English, and the only Hungarian I knew was *Halaszbastya*, which I couldn't pronounce.

"American?" the man asked.

Usually, I would answer that question cautiously, although the answer was pretty obvious to anyone asking. I nodded.

"You have something for the newspaper?"

I took out the tape. It was wrapped in a plastic Ziploc bag. The janitor's eyes seemed to widen. Nuclear secrets. Covert ops. I gave him the name of the editor, and he nodded his head.

"Not here. Monday."

"Can you make sure he gets this?" I asked, and the man nodded his head again. In my cross-cultural dispute-resolution class I'd learned that in some cultures—Asian cultures, predominantly—sometimes "Yes" meant nothing more than "I acknowledge that you are speaking to me, even if I do not understand what you are saying."

"Yes," the man said.

Dejda looked like she was about to vacate her body and spend the next twenty-four hours in some more interesting alternative reality. I wrote the name of the editor on some tape and stuck it to the Ziploc bag. The janitor took it and said, "Yes."

So much for the CIA, I thought, walking out of the *Sun* offices. Then Dejda grabbed my hand and whispered, "How many countries have you had sex in?"

Later, at a crowded little restaurant on Paulay Ede called Bohemtanya, we used our last *forints* on a dinner of spicy meatballs. They came on wooden plates with potatoes, hot mustard, and heaps of sauerkraut and red cabbage. We drank Austrian lager, cold but tame when compared to the Czech stuff, and *Egri Bikaver*, Hungary's famous Bull's Blood, a dollar a bottle.

The train back to Prague was empty until we got to Bratislava, where it filled with vendors heading into the Czech Republic to sell their wares. An old *babicka* came into our compartment with five enormous plastic bags full of flowers. She nodded to us and started to talk, quickly and in Slovak. We nodded to her and smiled, which prompted her to talk some more. Dejda listened intently to the *babicka*, but could only gather that she'd been grievously wronged at some point in history, but had made her peace with it and now viewed the transgression with rueful good humor.

Slovakia was the least economically stable of the "Vysegrad Four" countries, still led by the corrupt Meciar government. Its prospects for joining any of the international communities courting the Czechs and Poles and Hungarians seemed to lessen each day. Meciar had recently been quoted threatening that if Slovakia was not welcomed in the West, it would be forced to go East, back into the waiting arms of the Russian Federation.

The *babicka*'s flowers were tiny, white, and yellow, wrapped together in bunches of fifty and bound with a reed. A half an hour past Bratislava, there was a knock on the train compartment door, and then it flew open. The ticket collector stepped into the triangle of harsh light.

"*Listek*!" he demanded.

We produced our tickets. The *babicka* didn't have a ticket and offered the collector five of her flower bundles. She told him her story of being grievously wronged at some point in history, making peace with it, and now viewing it with rueful good humor. He declined the flowers but let her stay. When he was gone she fell into a looking-out-the-window trance; I would have thought she was asleep, but her eyes were open, watching the Slovak countryside slide by in shadows.

•   •   •

IN FOUR GAMES against Ewing that season, Shaq had scored forty-one points three times and thirty-eight once. It seemed like he was "sending a message." John Starks was the only guy who could win games for the Knicks, and he was just years away from stacking shelves at a grocery store. The Lakers were rolling behind Quick Nick, the best pro turned out by the perpetually-on-probation Bearcat program in years; they'd changed their pitch from "Showtime" to "the Lake Show," in an effort to escape the expectations that came with being the Lakers, and it seemed to be working. Poor Timmy Hardaway couldn't buy a win up at Golden State.

In Prague, the expat community was mourning the death of the English-language weekly *Prognosis*, which upon its founding had been the first expat paper in post-Revolution Czechoslovakia. One of their earliest issues had included a list of "useful phrases to know in Czech" for Americans fresh off the train. At the top of the list was "Don't shoot, I'm Canadian." The paper had lasted just under four years, becoming known for its provocative headlines as much as its impressive journalism. One article chronicling the fallout from Prague's burgeoning sex trade fell under the 36-point-font title MOMMA GOT PAID, DADDY GOT LAID, AND I'M AN ORPHAN. Long before *The Prague Post* appeared on newsstands, *Prognosis* was the expat community's literary lifeline, facilitating the city's transition into, as *The New Yorker* described it, a metaphor for itself. The proto expats who'd started it had been first on the scene, ahead of the cultural wave; they might have actually created it, as opposed to the rest of us who were just along for the ride.

In the NCAA, there was a revolving door at the top of the polls. UCLA, led by the O'Bannon brothers (Ed apparently recovered from his knee problems and was now playing the "glue guy" for a corps of youngsters, including Charles O'Bannon and Ty Edney), was currently ranked first in the Associated Press poll, chased by Jerry Stackhouse, Rasheed Wallace, and the rest of the Tarheels. At Michigan State, Shawn Respert was playing off-guard better than anyone in the country. Gary Trent, "the Shaq of the MAAC," got my vote for power forward of the year despite playing in a mid-major conference, ahead of Lou Roe and Joe Smith, but just barely. Joe Smith was carrying Maryland. Maybe Corliss Williamson, whose nickname was "the Big Nasty," was in the mix, too.

I had concerns about Lou Roe's ability to make the jump to the next level. Lou Roe was a man in college, but it was hard to see how his game would translate to the pros, where they were all men, and they were all big. You had to be a freak of nature to excel as an undersized forward in the pros; Barkley was a freak of nature—they said he could stand under the basket on one foot and jump up and dunk. Karl Malone was sort of a freak of nature, but more of a self-made one, built in the weight room, not in the celestial interstices. Lou Roe seemed like a hard worker, and I worried that he'd join the pantheon of great college players whose games didn't translate: Walter Berry, Mark Macon, Antoine Joubert, David Rivers—Pearl

Washington, for that matter. Alfredrick Hughes? Not sure anyone ever expected him to be a great pro, except me.

It was early March, and I checked and rechecked the single page of the *International Herald Tribune* sports section for stats, filling out my brackets and imagining the office pools and noon tips of the upcoming tournament. After October, March was my favorite month. For a couple of weeks, everyone wanted to talk about spring and basketball. I had never had any success in picking the tournament, but it was no deterrent: The Sport Bar Praha had a tournament pool, and I dropped 100 crowns on Maryland to take Kansas in the finals.

. . .

MY DAD AND I had mapped out the greatest dunks ever, but they didn't compare to the greatest *games* ever, which, because of the immediacy and emotion and the absence of compensation, were almost exclusively the province of college. The 1992 Duke-Kentucky game was probably the best game that had been played in my lifetime, the game that Laettner won on a turnaround foul-line jumper at the buzzer, taking Grant Hill's full-court pass with two seconds left. Just moments before, down one, a Kentucky guard named Sean Woods had taken the worst last-second shot you could imagine, an off-balance, one-handed floating bank shot from straight on, over the outstretched arms of the six-foot-eleven Laettner. The commentators were clearly aghast. One of them said, "Where did he find the . . . courage . . . to take that shot?" Duke and Kentucky had been trading punches all game, the clock was winding down, Mashburn had fouled out with 28, and Kentucky had to get a shot up. Woods didn't know quite what to do. He got into the lane, Laettner was in position (Laettner, who shouldn't have even been in the game, having stomped on Kentucky forward Aminu Timberlake's chest earlier in the game), and Woods left his feet, leaning in, and made it. And for the length of a time-out, that was all that mattered in the world.

That 1992 tournament had more than its share of photo finishes. It was the year Georgia Tech had won a game on a freshman power-forward's three-pointer at the buzzer, and Al Maguire had screamed "Holy mackerel! Holy mackerel! Holy mackerel! Holy mackerel!" I'd been in Europe, on trains and in hostels, but my dad had recorded the whole tournament for me on our newish VCR. We'd watched the games together, him for the second time, over the summer.

. . .

Motol 2: March 15, 1995

We played Motol on the Ides of March. They dressed in black and brought a big, wild, bald man who played with a rabid zest and threw in threes all game long. He hadn't been around the first time.

Before the game, Honsa asked me if I'd had a good day. He'd taken to asking that before each game. I had had a fine day: a lunch with my English employers, a chocolate bar with Dejda, a check on the flowerbuds (not quite there). Cameron, Lindsey, Shannon, and Fast Dave had come to watch the game, and sat at the top of the concrete bleachers. We'd been playing well. Everything seemed in place for a breakout game.

Midway through the first half, I'd already thrown the ball out of bounds twice, lost a dribble, traveled, and air-balled a five-footer. While bringing the ball upcourt, I shook my man with a juke and tripped over the long black loop of my own shoelace. My man picked up the loose ball, sauntered down the court, and laid it in.

Vykli was playing well, and Slava got so hot in the second half that he brought us back into the game with three consecutive threes, including one that banked in. Tonda played strong in the middle, wheeling and banking short jumpers and put-backs. Mondy came in and swatted two jumpers by Motol's star into the netting behind the hoop. We started to press and climbed back into the game. Tomas got a steal, raced downcourt for a right-handed layup, turned it into a jump shot, and missed it. Poli missed the put-back. I hit two foul shots to draw us within one, but we couldn't pull even. Down by two with a minute left, we pressed and they threw a deep bomb. Tonda was back, stretching for the ball. He collected it just like Peli had in the win before Christmas, but he couldn't hold it and it slipped through his fingers. Motol's deep man grabbed the loose ball, laid it in as Tonda grabbed at him. Hoop and the harm. They went up five and the game was over.

We were three and four in the second half of the season with four games left. Big Bob said that the team had decided to merge the A and B teams next season and play in a lower league. He had been playing with our B team during his suspension, and had decided to keep playing there after it expired. He said he didn't like the intensity of the A squad's games. In *The Prague Post*, they ran a story about the eight non-Czech players in the *Superliga* under the headline FOREIGN MEN CAN'T JUMP. The article detailed the struggles that the foreigners were having adapting to the Czech teams, and quoted Tracey talking about his frustration over only being loved for the occasional dunk. He sounded like he was out of Prague as soon as his season was over. It didn't really seem like his teammates would miss him.

I wondered if Vinohrady would miss me when the season ended, if they'd ever again allow an American to join them. I was trying to play better, to fit in and lock down on defense. Vykli and I had smoothed things over. He just wanted the structure of the plays maintained; he wasn't an improviser, and wanted to know that we were going to do what the play said we were going to do. The Czech ballers had grown up studying diagrams and play sheets, not watching World B. Free "create his own shot" or Jordan dunk on Kelly Tripucka. They played an ordered game. I was starting to figure that out, and not surprisingly, we were playing better and more together on the court.

Off the court, we were all getting along. Tomas and I met for dinner occasionally, where he'd talk to Dejda in Czech and me in English. I wondered sometimes what they were saying. Even Slava and I had found a way to coexist; we were complementary, in fact. Slava—slow, out-of-shape Slava—was Vinohrady's true point guard. When he was in the game, everyone played calmly, confident in the structure. When I was at the point, everyone ran around with their heads on swivels, not sure when a pass was going to hit them in the ear, or when a shot was going to careen off the rim and snap their fingers back.

And Slava was a leader—the players listened to him, laughed with him. He ran the locker room, and had even begun to include me in his pranks. After each game, Honsa would tell us what time the next practice was.

"*Trening*," he'd say. "*Zitra. Sedm.*"

Slava would look at me and say "*Rano.*"

Rano? That was morning. Seven in the morning?

"*No*," Slava would say, as he and Michal laughed. "*Sedm rano.*"

· · ·

Technika Strojní 2: March 23, 1995

We played Technika on a tennis court at Strahov Stadium, atop Petrin Hill, behind the castle and the miniature replica of the Eiffel

Tower. Strahov was where the national *Sokol* gatherings were held. Pink Floyd had played there in December.

Technika Strojní played in a tennis complex adjacent to the stadium. The backboards were hung from the rails of the spectator gallery. In warm-ups, I watched Technika's squad of meaty small forwards skip graceless layups off the rim and thought there was no way we could lose. Four of them had beards. No way could we be that bad.

Peli had returned to the team. The reasoning was unclear. As far as I could tell, he'd just appeared at the bus stop, changed into his uniform, and resumed swatting shots into the stands. I'd seen him on the street earlier that day and he hadn't mentioned anything. I was walking with Dejda down a side avenue near the laboratory where she did her mysterious experiments, and two men strolled by us, wrapped in scarves. After we'd passed, I heard someone calling my name. It was Peli, on his way to some afternoon class at the university. We'd exchanged high fives and back pats and some short, smiling gestures, and after we parted, Dejda had looked at me differently and pulled closer as we walked away. Was there anything better than to come across a teammate on the street?

Against Technika, Vykli and I pressed their backcourt from the tip. Slava didn't get in much; he might have been injured. Technika's point guard could only dribble to his right, and when we cut him off he panicked. On one occasion, he slapped Vykli on the jaw. No call. I took him to the hole on the next possession, laying the ball up as Peli cleared the lane. He came back, but we tapped the ball away, and Vykli fed Michal for a layup.

They couldn't play with us. All game long, we picked up turnovers and scored. Peli grabbed rebounds and scored. Tomas took passes on the wing and scored. But somehow, when the game ended, Technika had more points.

It seemed sometimes like we were the victims of creative scoring by the statisticians, but then we'd lost plenty on our home court. Sometimes Vykli and I got caught up trying to outscore each other and ignored our teammates, but most of our teammates had roles that didn't require the ball. We'd shown against Košíře that we could beat anyone when we put two halves together. Unfortunately, it appeared that anyone could beat us when we didn't. The end of the season was in sight, and we were still Maryland, unable to sustain.

. . .

ON FRIDAY, THE buds on the bushes near my apartment finally came out. I went down to the Old Town to run some errands, and a warm spring breeze curled around the corners on the benches outside the Kotva department store, where people lounged with fistfuls of *pareks* and wax cups of orange Fanta. The breeze smelled like wet earth. Young couples made out on the steps of the John Hus statue. The day seemed made for daydreaming, as maybe most days do when you can't speak the language well, only go to class eight hours a week and don't have a full-time job.

I went to the Jewish Cemetery in Josefov. The cemetery was tiny, packed into a corner of what had been the Prague Ghetto, under whose eaves and shadows Rabbi Loew had sculpted the Golem from river mud. Avigdor Kara was the first Jew put in the ground there, in 1439, and the burials continued until 1789. The bodies were buried one on top of another—some said ten deep—and many of the tombstones leaned precariously together like the teeth of an abused comb. People walked silently between them, leaving pebbles and small-denomination coins on their edges.

Outside the walls of the cemetery, tour groups choked the sidewalks. The Prague tourist season had started, and it would run until Christmas, with a brief respite in September. March and April were Italian-student months; they roamed downtown in thick, interlaced packs, redolent of cologne. When I'd first arrived, I'd sought out tourists; they'd made me feel less far from home. But after a few months, they'd grown tiresome. They were loud and aggressive; they didn't notice the looks cast their way by the locals, or if they noticed, they didn't care. The college-age ones filled the Sport Bar Praha and pulled their penises out after too many *svelte pivo*. They mispronounced *Kundera*. Some of the more-authentic *hospodas* had begun to implement a two-tiered pricing system: a beer for a tourist was 25 *koruny*, nearly a dollar. For a Czech it was 9 *koruny*, or roughly 30 cents. What the Czechs still didn't understand, apparently, was that a dollar was still too much of a bargain.

There was a sign at the entrance to the Jewish Cemetery that listed the price for CESKY STUDENTI. I dropped my coins and flashed my CEU ID.

"*Cesky studenti?*" the woman behind the glass asked.

"*Ja mluvim cesky, ne?*" I asked back. "*Ano.*"

She frowned, but gave me a ticket.

I'd picked up some things at the Shot-Out Eye. Save your two tiers for the Gamecocks and the Italians with lira to burn, *babi*.

· · ·

CEU's END-OF-SECOND-TERM EXAMINATION period coincided with both Jordan's return and the NCAA tournament, portions of which the entrepreneurs at the Sport Bar Praha were showing on "tape-delay," which was the delay between when their friends in other parts of the world taped the games and when they arrived in Prague by express courier. Occasionally, there would be a live game on one of the satellite feeds they got, but it would begin airing at midnight and end at 3:00 A.M. It didn't bode well for exams.

All of my NCAA tournament predictions were playing badly. I'd picked Syracuse as a Final Four dark horse, but they lost when their star senior Lawrence Moten called a time-out they didn't have. I had Moten pegged for that year's "Senior makes good" story. Now it looked like the "Senior makes good" story would involve Bryant "Big Country" Reeves, the Oklahoma State center. I hadn't seen much of Reeves, but in postgame interviews, he looked sort of goofy, with a tight flat-top on a wide, jowly head. The effect made him look like a thick screwdriver. He didn't wear his socks high or carry himself with regal bearing like Lawrence Moten. Moten had been heady for years before the time-out; had he learned nothing from Webber?

The examinations at CEU were being renamed "comprehensives," and the number of them we had to take was being doubled. Sometimes it seemed like, during this first year in Prague, CEU was making up its academic program as the year went along. The program's director had flown in last week apparently for the express purpose of expelling the one student from Kazakhstan for failing a test that she then passed on the re-sit. The school paid for her return flight to Almaty. Her departure was something of a mystery, and the rumor among the students was that the administration was trying to make the program appear rigorous for external accreditation examiners who were scheduled to visit. We all wanted accreditation; without it, we'd spent a lot of time pursuing something we couldn't really use. But we felt bad for the Kazakh girl. She had flat, Asian features and had spoken to few people in the first months of the program. She'd just begun to come out of her shell, and say funny, weird things, and smile a lot. I wondered what she would do when she got back to Almaty.

I got the feeling that I was as much an enigma to my classmates as the Kazakh girl had been, and that if given the choice they'd have sent me to Almaty and kept her. I didn't live in the dorm and thus missed out on a lot of the discussions and bonding that they shared. I had Vinohrady and my expat friends. They had their wars and their cynicism and their music. Early on in the first trimester, there had been elections for class president, and I'd thrown my name in the hat, thinking it would be a good way to meet people. I'd finished second to last in the balloting, and the last-place candidate had withdrawn in the middle of the campaign. Each person could vote for two candidates, including themselves if they were running. I wound up with three votes, total. Out of the forty-five students, I'd been my own first choice and two other people's charity vote.

It snowed on Monday, covering Friday's buds in three inches of cold slush. Our last examination was in Security Studies. The professor, the ancient Czech Otto Pick, left us with abstractions like, "What is power?" I sat still for ten minutes, trying to remember any of my notes from the semester. Power was Isiah Thomas's Svengali-like control over a roster featuring Rick Mahorn, Dennis Rodman, and Bill Laimbeer. Around the room, I could see at least two people employing crib sheets; one of them was Dagmar the Pole, who had tried to quit the program twice already. Dagmar was from northern Poland and kept threatening to hop the next train home. There seemed to have been a fairly large amount of cheating going on in the first term, and it looked like the comprehensives would see more of the same. It seemed to be symptomatic of a different cultural paradigm. When it came to totalitarian academics—or maybe when it came to scholarship positions in Prague—failing was not an option.

Ahead of me, a Russian named Anatol suddenly slumped in his seat, letting out a little sigh. Was this a ruse to distract the proctors while Dagmar made a break for the door? One of the classroom monitors came over, and then chairs were squeaking as people jumped up to have a look. We were ushered into the hallway and the exam was delayed for forty-five minutes. Some students returned to their rooms to stuff themselves with more relevant material. After a long wait, an ambulance-type team came to the classroom and took Anatol out on a stretcher. He looked pale but okay. He'd apparently experienced some sort of actual seizure, the details of which nobody could convey.

I used the delay to index my thoughts on power. I remembered Professor Pick saying, once, loudly for the microphones, "Power is a relationship." He hadn't followed up on it, or at least, I didn't remember the rest.

I was in a relationship and felt pretty powerless. Renee accused me of being "whipped" the other night as I headed out into the snow with my sneakers and a package of Lipton Cup-a-Soup stuffed into my backpack after Dejda came down with a head cold.

Whipped. Right.

I'd assumed Renee was jealous and had written her comment off to her problems with her gun-toting Czech colleagues. But then a friend who was planning a visit to Prague had written to ask what I needed from home. I wrote back "Brown sugar and Lady Bic razors," and that didn't sound good at all.

What did it even mean to be whipped? Could someone be whipped by something they'd invented? (Yes. Obviously.) Dejda and I seemed like we were on a two-way street, even if it was also a dead-end street. It wasn't like I was a disco-boy. I'd sent her home when she bugged me. Shit, she'd been ironing for me lately, and I'd already doubled the number of countries in which I'd had sex. She had her grandmother, who liked me and made me strudel and *knedlicky*. I had my teammates, and they'd already offered to kick Dejda on my say-so. All I had to do was give the word.

Most important, things had an end—an end that was in sight, even. Maybe that was the problem, what I was so worried about, why I'd leave my flat at night to brave the trams and the skinheads and the coal dust to get to Dejda's aunt's apartment in the *panelacs*. Things had an end.

It was a lesson I should have learned in the Jewish Cemetery: If you built something out of the mud of the Vltava, you'd better have thought of a way to keep it under control.

. . .

THE COMPREHENSIVES CAME to an end, and I invited my classmates over to the flat for lunch. About twenty of them came, and they brought their liquors and their cakes; I made a salad with chicken and olives.

Hele, an older East German woman who always looked sad, took me aside. "They didn't vote for you because they think the Americans always want to run everything." She said that the Central European students had banded together early on around their distrust for the West and their dislike of our Western instructors.

Huh? What about the Russians? America hadn't spent the last fifty years occupying them, after all. But the Russians, Yevgeni and Constantin and Dmitri, seemed to be as popular as anyone. Maybe they were a particular kind of Russian.

Many of my classmates asked about the apartment over the course of the party, and I heard more and more about the mysteries of the Hotel Olšanka. The Hungarian Csaba looked longingly at our closet kitchen. I was sure he could do more with it than salad. Dejda showed up and was a big hit with the guys. Irakli the Georgian soldier who swore he'd never killed anyone walked slowly around my apartment, looking at things with his dark eyes and nodding. As evening fell, they sang songs and finished the liquor, and then everyone left, en masse, and I could hear them talking and laughing at the tram stop around the corner.

• • •

Horní Počernice 2: March 31, 1995

We played Horní Počernice at home. Horní had the guard who'd worked us over when we'd played at Chvalkovická before Christmas. We'd been playing better lately, the Technika game notwithstanding. It would be nice to finish with a winning record in the second half of the season. There were three games remaining before the end of the season; Pankrac we could beat, and Meteor at home in the season finale looked possible. Horní was our only tough opponent left. If we could beat them, there was no telling how things might end.

If this were fiction, we would have beaten Horní Počernice, then fallen in some surprising and disruptive way to Pankrac, and everything would have ridden on the Meteor game. We would have won that, but not before surviving egregious foul calls and some level of brawl. I probably could have put up a three to win it, but I'd have seen Vykli out of the corner of my eye and passed to him for an easier layup. We would have embraced, with Slava and Honsa doing the same, and Big Bob would have run onto the court and dunked. Dejda would have been in the stands, wearing her velvet pants. Spring would have come to stay.

Alas, this isn't fiction. We lost to both Horní and Pankrac, Dejda and I broke up, the snow melted (but the wind was still icy), and by April 13, I stood on the corner of Na Příkopě and

Náměstí Republiky by myself, freezing in a cold snap, eating fried cheese.

Before the Horní game, Honsa announced that Vykli was done for the season. According to Honsa, Vykli had "difficulties" that were going to make it impossible for him to play. Vykli sat quietly behind the bench in a dark turtleneck, looking sad. He seemed physically fine.

Horní Počernice tore into us behind their star guard. He was gifted, his game economical. He dangled the ball out in front of him, but by the time you reached for it, he'd gone by you for a skying finger-roll or a pull-up jumper. He was the kind of guard who got offensive rebounds off foul shots by being in the right place faster than anyone else. In the first half, we were keying on him so much that he was able to thread passes through our focused defense to cutters back-dooring their men.

I laid off him a little, more out of caution than strategy, and his threes were coming up short. Maybe there was a weakness. Down low, a huge older man was throwing in rolling hooks and getting to the foul line, but we stayed with them early. I hit some jumpers and Michal worked his magic among the trees. Vykli roamed the sidelines with Honsa.

Mondy came in and crashed the boards. He had a special sort of rebounding technique: With both arms raised and eyes focused on the ball, he jumped into his man's backside or hip, pushing his man with the surprising heft of his midsection. Mondy could do that repeatedly, in swift succession, until he was virtually on top of his compacted opponent. When he'd compressed you into submission, he'd grab the rebound and throw the ball immediately back up toward the rim while falling to the floor with a howl. I'd never tried to box Mondy out, but it must have felt like trying to box out a snowmobile.

Even with Mondy doing his best, we couldn't keep up with Horní in the second half and lost by eighteen.

. . .

WITH THE EXCEPTION of the Kazakh girl, all of the students would be back for CEU's last term to whittle away desperately at their theses while spring became distracting summer.

UCLA beat Arkansas in the NCAA Finals—O'Bannons making good, with Toby Bailey throwing down a ridiculous two-handed reverse jam early on that seemed to knock Arkansas off its game. Jordan hit for fifty-five in his fourth game back, the single-game high score of the season. Jimmy Jackson had gone down with a sprained ankle, but Jason Kidd was collecting triple-doubles and leading Dallas as it chased Denver and Sacramento for the eighth spot in the Western Conference playoffs. Rumors of a rift between Jackson and Kidd, allegedly involving a woman, were cause for concern. In the East, Orlando remained the cream of the crop, even with a concussed Nick Anderson riding the pine.

I liked Nick Anderson; big, strong, and tough, he seemed like one of the few NBA players who Jordan couldn't intimidate. But Nick couldn't make his free throws. It was a mental thing, had to be. Nick was a great jump-shooter; he could extend back to three range whenever he needed to. How could a guy not be intimidated by Jordan and be intimidated by a foul shot? Grant Hill was a lock for Rookie of the Year. Before his ankle splintered, he seemed well on the way to the Hall of Fame. Jordan was shooting at only a .323 clip as he played his legs into shape, but if he could find his range before the playoffs, if the Bulls could absorb his return, and if Pippen and B. J. Armstrong didn't just explode at the power shift then they'd be a very dangerous team again.

. . .

Pankrác 2: April 7, 1995

Vinohrady could have been a very dangerous team, too. Unfortunately, the team that showed up to play against Pankrác had its head up its collective ass. We strolled into the Pankrác gym, checked for dead spots, threw some lazy layups off the backboards, and went to the bench.

The Mullet was in street clothes, if he lived on Chump Street—tight black jeans and a tight white turtleneck—and his long blond hair was slicked back and looked wet. Honsa announced that we had to win again if Vinohrady wanted to stay in the league the following season. It wasn't clear if he was serious, since he'd said that before. Vykli showed up in his uniform; he'd apparently been cured of his difficulties. He was sitting giddily on the bench next to Michal, happy to be back. Maybe Kratcha had lent him *Wang Dang American Slang*.

Off the tip, I broke down the right side and Slava fed me. I crossed over lefty, moved their man to the middle, and spun back right for a hanging jumper that kissed off of the boards. I reached in on their guard for a cheap foul as he plodded toward me like a Claymation figure. Pankrác fed one of their big, slow forwards. Tonda towered over him, but he pumped, pumped, pumped, took a step, and threw the ball up like he was launching a shot put. No chance to go in, but the ref said Tonda had fouled him.

On the next possession, Michal curled into the lane and flipped up a short shot that looked like it would catch the front of the rim. I circled along the baseline and timed my jump so that when the ball fell short, I was there to flip it back in. Another lazy foul of their guard, Number Eighteen. Moments later he found some space and drained a three.

Vykli and I switched on defense and he tried to break Eighteen's rhythm. There really wasn't too much rhythm to break, just the confidence of anyone playing in their home gym, but Vykli started grabbing and reaching as Eighteen held the ball above the arc. Eighteen threw an elbow into Vykli's throat; Vykli retaliated with a shove. A whistle blew. A knot grew. Eighteen put his hands to Vykli's throat. I pushed Eighteen. The Mullet was yelling in Czech at a group of my college friends who'd come to Prague to visit for a week and had been cheering loudly from the stands. They looked terrified.

Once again, it was hard to figure out exactly how we lost. We seemed to incur a disproportionate number of whistles in the second half. Pankrác could do no wrong. Eighteen cooled down, but the war of attrition down low took both Tonda and Martin out of the game. I had eleven in the first half, but, saddled with fouls, didn't do much in the second. During a time-out, one of my college roommates told me that the score girl, who appeared to be Mullet's daughter (or maybe his girlfriend), had been awarding Pankrác one point for each two she gave us. Whenever we scored, they did too. I passed the information on to Honsa, who looked at the scorer's bench. They were smiling at us. Honsa looked like he might explode, but then took a personal moment and came back and shrugged.

According to the scorecards, we lost by about twenty. We were three and seven in the second half, four for twenty-one on the year.

Meteor, in the last game of the year, came to Vinohrady on Good Friday.

Finale

DEJDA AND I split up because whenever I stayed at her aunt's flat and the phone rang, she'd go into the other room to take it. The only people calling her at five in the morning were calling from California, and I guessed she didn't want either her mom or her ex-boyfriend to know I was there. So for about five days I considered us split up. I don't know if Dejda considered us split up. She might have thought we were each busy. In any event, the weather was getting warmer, Czech women began wearing miniskirts that looked like broad belts, and I got bored of being alone at night. So when Dejda proposed a trip to Krakow for the upcoming Easter weekend, I said yes. Who didn't like Krakow?

We decided to catch the red-eye train on Friday night at nine-fifteen, arriving in southern Poland at six-thirty in the morning on Saturday. It was only after we bought the tickets at Cedok and Dejda grinned and whispered the eight words that green-lighted most of my NC-17 fantasies ("I can't wait to be alone with you") that I realized—*fuckshitbitch!*—that we played Meteor in the last game of the season on the same night.

God damn. How did I forget that? Hadn't the season, the finding and joining of a team, been the whole point of spending the year in Prague in the first place? It wasn't to get involved with some Czech (*half*-Czech!) woman and dick around. Certainly not if that meant missing games! Damn it. After everything else, the season was supposed to end with a simple and triumphant flourish. And I'd managed to screw that up.

I focused on this glitch. The question wasn't "How did this happen?" but "What are you going to do about it (jackass)?" I could simply cancel the trip. That would be unfortunate. The Monday after Easter was a holiday; it was the only long weekend for several months. The following weekend Dejda was headed to Slapy, and after that my dad came back to catch the one opera he had missed at Christmas. It felt like Easter was the last chance we'd have to go away together before the weight of summer and visitors and my thesis and our eventual, unaligned departures began to press. Krakow, as the spiritual capital of Roman Catholic Poland, would be *really* nice at Easter. And Dejda couldn't wait to be alone with me.

Still, Vinohrady had a game—its last game—my last game of what was likely to be my last swell season ever. I'd played in a funk for nearly half of the season, but I hadn't missed a game. We'd struggled through our long winter doldrums and had begun to show signs of greatness. Everyone seemed to be holding their heads a little higher since the Kosire game, like we were the dark horses of the *Přebor*, like we were Cleveland State, or Vanderbilt, some bad motherfuckers, the team nobody really wanted to play. I'd been locating my inner Byron Scott. Plus, Meteor wasn't that good. It would be nice to end the season with a win.

Our game with Meteor started at 8:00 P.M. in Vinohrady. The Katowice connector didn't leave until 9:15 P.M. Maybe it would be a fast game. Maybe there'd be a rail strike. I decided to make my decision on the fly.

•　•　•

Meteor 2: April 14, 1995

The referees were late, and it was 8:10 P.M. before we tipped. My black soul-filled hoop sneakers were at Dejda's apartment. I couldn't get a message to her and had to wear jogging sneaks. Big Bob asked me where he could get a pair. Bob was manning the scorer's table. I spoke with Honsa and told him about the 9:15 P.M. train to Krakow. He shrugged, like he was keeping his opinion to himself.

Although the game was at Vinohrady, we'd been preempted by an indoor soccer tournament on the main court, and were playing in a side gym with a wooden parquet floor and no three-point lines. It looked like some sort of dance floor, or a stable, to which someone had added rims. The rims were soft and old and had a slight forward lean to them; outside shots caught them and clung like metal filings. We had a full squad. Meteor only had seven players. Slava, Vykli, Michal, Tonda, and I started.

Tonda won the tip and we came downcourt. Slava went to Vykli, to Tonda, then back to Slava, who faked a pass to me and put up a foul-line jumper. The shot was long and came back softly over the front of the rim. I went up, tapped it left-handed just to keep it alive, and it dropped through the rim. Next play, I took a pass from Vykli and hit a turnaround jumper from the wing that used every bit of the rim before going in.

Hmmm.

The running shoes felt a little lighter than my three-quarter tops, and maybe it was all psychological, but I felt like I was getting up higher on my jump shots and out faster on the break. I got a jump hook to drop from the right block, and then banked in another from a step further out. Dejda showed up on the sidelines with a swollen backpack.

Martin came in and we worked the pick-and-roll. On the press, Vykli and I swallowed up the hapless Meteor guard and forced him into a turnover. Kratcha came in for Michal and blocked a shot emphatically. He gathered the loose ball and spun out onto the left side for a break. Vykli cut down the court in front of him. Meteor's sole defender went with Vykli, and I trailed in their wake. Kratcha sent a long bounce pass to me and then the lane was clear, as if by magic. I felt light and strong, the ball cupped low in my hands. My steps were right. I went up.

It wasn't a dunk, but turned into one of those special layups where you got whistles from the crowd. Kratcha shouted something. I hung a little longer in the air and tapped the backboard.

At the half Honsa confirmed that we were ahead, but he hedged when asked by how much. Meteor was staying close with decent outside shooting and occasional failures in our press that a blind man could exploit. The second half started, Tonda powered in a layup, and Mondy and I each got offensive rebounds off missed threes by Vykli on the same possession. Meteor switched to a zone and Kratcha hit me for a shot that would have been a three in any gym with a line. On the next possession, Kratcha kept the ball and drove baseline for a left-handed scoop. Michal reversed a layup.

There was no scoreboard, but it felt like we were ahead by ten at least. Maybe fifteen. Most of the season had felt like that. A Meteor guard picked me up at the top of the key. I crossed over on him right to left, went down the lane, let him catch up, then spun back to the right. He was reaching, so I elevated and—whistle—sank the jumper.

I went to the line to complete the three-point play and glanced over at Dejda.

She looked worried. Was she worried about me? No need, sweetheart. I was feeling as good as I'd felt all year. Feeling like I could have made a run at the CBA, or maybe the Italian leagues. What other countries were there?

She pointed at the clock hanging on the wall behind the rim like a moon. It was 8:55. Our train for Krakow, across town, left in twenty minutes. We should already be in our seats.

Shit!

I stood at the foul line. There were about fifteen minutes left in the game. Honsa had sent Jena to the scorer's table to sub in for me. Jena had even put his protective glasses on. I had picked up three fouls. If I made the free throw, there'd be a stoppage and I'd come out. If I missed, I'd stay in. I had seventeen points and felt like I was inches away from the zone, like I was finally fully integrated into the team. But Jena was already coming in, and we seemed to be pulling away. I might not even get back off the bench. There was no way Meteor was coming back—their guards were sucking wind even now. If I stuck around for even five more minutes, we'd miss our train for sure. We might not even make it now.

Decisions. I looked to Bob for the score, but he wasn't paying attention. I decided to leave it to the free throw. If it went in, then I'd be coming out anyway, could check the score, and would split with Dejda. The Vinohrady season would be over, except for France. If the ball stayed out, if it clanged off the backboard or fell softly away from the side, then I was where I was supposed to be.

Opposing fans used to hold up life-sized posters of swimsuit models to try to get Bird to miss foul shots. Chris Jackson would hit 400 free throws in a row before practice, making his teammates wait until he missed. The referee bounced me the ball. I took one dribble, let the ball spin in my hand until the grooves came up right, promised myself that I'd try to make it. I bent at the knee and let it go.

Swish.

Whistle.

Jena came in.

At the scorer's table, Bob confirmed we were up by double dig-
its. I nodded to Honsa, who nodded back, and accepted high fives
and low fives from the bench. Behind me, the game started again.
Slava, on the bench while Vykli ran the point, said *"Trening, zitra
rano, sedm."* Then he asked, "You will come to Argue-ville?" which
he thought was the name of the French town the international
tournament was in.

I nodded, grabbed my stuff, and ran out of the gym with Dejda.

We jogged down Vinohrady toward the train station, the sweat
drying on my arms. There were no cabs around this part of Prague 3
on a Friday night; they were all in Václavské Námĕsti or the Old
Town. At the Wilsonovo highway, we jumped the divider and dodged
puttering Skodas and Trabants. I had the bigger bag, but Dejda's
backpack threatened to topple her. We began to run toward Hlavní
Nádraží's parking garage, and then changed our minds and headed
straight down the tracks toward the platforms until we found our
train at *nastupiste ctyri*. All the compartments were occupied, and we
crowded in with two soldiers and two businessmen in bad suits.

It was 9:10 P.M. The game would have been nearly over, depending on the whistles. I wondered if we'd held the lead. We stored our
bags and settled against the window, Dejda leaning on my shoulder
and closing her eyes. She was scheduled to fly back to California in
just over two months. I looked out onto the dark tracks as the train
began to move, feeling like I'd stolen something.

Part Four:
The End of the Road

Biskupcova

AT 6:00 P.M. on Thursday, I opened the double-paned windows of my apartment and looked down Biskupcova, which stretched in a long crooked line out toward the pink horizon. There was a murmuring at street level as people in the neighborhood returned from school and work. Old women leaned on folded arms out of first-floor windows and chatted with the passersby. The evening was warm and sweetly scented. Along the sidewalk, the rows of long barren trees had begun to sprout their summer leaves. It was no longer possible to see what all the people were doing in upper-floor apartments across the street. The pale sidewalk extended off in the distance, like Gatsby's starry ladder, rising up to a secret place above the trees.

I looked at the ladder and thought dramatic things about Dejda and my family and the future, until something, a sound, started descending the ladder toward my apartment. Someone was dribbling.

Just from the sound you could tell the ball was rubber and overinflated. I could hear the pauses and the footsteps when the ball hit a crack and had to be chased down in the street. Two kids appeared, between the green curtains of leaves, young, bouncing the ball irregularly between them every couple of steps, exclusively right-handed. I thought about all the ball-handling drills I'd ever tried, the figure eights, the spider dribbles, dribbling while wearing mittens, with my eyes closed, with plastic handcuffs over the mittens. About hours spent whirling the ball around—first hips, then ankles, then neck, then hips again, like a satellite. About a couple of exceptionally restless nights in junior high school where I slept with my basketball, because I'd heard that Pete Maravich used to do that. About watching and watching again, in super slow-mo, Isiah's double back-and-forth against Alvin Robertson—*Alvin Robertson!*—in the 1989 All-Star Game that put Alvin so far back on his heels he couldn't even get his balance to wave at the ensuing jump shot. Or Jordan's unusual left-right-left crossover on Bird in the 63-point game. Or Timmy Hardaway's UTEP Two-Step on Mark Price and his hanging and-one follow. Every drill I'd tried to become a ball-handler, to learn each new crossover, each new spin. To hold onto what other people wanted.

B.B. King called his guitar Lucille, but I didn't know anyone who named his basketball. It wasn't that a ball was less personal; a shooter knew every groove and divot, every peel of frayed leather on his favorite ball. But the ball could be fickle, and it got passed around and lent out, and at game time you played with the one they gave you. So instead of giving it a name like Lucille, you called it the "Rock."

"Gimme the rock," you might say.

You'd scream at it to "Drop" or "Get down."

You'd call out, "Glass!" and pimp it out to the boards.

"One time," you'd implore to it. "Just one time."

I watched the dribblers, thinking about ways to split them, to make one lean right, the other guard left, and then knife between them, emerging on the other side, leaving them behind, taking the ball away to the hole. Then I caught myself, and thought "Grow up." The real world didn't revolve around one inflated leather globe. It was substantially more complex.

Krakow had been stunning; rain-soaked and full of flowers. Dejda and I had stayed in one of the smaller hotels on the outskirts of the Rynek, watching *MacGyver* dubbed in Polish and roaming the alleys near Wawel Castle. We got back to Prague to learn that Vinohrady wound up losing to Meteor by five. The season was over; Vinohrady finished with a record of four and eighteen. Next year, the team would drop out of the *Přebor*, back to the lower league from whence they'd risen the year before. We'd seemed so close to being competitive. Our worst loss of the season was against a team we would have beaten the first time around if they hadn't gotten a dubious last-second foul shot (my man, un-boxed), and we'd beaten the second-best team in the league by thirty-four. I swung between feeling guilty and overindulgent. I wasn't good enough to make us lose.

We kept practicing, focusing on the trip to France, although the trip had become pretty clearly less about basketball and more about the pleasures and relative novelty of going to France. The games were to be played in a town called Maurienne, near Albertville, in the French Alps. I couldn't find it on any of my maps.

In the meantime, I played in the occasional pickup game on the courts near my apartment. The court belonged to the local elementary school, and to use it we had to scale a seven-foot metal fence. Sometimes the schoolchildren played with us. Sometimes, older belligerent men in overalls joined in, running with the ball and shooting from behind their heads. They wore stained shirts and had spackling powder clinging to their shoulders and hats. It puffed off of them in clouds when they got fouled. Sometimes, the games ended in fights, in a crowd of people separating two others, in hard words and swears and plenty of Czech I was sure translated into "Take your foreign ass home." Once, a local said he was coming back with his comrades.

Years earlier, one of my middle school textbooks featured swirling crayon-like sketches of Prague and Budapest that made them seem like they were made out of smoke. The curriculum got less flattering in later years; Kafka and Dostoevsky and *Darkness at Noon* and *A Clockwork Orange*. Those books were full of vaguely sinister words like *pod* and *dum* and *prospekt* and comrade and collective. It was either a mark of the transition or of my own obliviousness that over the course of the year I hadn't thought much about Communism in any real terms. I'd thought plenty about it abstractly, as in "These are books written by and about opponents of Communism, which is bad." And maybe Prague wasn't really the right place to think about Communism, anyway, at least as an economic theory; it was as out of place as considering the merits of representative democracy on a reservation. My teammates never talked about their own experiences, or referred to each other as "comrade." I imagined that some of them, or their families, might have been Party members. Or maybe not. If I'd been paying closer attention, maybe I could have figured out which, but I doubted it.

In Prague, the only things I saw on a daily basis that reminded me of the country's recent past as part of a totalitarian regime were the private security guards lining the storefronts along Vaclavske Namesti. They looked nothing like the rent-a-cop version in the corners of the Gaps and Banana Republics in the malls of America. With their blown-out jackets and boots and scary guns, the Czech security guards looked paramilitary. They looked like they wouldn't need much of an excuse to shoot someone, and they weren't particularly concerned about repercussions. I didn't know why they made me think of Communism, other than the fact they were unsettling and seemed to suggest a certain disregard for individual rights and the process of law. But that could just as easily have been corruption, on which Communism didn't have a monopoly. Certainly, the

Pod Smetanou didn't make me think of Communism. It made me think of Big Bob and sausages and beer. And *Obecni Dum* made me think of Dejda, who made me think of comfort and sex and arguments.

. . .

DEJDA AND I had planned to meet for a picnic, but I was running late downtown and needed to find a bathroom. Fast Dave's brother had shown up in Prague—the latest of a never-ending string of visitors—and I'd gotten roped into listening to his woman troubles and ensuing transcontinental drive. It had required a lot to drink. Dejda was waiting across town, at the foot of St. Mikuláš.

I went to McDonald's, which was teeming with tourists and the young Czechs who could afford it. There was a sign near the door, in Czech, telling the locals that the hamburger prices were lower at the McDonald's around the corner. The restaurant was next door to a clothing outlet called Himi's Jeans, a Czech version of the Gap that sold *Miami Vice*-style jackets to which Czech youth seemed drawn. One was a black faux-satin number embroidered with the words USED COMPANY—CONZEPT LINE. Another just said TOP SCORE CLUB. The most popular one was an aqua and pink denim jacket with a Native American chief in profile on the back. Beneath the chief's flowing headdress, the jacket read DETROIT REDNECKS FOOTBALL CLUB.

I headed up the McDonald's stairs, past the security guards stationed to deter Gypsy kids from panhandling inside. Since it was a tourist McDonald's, it tolerated people coming in just to use the bathrooms if those people looked like tourists. I congratulated myself on my chameleon-like ability to blend. The tables were crowded with Italians, Germans, and homesick Americans with backpacks. They were impossibly slow on the stairs, and I rushed past them to the toilets.

But where were the urinals?

There were no urinals, of course, because it was the women's bathroom. I didn't realize that until a stout older Czech woman teetered out of a stall, hitching up her skirt. When our eyes met, there was a long moment of uncertainty. Had she made the mistake? Then we both rushed to the door to check the blue plastic icon. Yes, it was wearing a dress. The woman pointed to herself, to help me understand. Then she pointed across the hall.

"*Ti*," she said, indicating the blue plastic man icon. "*Tam.*"

You, there.

I nodded to her. We laughed for a second. I tried to apologize but it went badly.

"*Tam*," she said again.

I nodded again. I was trying to remember the Czech word for "I understand." It was *rozumim*, but I couldn't get it.

She stopped smiling. She was still holding the door to the women's room open. It was about to get awkward. I threw my head back, rolled my eyes, and said, "*Ti vole!*"

That seemed to relax her. It really was a useful phrase. She grabbed my hands and patted them. Then she started to talk. I had no idea what she was saying. I gave her about a minute and then pointed to my bladder.

"*Prominte*," I said.

She looked at me and then began to walk me toward the men's room. For a minute, I thought she was going to come in with me, but she left me at the door. I urinated proudly. It felt sort of like belonging.

Dejda, when I found her, was still flushed from the other night when the expat proprietor of Jama had offered her a job as a

"Jägermeister Girl." The position would have required Dejda to walk around his bar wearing shot-glass bandoliers and hip holsters. The proprietor's advice to Dejda was "The sexier you dress, the better." Dejda had been a tennis All-American at UC San Diego and had the body to prove it, and she seemed to be pretty pleased with the offer. But she was also leery of getting pawed; she'd recently had a meeting with an acquaintance of her mother's, a businessman who held the purse strings on some corporate biology grant. Five minutes in, the man had asked Dejda to sit on his lap. Women here, it seemed, still had to put up with some level of that shit. Renee had plenty of stories about workplace indiscretions that would have resulted in an instant lawsuit back in the States, and her bosses didn't even think she took an interest in her appearance. Dejda had responded to the Jama offer with "Oh my God" incredulity, but you didn't have to look too deep to see her happiness at the thought of making some extra money as a "Jägergirl," and just beneath that, to the anger and exhaustion at the hands of men and their schemes.

We had a picnic on the Charles Bridge, sitting in the shadow of St. John of Nepomuk, to the left of the center of the universe. I was supposed to have been in charge of getting provisions, but had been too proud of my bathroom exchange to remember. We bought some cheese and tomatoes and cheap wine and a round of brown bread at a *potraviny* at the end of the bridge. We cut the plastic top off of the bottle of wine and held it by the neck as tourists and pickpockets drifted past us, pausing from their respective endeavors to watch the sun sink behind Petrin Hill. There were less than eight weeks remaining until we left. The lights from the castle flickered off of the Vltava and Dejda said, "I have so many memories from this year, I don't know where to keep them."

· · ·

211

EXPATRIATE GAMES

HONSA CALLED A final team meeting, at which two were decided critical issues: whether or not to have two teams next season and whether or not to keep practicing three times a week. Honsa and Radek chaired the meeting from desks at the front of a classroom high in the Vinohrady complex. Big Bob sat up there, too, for reasons nobody made clear. Behind them, a *sokol* emblem hung proudly on the wall.

On the first issue, the players voted to consolidate the A and B squads into one super-squad. How this would help was unclear, since the B team had also only won four games. It also meant that six players would get cut outright next year in order to reduce the number of bodies and increase the playing time for the remaining players. The vote was controversial, and Honsa's face was redder than usual. I abstained.

The second issue was easier. Only Kratcha voted to continue practicing three times a week. The rest of the players gave themselves Fridays off.

With those two issues decided, Honsa distributed the final statistic sheets for the season. They were, predictably, comprehensive. The players grabbed for the sheets, eager to begin bragging. With Peli's departure, I finished as the team's leading scorer with 240 points in twenty-two games, or just under 11 points a game. Pete Maravich could rest easy. I also finished first in the minutes-per-point category, scoring a point every 1.975 minutes. I was glad I hadn't known that stat during the season; the pressure, and the math, would have complicated things. Vykli was second in both scoring categories, but finished with the highest cumulative grade average at 4.85. At 4.59, I trailed both him and Slava. Still, a big improvement from mid-season. Mondy and Martin were neck and neck in the fouls-per-game department, with Mondy coming out ahead at 2.9. Slava hit 35 threes to Vykli's 33, with both of them hitting at well over 50 percent. I hit 19.

At the far right of the stat sheet was a column headed *Nazor Trener*, where Honsa listed his summary of each player's season. I got Tomas to translate for me. For Vykli, Honsa had written: "Excellent shooter, but overly individualistic and prone to conflict with rivals and referees." Slava was an "Efficient floor-leader and great shooter, but hampered by fitness." Among the comments for Tonda: "Catastrophic physical condition." Under Tomas's name, Honsa had put "He is not here psychologically." I was worried about what Honsa had had to say about me. Tomas read it: "First-rate skills, but unfortunately not compatible with our style." Ouch. But no surprise.

"Still," Tomas continued reading, "a marvelously helpful addition to our team."

I thought I might cry. Not really, but still…

It was becoming clear that the team itself as a formal entity was close to disbanding for the year. The France trip was sort of team-optional. Neither Vykli nor Kratcha could go. They had to work and study for exams. Tonda had winced when he heard how much it was going to cost. Honsa himself was noncommittal. It occurred to me that this could be it. I might never see any of them again. I felt like I should say something. I owed them all so much.

"*Panove*," I said, repeating the greeting that had been on the play sheets Honsa had distributed back in September. "Gentlemen."

The players looked at me. I spoke pretty rarely, and spoke Czech even less often.

"*Dekujime mostat na hesky sezona*," I said, borrowing words from signs I'd seen, T-shirts, notes on Dejda's grandmother's refrigerator. "Thank you so much for a beautiful season." There might have been some French in there. "*Ti mam hrad*." I wanted to tell them I loved them, but "like" was the best I could do.

Poli said something that made the rest of them laugh and he pretended to give me a hug. Kratcha did the same. Vykli and I shook hands. He said he wanted to stay in touch. Us *advokatni* had to stick together.

I gave Honsa a T-shirt with the Chicago Bulls logo on it that said "Three-Peat!" He smiled his red-cheeked smile, the same one I'd seen the first time we'd met, in the locker room when I asked if I could try out.

"*Dekuji*," he said.

"*Ne*," I said, pointing at myself and then at him. "*Dekujime*."

"*Ti vole*," Honsa shrugged. "*Neni zac*." It was nothing.

. . .

MY DAD CAME back to Prague for ten days, although he spent half of it in Budapest and Pecs, a medieval town in southern Hungary. While in Prague, he took me to hear Verdi's *Requiem* at a chapel along the Vltava. We were waiting for Dejda at the foot of Václavské Náměstí. She was late. My dad was patient. Half an hour passed, and I didn't know what to do.

"How long do you wait?" I asked him.

"If you're going to wait," he said, "you wait until she shows up."

During the "Dies Irae," Dejda managed to fall asleep. My dad pretended not to notice, or maybe he really didn't notice. Meanwhile, I listened to the host of demons chanting "*Di-es ir-ae!*" It sounded like they were chanting to me. *Da, da, David,* they chanted. *Do your thesis! Da, da, David, fifty pages.*

After the concert, we went to dinner at the Knights of Malta. My dad had venison with croquettes. I had aubergine and thought of Mary's long calves. The next morning, we took the bus to the airport and made plans to meet in Boston in July.

Dad said, "Finish with a kick," and went home.

•   •   •

MAY FIRST WAS a national holiday in the Czech Republic, as it was in most of Europe. In Central Europe, the holiday had been long co-opted by the Communists as a "Worker's Day," and accompanied by large-scale Party-orchestrated celebrations in the streets and squares of the Russian satellite states. The post-revolution holiday was conspicuously devoid of Czechs, most of whom had gone to their cottages in the woods for the long weekend. Those stuck in the city headed, along with the expats and the tourists, to Petrin Hill to savor a day that started cold and gray but ended warm and gold.

I picked Dejda up from her biology lab and we headed to the red roofs of Mala Strana, the Little Quarter. Petrin Park sloped down from the hills of Strahov to the river and was dotted with statues and cherry trees and carved with paths. Halfway up was a statue of the Czech poet Karel Hynek Mácha, who, just before he died at the age of 25, wrote a poem called "May." His poem lamented an unrequited love, and on May Day, lovers went to his statue to lay flowers and hope that they never suffered his fate. Another May Day custom was to kiss your girlfriend under a blossoming cherry tree. That would ensure she stayed young and beautiful throughout the coming year. Dejda ran to one and puckered up, white cherry petals falling on her like the biggest snowflakes I was ever going to see. *A lot of fucking good this is going to do me*, I thought, and obliged.

•   •   •

WITH MAY, THE interminable NBA season came to an end and play-offs finally started. First-round matchups included the Lakers against

215

Sonics and the Bulls versus the Hornets. The Celts drew Orlando. Good-bye, Boston. The Celts of the 1990s bore no resemblance to the powerhouses of the Bird Era, except for Eric Montross, who was big and white. For a few years I'd taken pleasure in the Celtics' demise, but it no longer made me smile. Gone were the days when they would throw out Bird, Ainge, DJ, McHale, and the Chief and then bring in a guy like Wedman to drain improbable threes or Sichting to pick a fight with Ralph Sampson. The Celts always seemed to have some small guy ready to duke it out with a bigger guy: Sichting v. Sampson; Ainge v. Tree Rollins; M. L. Carr v. just about anyone. Of course, there was also the time when the Chief tomahawked Bill Laimbeer, but you almost couldn't blame him for that. It was a mark of how disliked Ainge was that when he fought with crazy Tree Rollins, who had about a hundred pounds on him, Tree Rollins bit Ainge on the finger, and people refused to believe it, and accused Ainge of biting Rollins.

The Celts' struggles were symbolic of the entire Atlantic Division's fall from grace, a fall that began with the "lost draft" of 1986. That year, the Sixers, who had won the championship in 1983, had the first pick as a result of some trade loophole. With Moses, Doc, a young Barkley, Mo Cheeks, and "the Boston Strangler" Andrew Toney, they were stacked. By the magic of the lottery and trades, the Celts had the second pick and looked to complement their starting five with some young legs. The Atlantic would have been set for another ten years.

But what happened? Harold Katz traded the number-one pick to Cleveland (who took Brad Daugherty) for Roy Hinson and Jeff Ruland, each of whom was past his prime. Then he traded Moses Malone and Terry Catledge and threatened to sell Doc. Exit Sixers. The Celtics, meanwhile, drafted Lenny Bias and two days later his heart exploded. Who was there to pick up the Atlantic? The Knicks?

New Jersey? When Bird stole Isiah's pass and fed DJ for the layup to end the murderous 1987 series, everyone cheered a little harder and a little longer, because it was clear that the Pistons (and, later, the Bulls) were ascendant, and the Atlantic as a force was a thing of the past.

. . .

PRACTICES HAD DWINDLED to a core of ten players. More often than not we played five-a-side soccer. They were all very good; Peli and Big Bob, improbably, were among the best. I was the worst, despite having played on my high school's varsity team for five years, including one as an 8th grader. Playing soccer with the Czechs felt a little like hoop in reverse: Whatever limited skills I had in soccer I owed to repetition, not imagination, and I had no touch. They all played more innately, the ball firing off their feet on shots and floating off on passes. One night, I got stuck in goal, ducking from the shots they hit at me. In the locker room afterward, when Bob got in the shower, Honsa grabbed Bob's camera and took pictures of him, naked. Mondy, also naked, jumped in and hugged him.

Outside, the lawn of Vinohrady was wide and green and empty. It looked like the sort of lawn you could run to the middle of, lie down, and vanish. Over a small hill to the left, I could hear a lawn mower and smell the wet cut grass. The sun was low in the sky, ready to drop beneath the horizon, and the light seemed soft and gauzy. I went with Bob, Tomas, and Jena to the Pod Smetanou. I still owed Bob a case of *Velkopopovicky Kozel* from that ill-advised wager back before the season began. Tomas let me drive his Skoda to the pub. I hadn't been behind the wheel of a car since leaving Boston. The Skoda was a manual transmission and rode heavy, and on the cobblestones we rattled without pause, but just sitting behind the wheel made me feel like I could fly.

We drifted through the back streets of Prague 3. Tomas was nervous because the cars on either side of the street were parked with their tails out, creating a narrow lane within which to drive. In Czech, the word *Skoda* meant a lot of things, including "too bad" and "damage." The pale moon was rising in the eastern sky, shining down on the castle. Bob said that when Basketball Marek had traveled in the United States two years before, "he crash four cars." He rolled his eyes. Marek! Bob seemed to think Marek's troubles were entirely connected to the alleged size of Marek's dick.

. . .

PRAGUE HAD BEEN packed with tourists and Euro spring-breakers each day since Easter. The crowds swelled downtown. I watched a gang of Gypsy women mug a pair of well-heeled German couples at the 22 tram stop outside the Světozor Theater. The Gypsies had waited until the tram arrived and then melted out of the shadows to form a group that waited with the Germans to board the tram. When the doors opened, two Gypsy women got on and stood in the doorway, arguing with the driver and creating both a distraction and a bottleneck. The Germans were trapped in the pack behind, trying to squeeze onto the tram. While they did, the Gypsies behind them rifled through their coat pockets and waist pouches. It would be impossible to tell who was grabbing what. Just as the tram doors closed, the Gypsy women at the front squeezed off and the Germans squeezed on, relieved to be out of the scrum but, as they'd discover five minutes later, minus their wallets.

Renee had decided to move out of our flat. She'd found a cheaper, bigger place in Smíchov with a television and a phone. Her move left me in a bind. Our rent was about twice what I could afford. I'd need to either find a new roommate, get the landlords to lower the rent, or move out. Dejda proposed that I move in with her. I thought about that. We would be living together. Was that a big deal? I wasn't put off by the moral aspect of it so much as the physical aspect. What about my stuff? What about my razors? Would I be able to leave them on the sink? And I was a little afraid that we'd get on each other's nerves pretty quickly. Just the other night, the night we'd taken Tomas's Skoda for a ride, I'd come home later than I meant to and there was a distinct chill in the dark bedroom. A note by the light read, "Thanks for being on time, Dork-face."

Dork-face? Was that the price of entering fully into a semi-adult relationship—being called *dork-face* in your own bedroom? It would no doubt feel worse being called dork-face in Dejda's aunt's bedroom. I didn't want to be called dork-face anywhere. It seemed more prudent to talk to my landlords first.

The Lakers had gone up two to one on the Sonics and played Game Four in the Forum. Boston, after losing Game One by 47 points, won Game Two in Orlando. The Bulls and Charlotte split the first two, with Jordan going for 45 and 32 points, respectively. Denver, with a backcourt of the six-foot-seven Jalen Rose at point and the five-eleven Abdul-Rauf at off-guard, looked like it was headed out of the playoffs pretty fast.

Jan Wiener

PRAGUE CELEBRATED V-E Day on May 8 with celebrations marking the fiftieth anniversary of the end of World War II. Prague Castle was hosting an exhibition of Czech Resistance. One of the visiting honorees was Jan Wiener, whose offhand comments about finding him in Prague and not backing out still felt like challenges, even though he hadn't meant what I'd thought he meant, either time.

During my first visit to Prague, I'd borrowed the book Jan had written on the assassination of the World War II German *Reichsprotektor*, Reinhard Heydrich—really, I was looking for any way to stay in his orbit. In the book, the story of Jan's own childhood was intertwined with that of the doomed assassination, and was just as harrowing. Jan had been born in Prague in 1920. His family was Jewish and, when National Socialism took power in Germany in 1938, Jan was sent by his mother and grandmother to live with his father in Yugoslavia. The family's belief was that Jewish men, especially those of fighting age, would be targeted, and it was safer to be out of Prague. Jan's mother and grandmother stayed behind, and it was the last time he saw them.

Jan had to get permission from the local authorities to leave the country. The process required that he submit a list of the items he was taking. He had six pairs of shoes on his list. In a moment of cruelty that Jan never forgot, the Czech official in charge of visas had sneered at him: "Little Jew, you won't have time to wear out one pair."

In Yugoslavia, Jan and his father passed their waiting time by playing chess and drinking plum brandy as the war began to surround them. Soon it was clear that the rest of the family would not get out of Prague alive, and that the war would find them in their exile. Jan's father, exercising the only control he felt he still had over his life, decided to kill himself with poison. He urged Jan, then twenty years old, to do the same. Jan refused, and his father made one last request: for Jan to stay with him after he overdosed, to make sure he died.

Jan's father gave Jan a dose meant to put him to sleep, which Jan accepted. Then, alone, Jan's father administered a more potent dose to himself. In the morning, Jan stayed as long as he had to. Then he ran, slowly during the day and fast at night, across rivers and borders, under trains and mountains. He was caught in Italy hanging onto the bottom of a train car, by the toilet hatch; a soldier with a mirrored pole spotted him. Jan was sent to an Italian concentration camp. He escaped and was recaptured, emaciated from days on the run. His fellow prisoners made him a feast of the camp dog when he returned. He escaped again, and was liberated by Allied troops advancing up southern Italy. After that, he went to London and began flying bombing missions back over his beloved Czech Republic.

When the war ended, Jan returned to Prague to find the collaborator who had ridiculed his packing. The official was still in government and didn't remember the young Jew even after Jan dragged him across his desk by the neck and cocked his pistol at the man. The official begged for his life. Jan broke the man's nose and left him there.

• • •

TIME WAS GETTING short. There seemed to be so much still to do. Dejda got a little manic and pulled me around like a puppy. Cameron and Lindsey rented a car and drove into Southern Bohemia. They were planning to leave Prague by the first week of July. A month earlier, they'd adopted a dog, a German Shepherd they named Matti. Matti's fate was unclear. Shannon had moved in with Joel, a platonic arrangement, initially, of complementary dry wits and relative maturity. They had a dog, too. Dejda, who was neither dry-witted nor all that mature, wanted a dog, but decided that she'd settle for a weekend of wine tasting in Moravia instead.

Moravia, which made up the eastern half of the Czech Republic, was dotted with small wine-making cities with names like Valtice and Břeclav. But they were far from Prague. I looked into renting a car, which would have cost 3,600 crowns for the weekend. That was slightly more than Dejda made in a month at the biology lab. A dog would be cheaper.

Dejda wouldn't be dissuaded. On Saturday morning she decided that we should hop on a bus to Brno, the capital of southern Moravia, hometown of Kundera and Jaromir Jagr and launching-off point for vineyards. When the NHL players went on strike in 1993, Jagr returned to Brno to play with a team called Poldi Kladno. The local soccer club, Boby Brno, trailed only Prague's Slavia and Sparta in the national standings. I didn't know much about its hoop teams.

We have to go now, Dejda had said, as we lay in bed at her aunt's apartment. We don't have time to waste. Generally, when a girl says that to a guy, the guy should think twice—but in my experience, I never did. Off we went to the bus depot.

The bus rolled out of Prague, and in half an hour we'd left the city behind. Unfortunately, there were three more hours of driving after that. By the time we got to Brno, Dejda had forsaken her recent vow to eat healthy and bought three cones of lemon *zmrzlina* and slices of pizza topped with sauerkraut. I'd gotten used to the smells of the municipal transport food kiosks—deep-fried fat and cigarettes—and now it was a comfort after the long bus ride. We'd paid 66 crowns—slightly more than $2—to get to Brno, halfway across the country. Now we paid 20 more crowns and hopped on a rickety bus to Mikulov, a tiny village on the Austrian border. It rose off of the smooth Moravian plains like a red-roofed blister. Mikulov, Dejda told me, was famous for its wine cellars, a fact she'd apparently picked up on a poster in the Brno train station. We had no room, no map, no guidebook, and little money. But it was a sunny day and we were scheduled to get into town by 7:00 P.M. How hard could it be to find a room?

Very hard, as it turned out.

Mikulov had an eerie, almost empty feel to it when we finally arrived. The main square was deserted. This made it hard to believe the staff at the first three guesthouses we tried when they told us that everything in town was full. When the clerk at the fourth house told us the town was packed solid, we started to believe it. Apparently, every hotel and boardinghouse was full of Austrians, who'd crossed the border to spend the long weekend tasting wine, flaunting their Euros, and wandering in the hills.

It was getting dark out. Dejda started to mope and mentioned sleeping in a field. I'd figured out that moping, like snoring, was something you could do only in pairs, and then only if you started first. I wasn't sure if that was really the case with snoring, but I'd never seen evidence to the contrary. Dejda could be a champion moper, and even my promise to have her safe in a room within the hour didn't cheer her up. She rolled her eyes and sighed like it was my idea to get on the bus in the first place. *We don't have time to waste.* I couldn't believe I'd fallen for that.

We headed down to the Hotel Rosa, a gingerbread-house *pensione* that looked way out of our price range. I had a credit card that I'd painstakingly avoided using all year long, but threw it down and asked for a room. The sight of plastic nearly got Dejda to smile, but then the hotel clerk said that there were no rooms available. Dejda started to plead in Czech with the clerk—she said something about Prague and Austrians and what sounded like "husband"—and looked authentically close to tears. It was impressive and a little frightening. The clerk frowned, but made a couple of calls. Ten minutes later a marionette of a man—small and thin, with limbs that seemed to each be moving independently—pulled up to the Rosa in a red Skoda.

Ano, he nodded; he had a room for us.

Dejda stopped moping as the man drove us in his small car through the darkening town. He introduced himself as "Placic" and his small Craftsman-style house as "At the Green Tree." He lived there with his wife and daughter—the sight of whom was no small relief; in the already eerie Mikulov, Placic and his Green Tree had started to seem a little elven to me. Our room, at the top of the stairs, looked out over a small garden full of lilacs and cherry trees. Placic charged us 400 crowns—about $14—a night, gave us maps, and showed us how to find the best local cellars, which he circled. Mikulov claimed to be the ancestral home of viniculture, and its cellars were carved into the limestone hillside.

"Hurry," Dejda said, toggling back from morose to enthusiastic. "I'm starving."

Jesus. I was still checking my watch to confirm that, yes, within the hour I'd found her a room. You'd think I would've gotten some points for that.

We dropped our bags and headed out to the closest circle on our map. Placic had marked the Pod Kozim Hradkem *sklipek* with stars, and dotted a line to it from his house. The path took us to a long gravel trail, up a hill. We had no idea what would be at the top. I was hungry and the night was moderately warm. Dejda had her second wind. I followed her swaying hips up into the Czech hillside. The trail ended at a small rose garden where people were sitting in the shadows and sipping from plastic water jugs. They smiled at us like we were in on a secret. It was sort of like what I imagined heaven would be like.

We pushed open the door of the *sklipek*. The interior was cave-like and full of Czechs singing songs. A red-faced man with an enormous neck was playing guitar. Dejda and I stood in the door-way, unsure of what to do. There wasn't a bar, but the proprietor came over to us like he knew us and directed us to a back room. We went along. The back room was cool and full of wooden casks with small holes in the lids, plugged with cork. The proprietor took a long glass tube with a bubbled top off of the wall, dipped it into one of the casks, and drew a breath at the other end. Wine flowed magically up into the tube, pooling in the bubbled reservoir. Then he pushed a breath out through his cheeks and shot a thin stream of wine into two small glasses. Concerns about sanitation took a backseat to the romance of the craft. The wine was dry and cold.

I finished the bottle of *Dobra Voda* we were carrying and we filled it with a Moravian white from another cask. The proprietor brought us back into the main room where we sang along with the other patrons, swigging from our bottle, long past the eleven o'clock closing hour and deep into the night. As we left, the proprietor refilled our bottle and gave us a second one for the road, and we skidded down the gravel trail, laughing, until Dejda stopped to pee behind a bush.

The next day, Placic offered to take us to the start of one of the local hikes, a twelve-kilometer route along a nearby ridge. Dejda was cocksure, piece of cake.

"I hiked Mt. Whitney twice," she said, as if I should be impressed.

Yeah, well, I played three-on-three with Kevin Duckworth when he was 300-plus pounds and he still blocked my shot. Where was Mt. Whitney, anyway?

We drove north out of Mikulov, past the green Holy Hill that rose above the little town. On top of it, the small, white chapel Svatý Kopeček perched like a nipple upon a huge breast. Every year the townspeople made a pilgrimage to the top of the hill to pay their respects to the Black Loretto Madonna. I wondered if Mikulov had been the model for Škvorecký's Kostelec, the little town where Danny Smiricky first heard about the miracle, and if Placic would tell me if I asked. We rounded rocky outcroppings and long valleys full of vines and yellow mustard, heading toward a town called Pavlov on the edge of Nové Mlýny Lake. Placic dropped us off alongside Pavlov's conical central tower, pointed to the red-marked pole where the trail began, and drove off.

Maybe this was how he'd freed up his room last night.

The hike started at the base of a string of solitary hills rising out of the plains. Each one was topped with a small castle crumbling back into its limestone base. From the top of the first hill—Sirotčí Hrádek—I could see far into Austria. We were in the middle of nowhere. The metric system again . . . I wasn't sure how far twelve kilometers really was.

We walked all day, pausing at the crests of several hills to eat the ham and cheese sandwiches Dejda had made from breakfast and stuffed into the corner of her backpack. We'd brought one bottle of *voda* and another bottle I thought was full of *voda* but was full of wine instead. We stopped often and sipped from it. I asked Dejda if she had stopped this often when she climbed Mt. Whitney, either time.

She said, "No, but I was with a tall, athletic guy."

Three hours later we were back in Mikulov, sore and dusty, sitting at a table in the rose garden at the Pod Kozim Hrádkem. The proprietor, for whom I had started to feel a very deep affection, brought us plates of spicy *gulas* and *smazeny syr* and more small glasses of cold, bright wine and water. The chef came out and sat at our table, talking to Dejda. He seemed happy to be talking to a non-Austrian. We got another two liters to bring back to Prague. The shower at the Green Tree washed the hills off our legs.

In the morning we hustled out and Placic drove us to catch the train to Znojmo, the fortified border town I'd missed out on after the Košíře game. It was killing me, not knowing what was in Znojmo. The name made it sound enchanted, like the kind of place where the snow wasn't cold. Znojmo sounded like the name of a very old uncle who was nonetheless mysteriously spry. Our train took two hours to traverse the forty-five kilometers between Mikulov and Znojmo, snaking lazily through the yellow and purple quilt countryside and the occasional sleepy town. The sky was clear bur ominously heavy and the train was sweltering. The skin at Dejda's neckline looked shiny and damp. It occurred to me that we could take a quick detour to Austria.

In Znojmo, as in Mikulov, most of the inhabitants were out hiking. Dejda and I headed down a trail to the banks of the River Dyje and spent a lazy hour reading a collection of Roald Dahl stories she'd traded for at the Green Tree. We hiked back to the town just as the sky cracked open and huge sheets of rain fell down onto frosted Austrian women carrying cakes. We hid in a doorway, feeling wet and good, until it was time to make a dash back to the bus station, to an overcrowded bus back to Prague. The trip took four long hours, and for much of it, many of the passengers stood in the aisles and swayed.

• • •

BACK IN PRAGUE, my landlord wouldn't lower the rent. I wasn't sure why I thought she might. So far, my powers as an advocate were unimpressive, especially in Czech. I went to the Hotel Olšanka for dinner, wondering when the MCATs were offered and if there was still time to sign up. The Hotel Olšanka's glistening new Western-style cafeteria was still empty—most of the other students had found nearby restaurants to frequent—and you could load your tray with as many plates of rice and *zelene* and *rohliks* as you could carry and still come back for sugar-dusted *palacinky*, rolled up like hand towels in an aluminum tray.

The only other student in the cafeteria was Janko, the thirty-five-year-old Montenegran who didn't go home for Christmas because he had been called up for military service. Janko was worried about his future. He was waiting to hear from the UN High Commission for Refugees, to whom he had applied for employment. He was laughing because a couple of years earlier he'd considered applying there for asylum. The UNHCR needed Serbo-Croat speakers in Germany to handle the influx of refugees and asylum-seekers. Janko thought it would be an ideal job for him, except that he didn't like dealing with Albanians.

He was writing his thesis on Montenegro's position on international diplomacy, and hadn't started it yet.

After the Mikulov wilderness adventure, eating at the cafeteria depressed me, and as I rode the tram home I started reflecting on all the types of people I didn't like. The list got long fast. Red, fleshy people who looked at me accusingly. Slow people. People who couldn't spell. Men in purple trousers. Men who smelled like cheap tobacco. People who looked like birds. Bony teenagers with shaved heads. Men with thick ankles. Women in poorly-thought-out outfits. Amazingly, there was one of each on the tram.

The evening had the cool heaviness that didn't even promise rain. Practice wasn't until Wednesday. *Ctvrtek*. Cameron was in Budapest, no doubt trying to clean up whatever mess I'd made with the data tape. Somebody had to pay. That's how it went in the CIA. Lindsey was busy. Dejda was meeting friends at the train station. Renee was in Italy, and didn't live with me anymore anyway. It would have been a good night to do some work. Instead, I went home, brushed past the postings and fliers of Czech commerce taped in our lobby, and fell asleep reading Skvorecky's *The Engineer of Human Souls*, a book I enjoyed even without understanding it.

At 5:00 A.M. my doorbell rang repeatedly. I was dreaming about the first girl with whom I'd ever fallen in love, a girl whose appeal was magnified substantially when viewed through the prism of distance. The doorbell kept buzzing. Had Renee come back from Cinque Terre to reconsider? A noise was moving through the apartment. I got up to go to the door and stepped into two inches of water. The noise was the tap in our bathroom, which was on full-blast. The doorbell was my downstairs neighbor, a sleepy, angry, damp Czech. This did not look good.

He started shouting when I opened the door. I couldn't understand him and paddled over to shut off the tap.

"*Jeziz Maria*," I said, over and over again. "*Ti vole*."

I thought back to the previous night, when I'd gone to brush my teeth and no water had come out of the pipes. At the time, it had seemed like just a problem with the flat—the kind of thing to be expected in a Soviet-era apartment block. I'd work it out with the landlords. It turned out that the water had been shut down throughout the Zizkov neighborhood, and it had come back on at 4:30 A.M. One of those flyers on the door, the ones I'd glanced at but ignored because they'd been in Czech, had probably mentioned it.

I was pretty sure I had turned off the bathroom tap tightly. Pretty sure.

I raised my palms up in a way that I hoped conveyed the sentiment "I don't know what has happened here" and began to mop up the water with our bath towels, wringing them out in the shower. The neighbor stayed in the foyer, yelling, watching me, his face incredulous. How could anyone be so dumb?

"*Skoda*," he said, meaning either "too bad" or "damage" or both. "*Skoda, zaplatit.*"

He was the first of a long line of morning visitors, followed by the building handymen, bleary-eyed guys in blue overalls who looked at my mess and told me to open the windows so that the air would help dry the water. After they left, my landlord showed up and asked if I'd left the tap open.

I said I didn't think so.

She looked skeptical.

Finally, there was a long ring at the door and a little old woman asked me to follow her downstairs. Her apartment was half the size of mine and had four clocks ticking loudly on the walls, milliseconds apart from one another. *Tic-tic-tic-tic-tic-tic*. They made it sound like time had accelerated. *Tic-tic-tic-tic-tic-tic*. The old lady's lace curtains draped over the windows, and yellow light the color of old paper filled the room. The wallpaper was peeling away at the edge of the ceiling and rivulets of water were running down the walls like tears. A rug was rolled to the side of the room. The old woman's hands were shaking and she dropped her cane twice explaining to me that she had no money to fix the damage. Who will pay for the damage?

I kind of thought I knew the answer there.

She asked me if I spoke Czech.

"*Bohuzel*," I said, "*ne.*"

She asked if I understood her.

I said, "*Trochu.*" A little.

She patted my hand and ushered me out.

． ． ．

I GATHERED MY expat friends and some teammates together to go and hear the Original Prague Syncopated Orchestra at the Národní dům na Vinohradech. The Original Prague Syncopated Orchestra dressed formally and the tenor sang through a fragile-looking star microphone. The mid-May sky was Hollywood-blue above Náměstí Míru, the Square of Peace. Along the roundabout around St. Ludmila's Church, cars circled off into the city. Inside, the orchestra shared the second floor with a ballroom dancing class for teenagers. Bob and Mondy wandered off in search of dates. The band played a song called "Where Is My Sweetie Hiding," and I closed my eyes and imagined some future place where everything was already done.

Dejda's flight home was set for June 19. Reserved, paid for, non-refundable. She'd be in San Francisco later that day. She said she had been hoping to leave on June 26, the last day her yearlong ticket was good for, but all the flights were booked.

When I'd first come to Prague, I kind of hoped that things would build toward a resolution, that everything would come to a head at the end of the season. That it would feel like something had happened, and had ended, and it would matter. I thought I'd learned how to handle transitions, but I hadn't really. That was easy to tell.

We spent pretty much every night together. I'd wake up in a tangle of her hair; she'd tell me about her dreams. In one, we'd gotten the dog she'd wanted. Dejda was playing with it, and it started scratching at the door, wanting to get out of the room. She went to let it out, but, in her dream, I said no.

· · ·

THERE WERE THE ongoing NBA Playoffs to distract me. The Lakers couldn't get it done against San Antonio and David Robinson. Vlade missed two free throws that cost them a game; they were down three-two instead of up. Jordan was wearing number twenty-three again, after Nick Anderson had said, "Forty-five isn't twenty-three." The Magic were up three to two in that series and were going to win it. The Pacers, behind Reggie Miller and the Davis Boys, had manhandled the Knicks. Starks was fading and Ewing was hurt. Phoenix and Barkley led Houston three-two but couldn't put them away.

The members of Vinohrady were still getting together for movies or concerts, but Honsa was rarely there. Tomas was plugging a trip to the mountains. Mondy was plugging a trip to the States. Robert was studying for his law exams. Big Bob was saving money for an REM concert in June. Notwithstanding the flood, my landlord had granted a one-month decrease in the rent in exchange for my agreement to leave as soon as the month was up. It seemed like a good trade, especially as she was apparently using the flood as an excuse to renovate and remodel some of the flats. And I think I was paying for most of it. I never saw the older lady again, although her door got a fresh coat of paint and a new peephole.

I shook Dejda for a day to get my bearings, and hopped on a train to the silver-mining city of Kutná Hora, an hour east of Prague, a city that had once been full of Italian laborers until the mines ran dry. It wasn't the luckiest of cities, having suffered through the Hussite wars of the fifteenth century and the Thirty Years' War of the seventeenth, bouncing back just in time for a massive fire in 1770. What remained of the original town was dominated by the Kostel Svate Barbory, a massive buttressed cathedral named for the patron saint of miners. Construction had begun in 1388. Inside, frescoes depicted the ghosts of mine workers searching for riches in the earth.

Near Kutná Hora was the smaller town of Sedlec. In 1278, the local Cistercian brought holy soil back from Jerusalem and spread it across the grounds of a small chapel; over the ensuing decades, the religious elite of the Czech Republic had lobbied to be buried there. The cemetery had quickly become overcrowded and, eventually, bodies were stacked like cordwood along the side of the chapel. This was neither graceful nor sanitary, and eventually the chapel commissioned the Czech sculptor František Rint to make better use of the bleaching bones of the faithful. In the crypt of the chapel, he'd set about building pyramids of skulls and chandeliers of femurs. Eventually, the pyramids rose to the ceiling. I joined in with a tour group of Canadian schoolchildren, who giggled and groaned and took photos, the caretakers scowling even as they sold another ticket at 25 crowns a pop.

· · ·

THE ROCKETS CAME back to beat Barkley and led the Spurs two games to zero. The top four picks in the NBA's July draft could be underclassmen, which was still a rarity, and if Golden State got Joe Smith to hit the boards, it might have something. Barkley said he was retiring, but nobody believed him. Jordan said he'd come back after the Bulls were eliminated by the Magic. My sister graduated from college and my parents gave her my old car, the Festiva I'd skidded onto Jan Wiener's lawn. Dejda had gone to France for ten days to visit another friend of her mother's. It was not the section of France where Vinohrady's putative "tournament" was supposed to take place. After the tournament—if there was one—there'd be two weeks until Dejda left, and a month until I did. Dejda was making noises about staying on if she could find a later flight, but they were the sort of noises people made to avoid thinking about other things.

People were asking what would happen next. Lindsey wanted to know if there would be a formal sort of breakup. Shannon wanted to know why we couldn't just stay together, despite the distance, if that's what we wanted. Neither of those seemed very realistic. We didn't have that sort of thing. I decided to consider my options on the way to the tournament, knowing that the minute I was safe with the team and away from the demands of the future I'd consider everything but.

The Road to France

Maurienne Internationale, May 31 to June 5, 1995

At the last practice, Slava had told us a time on Wednesday to be at Nádraží Holešovice. When the time came, I packed my basketball stuff, a change of clothes, some deodorant, and my Walkman, voided my bowels thoroughly, and locked up the flat on Biskupcova. I had been living by myself for a week by then; the apartment was clean, empty, and lined with books on Czech state-owned industry and urban America pickup courts. It was sunny and early in the afternoon, dusk still hours away, and I caught the tram from Strašni all the way to the station. If, as I suspected, the trip didn't happen, I could ride the tram all the way back.

At five 5:45 P.M., the team had gathered in the parking lot outside the train station: Slava, Michal, Martin, Jena, Tomas, Radek, and I were joined by a tall, thin man named Jirka, a mid-sized man whose name I never heard, a short, heavy man named Honsa (but not *our* Honsa), three teenagers from the Sparta youth team, and a slew of serious-looking young women carrying sports bags. The other players were dressed for a vacation; Martin was wearing flowered Hawaiian shorts. Michal had on a fanny pack. Slava wore the red, blue, and black tracksuit he wore to every game, and seemingly in everyday life. They all had sleeping bags.

I felt two things: (1) the thrill that something was actually going to happen; and (2) curiosity, because they all had sleeping bags.

Slava was on his cell phone, a bulky flip-down model that looked like a toy. The other players gathered around him. I asked Tomas why they had the sleeping bags.

"For sleeping," he said, and looked at me like I was crazy.

We waited an hour, Slava holding court in a knot of people. At 6:45 P.M., a short, white bus with red and blue side panels—the Czech national colors—flew down the driveway at the far end of the parking lot. Two police cars, their sirens howling, pulled in behind it. Maybe we were getting an escort?

Slava waved to the driver, who pulled over 100 yards away. The police cars bracketed him. Slava walked down to the bus and spoke to the police officers. It appeared that our bus was being cited for reckless driving before it even got out of the parking lot—indeed, nearly before it even got *into* the parking lot. Slava and the police officers were engaged in some sort of negotiation; the trip, which had looked possible a moment earlier, appeared in doubt. And that no longer seemed like a bad thing.

Then the police officers got back into their cars and left. Slava hopped into the bus's open door and it rolled the 100 yards around to the rest of us, Slava grinning like the captain of a Royal Clipper. "You castrated ox," we shouted, as he jumped off and grabbed his bag. Tomas and I stepped onto the idling bus and looked down its narrow aisle.

Concern one: No toilet.

I'd been bothered by the sleeping bags, nervous about the reckless driving, but the lack of a toilet got me really worried. It was a long way to France. The large windows on either side of the bus didn't open, but small slats at the tops slid forward to allow six inches of air to flow in. There were two drivers. One had the slouch and demeanor and the droopy mustache of some sort of malevolent animal; the other wore the baggy gray pants of the incontinent. They opened the bus's luggage compartment to load our bags— mine was small enough to carry on—and shoved aside seven cases of *Staropramen* beer. *Staropramen* meant "Old Spring." The beer was accessible from inside the bus through a small lid-like trapdoor near the driver's seat.

Each driver pulled a can from the plastic sheathing the cases and cracked it open.

Michal said, "To drive well, they must drink." He was smiling, but I don't think he was kidding.

I grabbed a seat halfway down the aisle, next to Tomas and just in front of Slava. Tomas said that the trip to France would take fifteen hours. I still wasn't sure exactly where we were going. Slava said that the tournament was in a town somewhere between "Argue-ville" and Grenoble, but that we were making stops along the way. He had carried on a cardboard box, which he placed next to him. In it, he had three bottles of RC Cola, two liters of iced tea, a carton of orange juice, a carton of milk, and six bottles of rum. As the sun set and the bus pulled out of Nádraží Holešovice, Slava and Michal, seated across from one another, began a duet, which was quickly picked up by the other players. The drivers shut off the bus's interior lights, and I said a short, silent prayer. All around me, as we rolled off into the night, people I didn't really know sang in a language I didn't really understand.

· · ·

GETTING TO FRANCE took substantially more than fifteen hours. By the time we pulled into Grenoble on the morning of June 2, we'd been traveling for a full day and a half. I'd drunk more rum, sung more Czech, pissed in more countries, and learned more about Tomas than I ever would have imagined possible.

On the first night outside of Prague, we hit a gigantic thunderstorm, complete with blinding bolts of lightning. I was determined to avoid the rum until we crossed over the German border. I wasn't sure why, but it seemed like a good idea to keep my wits about me. Also, I wanted to remember the moment when I could start to think of myself as an international basketball player. So far, I'd been limited to Prague or its suburbs, but once we crossed into Germany, we became something more: national athletic representatives, mercenaries, barnstormers.

We stopped for dinner at a restaurant outside of Plzen. The rain was clamoring outside and it was late for Czech restaurants, but somebody knew the proprietor and he seemed happy for the business, passing out plates of *kureci prsa* and *zelene*, yeasty blond beers and rolls. The women sat at their own tables, reluctant to join us.

We'd been on the road for hours already, and I'd hoped we were staying in Plzen for the night. I was wrong. That was why there were two drivers, to push through the nights. We got back on the bus and the storm seemed to intensify. Hours passed. The bus moved very slowly, rolling through the dark fir forests of Bohemia. The lightning illuminated our path. Around 2:00 A.M., I began to hallucinate. I saw a great empty A-frame gas station and a sign with words in Czech, English, and German. The lightning flashed again and where the A-frame had been I saw, lit starkly on a patch of grass, a Dalmatian mounting what appeared to be an Irish setter. I rubbed my eyes and looked over at Tomas, who was next to me. He smiled and gave me the thumbs-up.

The bus shuddered to a stop and we heard stern voices at the door. Michal and Jirka gathered our passports and vanished up front. What a dumbass, I thought. I just gave my passport away again.

Slava, sweaty and grinning, turned around in the seat in front of me, holding another bottle of rum. He wrapped his meaty hands around my neck and whispered, "Daveed is the best; he is from the West." The bus started to roll again. It wasn't stopping. We were in Germany. I took the rum from Slava, swigged deeply, and closed my eyes.

. . .

IN THE MORNING, my legs felt like wood. I'd tried to get diagonal for sleep, extending my feet as far out under the seat in front of me as I could. It hadn't helped. I was so worried that the drivers would fall asleep that even if the seat had been a La-Z-Boy I couldn't have gotten any rest. Some people stretched their sleeping bags out in the aisle. I borrowed a Sheryl Crow cassette from Tomas and listened to it eleven times.

As the sun rose, it became apparent that the drivers had very little idea of where they were going. I should have figured that out earlier, when they got lost after dinner in Plzen. Plzen wasn't a big city, but in our short foray there the previous night, we'd wound up heading the wrong way down a one-way street and circling a parking lot. A Czech bus driver getting lost in Plzen seemed a little like a landscaper getting lost in a public garden: plausible, but it didn't inspire confidence.

Once we left the Czech Republic behind, however, the holes in our drivers' professional skill sets became apparent. We were still in Germany, on the autobahn, and every couple of miles the driver—whichever one was driving at the time—would pull onto the shoulder and study a map. I had moved to the back of the bus after they'd driven it the wrong way down the one-way street and now had a bird's-eye view of the oncoming traffic, small black sports cars and semis whistling by at ninety miles an hour.

At one point, the bus began to cruise down an exit ramp. About halfway down it, the driver realized that it was the wrong exit ramp and stopped the bus. Then he began to back up. Cars whipped by us, honking and swerving. Michal was next to me in the back, shouting things up to the front, and I realized that he was calling out instructions to the driver, and that the driver, in turn, was relying on Michal to know when to cut the wheel and get back on the road. My anxiety about the lack of a toilet became acute, as I was about to shit my pants. I focused on staying quiet and not distracting Michal. He had an important job.

We waited for a lull in the traffic flow. When one came, Michal shouted to the driver. The driver cut the wheel, shifted from reverse to drive, and began to roll across the off-ramp and back on to the highway. As he did, two tractor-trailers came around a curve in the highway behind us, 100 meters back and gaining.

Michal screamed.

Slava ducked behind a seat.

Bohuzel, I thought. *We are going to die.*

The tractor-trailers' horns blared. One of them angled dangerously onto the exit ramp and the other one rode into the left-hand breakdown lane and flashed passed us.

"*Do prdele!*" the driver shouted at it.

Our bus rolled back into the right lane of the autobahn and snuck off down the road.

I asked Slava if he knew the names of the drivers. "One," he said, in English, "maybe Indiana Jones. One, maybe Jesus Christ Superstar." He laughed, showing off gaps in his teeth. Then thought for a second and said, "Fuckshitbitch, I don't know."

We didn't stop for longer than ten minutes until we got to Bern, Switzerland, and then only to piss on the shoulder while the women's team looked for flora that could accommodate six-foot power forwards. At noon on Thursday, nearly seventeen hours after we'd left Nadrazi Holesovice, the drivers pulled into an autopark near the Bern bear pits and announced that their contract required them to rest for eight hours. We were so close to France that it felt like a strong wind could have blown us there, but they refused to budge. We got off the bus. They closed the doors and told us not to come back until eight O'clock in the evening.

We were cut loose in Bern under a light drizzle. It didn't feel like a sacrifice to get off the bus, which by then smelled like body odor and sausage and canned goods, but we didn't really have anywhere to go. In the pits beneath us, thin bears with elongated snouts walked out of cubbyholes and cast desultory glances up at spectators. The bears looked beaten down, more like mutant dogs, large-snouted Appalachian dogs, than like the bears I'd seen in movies or zoos. People along the rim of the pits threw them carrots, which they caught in their elongated, desultory teeth.

We walked tentatively across a long bridge toward Bern's downtown. Far beneath, the swollen Aare was brown with mud. We stayed close together, half asleep, Czechs loose in a foreign capital, one whose political track record was spotty. The streets of downtown Bern were precisely cobblestoned and lined with expensive shops. We looked in the windows and talked amongst ourselves.

I checked my wallet. Back in Prague, I'd changed 900 Czech crowns into 150 French francs at the American Express office. In Bern, 50 French francs became 11 and a half Swiss francs. Tomas and I separated from the rest of the team, went to a movie called *Shallow Grave*, and fell asleep.

Afterward, we walked through the city. Above a stone arch at the main intersection a large clock shone like the moon. Cars purred and hummed. Like Prague, the downtown Old Town was tucked into the bend of the river. It had been raining in Bern for days, and the Aare had risen to the doorsteps of low-lying buildings. Tomas and I stood near the banks and looked back toward the high arched bridge. From far below, we could make out Slava standing at the very midpoint.

We yelled to him, "Together, we jump!" but he was too far away to hear it.

Periodically we'd run into other members of the team, wandering around. We all looked exhausted and slightly wild. Swiss people on the street gave us a wide berth. We walked back to the bus and found the rest of the team gathered around it, eating bread and sausages they'd dug out of duffel bags. The rain had stopped, and across the river Bern looked rich and exclusive. Jena had bought a small bar of chocolate; nobody else had spent any money. As evening fell the drivers opened the luggage compartments and we drank *Staropramen* for 5 crowns a can.

Our next stop, at midnight, was Lyon. Nobody was sure why we were stopping again; the drivers said it was so that they could sleep. What the fuck, I wondered, were they doing for eight hours in Bern? Not shopping. Not driving.

I'd grown to loathe our drivers, a sentiment apparently shared by most of the women's team. Lyon was like Bern, precious and expensive, and it was midnight. We walked around the city, past empty, thumping discotheques and all-night pizzerias, toward a church marked with a red neon cross high on a hill. From there, we could see over Lyon, a city that seemed to be built on terraces. The Czechs took photos of the dark sprawling landscape, pictures that were too dark to ever turn out and didn't need to. Again we window-shopped and prayed for sleep. Two hours passed and the drivers didn't open the door. Finally, the women's center, a formidable-looking blond girl, pounded loudly on it, and they let us back in.

In the morning, we reached Grenoble. I opened my eyes at around 7:00 A.M.; outside the bus window, the sun was blinding. I heard Slava say, "*Tady*." Here.

I closed my eyes and prayed that we were done with the bus. When I opened them again, I could make out the front of a French high school. It was 8:00 A.M. and students were arriving for classes. We fell out of the bus and stood aimlessly on the sidewalks. The students looked at us curiously but kept a safe distance, like we were some visiting delegation of orangutans.

I still hadn't been able to get any real sleep, and every single part of my body hurt. My head throbbed, my back was sore, my bowels felt impacted, and, Slava's assurances notwithstanding, we were clearly not where we were supposed to wind up. I couldn't even ask him to elaborate. I didn't know the Czech word for *clarify*. If we weren't even there yet, the ride back was going to kill me.

Tomas seemed much more rested. He seemed like he enjoyed camping. Maybe it was just a Czech trait, rolling with hardship. "Come on, Daveed," Tomas said, smiling. He was almost always smiling. "Come on."

Slava, Tomas, Jena, and I walked into Grenoble. I rubbed the smooth leather of my wallet like a talisman, resolving to buy anything that would make me feel better. We passed a *patisserie* and I bought a baguette and some cheese; Slava bought a round of Brie wrapped in foil. We tried to eat them but our jaws were sore. I put the bread under my arm. Slava stuffed the cheese in his bag.

"Toilet?" Slava asked me.

"Shit yeah," I said, nodding.

He nodded back.

We made our way across the city center and found an open café with patio seating on the main square. I waited outside and ordered a *café au lait* while Slava went in to use the bathroom. He was there for fifteen minutes. While I waited, the waiter brought me my coffee in a deep white mug. He put sugar and water on the small marble table.

The coffee was hot and sweet. It warmed my stomach and with each sip, I could feel my strength returning. It didn't feel like overstatement to say that the coffee saved my life. I ordered one for Slava and took my toothbrush out of my backpack. Slava returned, his hair wet on his forehead. He smiled and settled into a chair.

The bathroom was large and clean. I brushed my teeth and washed my face and luxuriated in a bowel movement. I wet my hair back and brushed my teeth again. I changed my underwear and shirt. The waiter knocked on the door, and I came out and ordered another *café au lait*.

Slava said to meet at the bus at 3:00 P.M., and then he and Jena wandered off. We were scheduled to play a game that night, at 5:00 P.M., after two nights on the bus and three of the six bottles of rum. Nobody seemed to know who or where we were playing, but it no longer felt like it mattered. Tomas and I sat at the café for a long time, watching the stunning women of Grenoble walk past us.

"*Holka*," Tomas would say as one walked by. "*Hesky holka.*"

After the second coffee, we left and hiked up the lush limestone mountainside abutting Grenoble. The hike took us through leafy passageways and narrow tunnels. Somehow we ended up above a gondola, looking down onto the rust-colored city. We agreed that we would live in France if they'd let us.

The rest of the team lounged outside of McDonald's. Radek sat on the curb, cradling his head like an egg. The younger players and women huddled at a table around their bags. All around them, Grenoble's fancy shops offered their wares. The commerce was overwhelming; toasters, rugs, sundresses, pots and pans. Beautiful women roamed in and out of the shops. They came in all shapes and sizes and looked utterly unapproachable. At 2:30 P.M. we walked back to the bus along Grenoble's long boulevards, Tomas whispering "*holka*" every few steps.

Our first game, a warm-up game, was against a Grenoble-area men's club team. The official Maurienne tournament didn't start until Sunday; it was one of those all-day, twenty-team elimination marathons. We'd been divided into two squads: a youth team and a "more experienced" squad. Jirka and not-our-Honsa played with us. Radek and Jena played with the youth team, whose best player was a strong young point guard named Kris. Kris spoke English well, and said he'd just gotten back from the Five-Star basketball camp in Pittsburgh, where he'd played with black guys for the first time. He said it like it was a rite of passage, which, for a young Czech basketball player in 1995, maybe it was.

The gym was in a town called St. Pierre. All we saw of it was the court, which was large and shiny and had new breakaway rims. The building looked like an airplane hangar or a Quonset hut; inside, it had an impressive scoreboard and hot-water showers. We were so happy to be there, the game was nearly an afterthought.

Then our opponents arrived. They were large and fleshy, with healthy cheeks and good haircuts and shiny, baggy gold uniforms. They hotdogged through two-line layups as their girlfriends whistled from the stands.

We stomped them. Slava hit a bunch of threes, the French defenders writing him off as a non-threat. Jirka played big on the block, he and Martin controlling the boards like Slavic Bash Brothers. Tomas got his mid-range game going and I hit an assortment of drives and pull-ups. The rims were so soft that every shot caught on them.

Late in the game, I was the lone Czech back on a three-on-one break, a St. Pierre small forward bearing down the middle of the lane with men filling the lanes on either side. St. Pierre's resident wild man was on the right. On the left was their star, a long-haired off-guard who'd been hitting flat threes all game. 'The small forward looked to the wild man, the ball cuffed in his right hand. He was going behind his back. I jumped the lane and his pass hit me right in the hands. The crowd whistled in scorn at him as I headed the other way, their three-on-one now our four-on-two. Martin, Tomas, and Michal hovered around the St. Pierre basket. I considered which pass to throw. Maybe a crossover to the left and go behind the back to Martin? Maybe the Magic-Johnson-to-Byron-Scott around-the-waist scoop to Michal for the layup? Maybe a fake swipe like Maravich and tap the ball out to Tomas for a three?

The French defender stepped forward from his foul line and I bounced the ball off my foot, lost my balance, and crashed into both him and Michal, all of us going down like candlepins. The ball went to Tomas, who banked in a twelve-footer. We won by nine.

Afterward, the St. Pierre players were congratulatory and hospitable, encouraging us like we were refugees. They did not seem to mind the loss much, and appeared more than consoled by the fact that they remained French, and we did not. We sat with them in a dining hall off of the gymnasium complex and ate ravioli and bread and drank red wine. Most of the Czechs didn't say much, but Tomas spoke diplomatically to the organizers, in French, and we were soon invited to come back the next year.

After dinner, we went back to the gymnasium. The French players left and the organizers began to take cushioned pads off of the walls and lay them flat on the court. Slava and the rest of the guys went to get their sleeping bags; the women got on the bus and it drove away. We were sleeping on the court.

Michal lent me an extra blanket and I stacked two mats on top of each other at the St. Pierre foul line. We were high in the mountains and the night air was cold, but the gym was quiet and it wasn't a bus. I fell quickly, deeply asleep.

. . .

IN THE MORNING, we cleaned up in the locker rooms, mopping our armpits with paper towels and scavenging leftover pieces of bread from the cafeteria. Outside the gymnasium, the air was clean and cold and the sun slanted through the mist. Tendrils of rosemary and lavender stretched out just off the roadside. The bus returned with the women's team and we loaded up our gear. I tore into the bread I'd bought in Grenoble, sipped from my bottle of *Dobra Voda*, and watched my teammates stretch and pass basketballs around and wipe the sleep from their faces. We were the circus, a curious, self-contained organism that rolled into places we didn't know and didn't understand to do a show, and then rolled away.

We headed to a town called Saint-Jean-de-Maurienne for the Twenty-fifth Maurienne *Tournai Internationale*. Maurienne was even higher in the mountains than St. Pierre, a town where the French seemed to be breeding basketball players. It had a central athletic complex that seemed to sport multiple full basketball courts. The walls of the local café were covered with photos of past teams, and the trophy case at the gym was full of shiny hardware. The main court, inside another airplane hangar, was impossibly lavish: two scoreboards, around-the-court seating, labyrinthine locker rooms, polished wooden floors, and Plexiglas backboards with breakaway rims. It looked like a high-end college complex, like the practice courts at Boston College.

EXPATRIATE GAMES

It was Saturday, and our "more experienced" team hadn't drawn a game until Sunday. We watched the youth team lose by two to a fantastic local French squad that would have killed Vinohrady. The French kids threw down dunks and stuck long three-pointers. Kris played like a star, hitting drives and jump shots and living at the line. He finished with twenty-nine. Jena got one of his sweeping layups swatted out of bounds—"*Tobe do oci*!"—by a whip-quick Maurienne guard who could sky. The Maurienne team looked well coached and well conditioned; they played with poise and pizzazz. Like the Radotin Under 17 squad, the Maurienne team looked as good (if not as tall) as any high school team I'd seen at home, and better than most. But maybe I just hadn't seen enough high school teams at home. Maybe if I had, I would have switched to golf.

After the youth team game, we went to a small café in town for dinner. The only other people in the restaurant were players from an Italian team. The room was quiet as we waited for the food— pasta and red sauce that just appeared; nobody ever dropped a bill. The Italians talked amongst themselves, glancing at our table. We did the same back. I'd taken Italian in college, but it was worse than my Czech. *Ecco l'uomo*, I could say. "Here comes the man." And *uscita spesso*—"Do you use it often?"—which I'd once made the mistake of saying as my friend Mike's Italian aunt showed us the bidet in her bathroom.

Although the food didn't look particularly exceptional, it just tasted *better* in a way I couldn't figure out. We were exhausted, and on an adventure, and the pasta seemed to be perfect pasta, and the sauce more potent and pungent than any other sauce, ever. The waitress poured red table wine—probably nothing special . . . it just tasted that way—and the Italians, who were passing around a bottle of something they'd brought with them, began singing, tentatively at first, and then with increasing unity and volume.

Slava was looking at Michal. I couldn't tell what the Italians were saying, but when their song ended, they seemed to pause and wait for us, looking over without quite looking. I was watching them, wondering what they'd sung about. It hadn't been *l'uomo*.

Suddenly, I heard a low Czech voice rising from our table. It was Slava, and he'd started to sing. Within seconds, the rest of the table picked up the song. The volume rose to the level of the Italians, and then even higher. I listened to the words and tried to pick up the chorus.

The Italians seemed intrigued. They began smiling. Our song ended with a loud "Ho!" and they immediately launched into another song, louder and more profane-sounding.

I leaned over to the quietest of them and asked him what the song was about.

He shrugged and made universally understood hand gestures. "Is sex," he said.

When the Italians were finished, Slava led the Czechs in a retort that seemed to be about beer. After that, the songs shifted to national anthems, folk tunes, and World War II medleys.

Our French hosts brought the food and said little.

Finally, the Italians launched into a cover of a popular disco hit that advised, "You gotta lick it before we kick it." It seemed like surrender. Vinohrady turned its attention back to the pasta. When the food was gone, the Italians invited us to a nightclub in Albertville.

"*Discotheque Actuelle!*" they shouted, clapping us on the back.

"*Discotheque Actuelle!*" we shouted back, but we were going nowhere.

The bus drove us to what seemed like a local middle school, a large brick building with rooms full of cots. We grabbed our bags and claimed beds. The women's team, long absent, reappeared and settled into a room nearby. The bathrooms were next to one another, and the younger players tried to time their trips with the more attractive of the women's small forwards. Sixteen cots lined the walls in our room, and they felt like featherbeds. Disembodied Czech voices floated through the dark, along with laughter and farts and then snoring.

Sunday came and we were finally going to get onto the court. Our first match was at 10:00 A.M. I woke up at 7:00 and stretched in the cold Alpine air, dug bread out of my backpack, and changed into my Vinohrady uniform.

We played on an outdoor court against a lesser French team. It was raining lightly and the court was slick. Tomas conveyed the rules: Games were played in two twelve-minute halves and each player got three fouls before they were out. Behind our court, snow-covered mountains rose into cloudbanks. Under a tent near the main gym, volunteers grilled sausage and onions, the scent heavy and mesmerizing.

Slava and I started together, with Honsa and Tomas coming off the bench. The team we played wore purple uniforms and played haughtily, which was to become a motif. I picked up two quick fouls and didn't even know what language to complain in. Martin and Jirka did their twin-towers number down low, Slava wobbled up and down the wet court, and I got a couple of jumpers and a breakaway to go. The game was over before it started, and we won by eight.

We lost our next two games, including one in which we were down two with ten seconds left and I went for the win with a long three that rimmed out and left Michal open under the hoop. The rain had steadied and then stopped just as our third game ended. Across the three-court parking lot the Italian team was brawling with our French hosts. *Discotheque Actuelle!*

Everyone was picking up fouls, the referees apparently wanting to limit the number of international incidents. Of the first three games, I fouled out of two. In one of them, we wound up playing three on two because everyone else had fouled out. We retired to watch the women's team whip everyone, running crisp offensive sets and knocking down threes and foul shots. Kris and the youth team were losing in the main gym. It looked like we'd get one more game after lunch.

Jirka, who spoke strong English that he'd kept to himself until Grenoble, announced, "I don't wanna play! I'm tired." Slava was back in his sweatsuit, reclining with a carton of milk at the back of the bus. The rest of us slipped off to explore Maurienne.

We found train tracks. A bullet train flew by, long and massive and fast and unlike anything in Prague. The Czechs whistled at it. I decided to take the bullet train back to Prague when it was time to leave. Jena and Tomas led us back to the café and a lunch of chicken and *pommes frites* appeared. We wolfed it down and I broke out some middle-school French on the owner.

"*Avez-vous un peu de pain, Monsieur?*"

He was a robust mountain-type man, with a thick mustache and a wide waist. "*Pain?*" he asked.

"*Oui*," I said, nodding, rubbing my stomach. "*Pain.*"

He picked up a cardboard box on the floor. It was lined with plastic and full of the heels of baguettes. My God, I thought, in France they throw their bread away. I grabbed a handful. The bread was cushiony and, like the coffee in Grenoble, just seemed better than it should be. It seemed to have regenerative powers. The texture was springy and durable. I chewed it slowly, savoring.

"*Pain*," I said to Tomas. "*Vyborni.*"

He was unimpressed.

. . .

WE EXPECTED TO have only one more game after lunch, against a young team of Maurienne B-siders. They were led by a stocky guard who drove brazenly, foolishly, into Martin and Jirka, waiting down low to close his lanes. I picked up two quick fouls and sat most of the first half, in danger of fouling out of my last game as a Bohemian. We led by five at the half, behind Slava's deceptive scoring.

I went back in to start the second half, for what I think everyone assumed would be thirty seconds of ineffectiveness, and began penetrating and dishing off. The young French players were primed to block shots—a bad habit imported from the States, no doubt—and they left their feet at the slightest shrug. Slava had been hitting long threes, and the French team had extended its man-to-man. I took the ball past my man, to the foul line, and dropped passes down to Michal and Martin. We swallowed them up with a zone, and they began to fade. Their guard got a three to fall at the buzzer, but we won by ten.

The win set up what could have been a showdown with our own youth squad, but they lost at the buzzer to an Austrian team after Kris fouled out with a minute to play. The margin would have been bigger, but a lanky fourteen-year-old Czech with hands like spatulas stepped up in Kris's absence to do an incredible Sean Kemp imitation. As we waited for their game to end, Jirka and I tried to dunk things. Jirka got a tennis ball to go down. I was feeling the power of the bread, and John-Starks-dunked a soda can.

The court had dried and we went zone against the Austrians, courtesy of Kris's scouting report. The Austrians had no scorers, but they had some slithery small forwards, and they matched up well with Martin and Jirka. I got a three to fall; Slava hit two of his own. Michal made his moves, and the women's team came over to the sidelines to watch. Martin and Honsa fouled out, and then Michal joined them. The Austrians lost a forward and an off-guard, and we came into the final minute playing four-on-four. With six seconds left, they tied up the game.

Slava inbounded to me at their three-point line. I drove past one of their guards, toward another. Jirka came free down low. The clock was ticking down. I needed to get a shot off. What had Dejda said about Mikulov? *We don't have time to waste!*

Ah, but I'd fallen for that too many times already. I pulled up at the foul line, but pumped and hooked a pass around the Austrian defender to Jirka, low on the blocks. He took the pass and reversed a layup at the buzzer for the win.

· · ·

IT WAS FIVE o'clock in the afternoon. We were leaving as soon as we lost. The ride home, if it took us as long as the ride to France, seemed like it would get us into Prague sometime in August. Slava talked to an official and announced that there was one game left. It was against the Maurienne squad that had beaten our youth team the day before, led by the fantastic guard who'd blocked Jena's layup so resoundingly. They had apparently lost to the Italians, who were playing in the finals inside the main gym.

The Maurienne squad sauntered to the court, resplendent in gold shorts and matching wristbands. They warmed up contemptuously and eyed us with disdain. Their star didn't start; he seemed to be roaming the tournament, playing with any French squad that needed him. We got some baseline stuff to fall, and they couldn't hit their contemptuous finger-rolls, too intent on slapping the backboard after releasing the ball. I got a semi-break but ran into trouble, and a Maurienne guard with almond eyes and razored sideburns tied me up. He muttered in French. I muttered in Czech. He won the jump, and Not-Our-Honsa subbed in for me.

Maurienne couldn't score, and the mystery of it seemed to be annoying them. The star guard came in and played less than four minutes; he reached on Slava, then charged, then drew a tech arguing. Just like that, he was gone, relegated to the sidelines where he quickly wandered off to sign autographs and sneer.

Not-Our-Honsa got a steal and led a two-on-one. At five-foot-ten, he weighed around 220. The contemptuous Maurienne defender couldn't believe that Honsa would dare keep the ball and go to the hole—which is just what he did, rattling the backboard with a layup that hit like a bullet train. We howled on the sidelines and Honsa flashed a wide smile. He fouled out on the next possession.

I replaced him and hit a quick three. The half ended and we were up, 26–12, staying quiet, just like we had against Kosire. The Maurienne girlfriends were watching the game, festooning us with Gallic abuse. It must have been a bitter pill, watching their elegant boyfriends, with their well-groomed goatees and sideburns and curling lips, getting walloped by Team Budvar, unkempt and uncouth.

The second half started and Slava led a break. Slava couldn't get to sixty, but he went from zero to forty fast. I was on the right, and he hit me with a pass. I was just about to go up when a voice in my head whispered, "Pump."

Pumping was for chumps. Real ballers went up. Shit, I just John-Starks-dunked a crushed-up soda can. I wasn't going to start listening to that voice now. "Pump," it said again, firmly. We were in unfamiliar territory. I decided to listen.

I pumped and two Maurienne defenders flew past me, one on either side and each about cloud-level. They could jump. Maybe the air was thinner? Whatever it was, the ensuing lane was clear and I laid the ball in. Not-Our-Honsa roared from the sidelines like a sea lion.

We stalled; I got hit hard in the nose by the Maurienne small forward and fouled out a minute later. It didn't matter. Slava and

Michal guided us to an easy win. The contemptuous Maurienne squad stormed off without handshakes.

. . .

AFTER THREE NIGHTS on the bus, six bottles of rum, seven games without our full squad, and too many *Staropramen* to count, Vinohrady left Maurienne with a third-place trophy. The women's squad finished third as well; their trophy was inappropriately smaller. The Italians got themselves ejected from the finals by picking up three technicals in the last twenty seconds. The contemptuous French spectators whistled and howled at them as they hoisted their coach on their shoulders and sang on the way to the showers. The Italians didn't give a shit. They seemed immune to the French contempt.

We headed to the bus, and back to the highway.

The ride home passed relatively quickly (although it still took eighteen hours), the drivers homing in on Prague. I spent most of it decoding Slava's cryptic pronouncements on the state of America ("Boston Bruins," he said, somewhere near Munich, "full of . . . ham") and dreaming about canoes. I talked to Tomas about women.

"They are not like us," he said, shaking his head and sounding like Fitzgerald talking about the very rich. I tried to explain how I felt about the end of the road—for Dejda, for the season, for everything I could see.

"Why does it have to end?" Tomas asked, referring to Dejda. "Do you love her enough to marry her?"

Jeez. That kind of thing hadn't really entered into my calculations. It was crazy talk.

Would it ever, though? And where? And with whom?

For about a year in college, and sometimes in Prague, I'd carried around a paperback copy of Nick Hornby's book *Fever Pitch*. It was a small book about Hornby's lifelong obsession with Arsenal, the English soccer club, and how the obsession subjected him to all sorts of torment and heartbreak. "This terrible tyranny of place," he said, talking (I thought) about how people, when they're desperate for something to grab onto, get stuck forever with what's local to them. I'd thought I'd resisted the terrible tyranny of place by never grabbing onto something and staying portable, but of course I had it entirely backward. That was probably true for everyone.

At the German border our bus joined a line of cars waiting to pass through the checkpoint. Kris and a couple other members of the youth team got off the bus and ran into the woods on the side of the road. We passed our passports up to the front and the German border guards stepped into the well of the bus. They had firearms. A few minutes later, we were through the checkpoint and rolling into the Czech Republic. After about 100 yards, Slava shouted something to the driver. The bus pulled over to the side of the road and Kris and the others ran out of the woods on the Czech side and got back on.

As we rolled toward Prague, Slava announced that there would be one last "team night" on June 8, when the season would officially conclude. I arranged to call Tomas to set up a dinner within the week. We pulled into the Andel metro station at 5:00 P.M. on Monday. I got back to Biskupcova at 6:00 P.M. and took a long, hot shower. Dejda's ride dropped her off outside at 6:30. It was June 5. She boarded a plane in two weeks, the same two weeks during which I has a thesis to finish. I carried her bags to my door; she climbed onto the bed and pulled off her shirt.

Back at home, Shaq and the Magic were set to meet Hakeem the Dream, Glide, and the rest of the Rockets in the NBA Finals. The games would be shown live, at around 3:00 A.M., at the Sport Bar Praha.

Ruzyně

THOSE TWO WEEKS passed quickly. As if in response to my internal narrative, Prague was in its full start-of-summer splendor. Tourists choked the streets and the sun stayed long in the sky. Monday, June 19, started with a 4:00 A.M. alarm for an 8:00 A.M. flight out of Praha Ruzyně, taking Dejda back across the Atlantic, to San Francisco Airport and the golden waiting hills of Palo Alto. On Saturday we'd gotten beer and a pizza at the Derby and decided to price transcontinental flights in the fall, even though we knew we wouldn't. It felt good to say, and to believe a little. Dejda had begun to cry at her grandmother's flat on Sunday, saying good-bye to the old woman who'd knitted the holes in our sweaters and fed us dumplings until we could roll home. She wept on my sleeve and into my collar on the tram ride back to her aunt's apartment in the *panelacs*, her body shaking quietly.

"It's hard for me sometimes," she said, "finding people to hang out with."

I gave myself something to do and packed her stuff. I packed T-shirts I'd lent her and bras I'd never seen. Dejda's eyelids were puffy and red and her golden hair was matted down on her forehead. Every few minutes, her wide shark teeth would pop through in a smile, always followed immediately by a cascade of tears. She said she wasn't ready to leave, but I think she was.

I looked out the window of Dejda's aunt's apartment, high up on the *panelac*. From there I could see all the way to downtown Prague. A flat beam of sunlight shone down on the city, through the clouds, and I thought *I cannot wait to get out of here*. There was just no good way to stay. It was a wonderful and terrible thing to feel.

"Do you love her enough to marry her?" Tomas had asked.

I loved her enough to maybe think about marrying her in maybe three or four years. Did that count? I loved her enough to hate it when she left.

We lay awake as long as we could, but morning came anyway and Dejda's aunt's Skoda came with it, and the road to Ruzyně was gray and flat and open. Dejda's aunt had some question about whether I'd come to the airport, but of course I was coming. The suitcases weighed a ton. I decided to sneak into the terminal with Dejda, which turned out to be even easier than sneaking into the Czech Republic from Germany; it required only a look of harried impatience. Dejda's aunt kissed her cheeks and left. We sat on a bench and waited.

What was there to do? Dejda was crying. My shoulders were getting damp. People passed us and looked away. I remembered the girl at Logan, with cheeks like snowdrifts, on her way to Spain. It had been so long, I thought.

Dejda rested her head on my shoulders. We talked about our first real date, at Jama, when we'd told lies to drunken tourists about being newlyweds.

And then, on a bright, clear morning, she got up and left.

Milan Kundera, in his essay "Sixty-Three Words," described the Czech word *litost* as "a peculiarly Central European emotion of regret and unfulfilled longing," the human product of centuries of exclusion from the beloved West. *Litost*, that Central European indulgence, was not what I felt when Dejda walked away and flew halfway around the world, but it jumped into my head anyway. I wasn't sure what I felt, but I spent a few long minutes sitting on the bench, thinking about it—sad, for sure, but also weightless and empty and wide open.

Ice Cube was cued up on my Walkman for what I'd assumed would be a tragic bus ride back to town. I pressed PLAY.

No barking from the dog, no smog, and Momma cooked a breakfast with no hog.

Damn right, Cube.

I went outside, climbed onto some restricted observation terrace, and waved at all the wrong planes, and then a big British Airways flight took off down a distant runway and I barely saw it go.

The Magic got blown out in four games by Hakeem and the Rockets, who repeated as champs. Shaq hadn't developed yet to where he could guard the Dream, and big Penny couldn't do it alone. In Skvorecky's *The Swell Season,* young Danny Smiricky chases jazz, women, and freedom through a long summer in a small town outside of Prague as the clouds of World War II gathered around him. The girls were eternally just beyond his grasp, freedom eluded him for a half-century, but the jazz he captured and savored, and while it didn't replace the other two, it made their absence bearable. The last story in the collection, "Sad Autumn Blues," ended with Danny belting out a mournful sax solo as his girls danced with their boyfriends and the Nazis shot his bandmate's father.

My swell season ended with the Magic fading in the Finals, the girl flying back to her old life, and the Vinohrady Bohemians scattering in the summer heat to Prague's dank *hospodas* and hillside campgrounds. At CEU, all the students got their theses in on time, including me. Fifteen thousand words on Czech Large-Scale Utility Privatization. My friend Joel, the privatization specialist, took one look at it and said, "I hope you'll keep studying so that eventually you'll understand how naïve this paper is." Or maybe he didn't say that, at least not out loud. A Bosnian woman named Una took the top academic honors; rumor had it that she had fallen in love with one of our lecturers and would be joining him in The Hague in August. Dagmar, the sweet, hulking Pole, handed something in, but nobody was sure if he'd qualified for a degree. Graduation ceremonies took place on a stage hidden away at the far end of the Hotel Olšanka, and the school threw a postgraduation dinner party on a boat that floated down the Vltava. Space was limited, and they conducted a lottery to determine which guests could come aboard and which ones had to stay ashore.

The promised Vinohrady team night never materialized, and the season ended, unofficially and without fanfare. We hadn't won much, and hadn't managed to stay in our division. When I last saw Slava, he was heading for the trams at Andel, the Maurienne third-place trophy in one hand and his round of Brie in the other. Michal, our slithery scorer, had gotten into the passenger side of a BMW and driven away. Big Bob was heading to Spain for a week. Vykli was still studying, and would be forever. I saw Tomas a couple of times for dinner or drinks; he'd managed to sort things out with his ex-girlfriend Martina despite her vow never to see him again. Cameron was weighing Hungary against business school in New Haven. Lindsey decided to take their dog and head back to the Pacific Northwest. Maybe they were exempt from the terrible tyranny of place. Fast Dave vanished with Femka into the dust of the highway, hitching his way toward the vineyards of Greece. I gave him my hiking boots, Mikulov chalk still stuck in the treads. Most of the CEU students had sorted out employment with another Soros-funded institute, the Open Media Research Foundation. They would be staying in Prague as long as they could. Yevgeni, the crazy boy from Siberia, got into Columbia.

The law school I'd gotten into began classes at the end of August. I tried to find an earlier flight home, but there was no way, on

Sabena, to get around a bottleneck in Brussels. I'd chosen July 14 over July 3, and now couldn't get the July 3 flight back. At home, my dad had gotten the Miata out of its winter storage; my sister wanted someone to watch MTV with.

I wandered through downtown Prague, over its golden cobblestones and thick bridges, through symbiotic crowds of tourists and Czechs and Gypsies. I saw a crazy old *babicka* hiding behind a stone pillar, peeking around it, looking for some ghost, some imaginary pursuer. I snuck around to be in front of her, put the telephoto lens on my camera, and tried to take her picture. She saw me and shrieked and scuttled off down the sidewalk, and then I was her ghost. I sat on stoops, admired the stream of halter tops cascading along the squares and boulevards, the braids above them and breasts beneath. *Holka*, Tomas would say. Played some pickup hoop on dusty outdoor courts with chumps and Israelis. I grew a beard.

I was flying on a Monday. On Saturday, I lay on a flat single bed in Cameron's spare room, where I'd been living since the end of June. Cameron's landlords were hosting two beautiful French architectural students upstairs and the house was full of noises. It was hot out and the doors and windows were open. I'd been living out of a bag for two weeks and was a little woozy. I closed my eyes and asked God for some sort of sign that I'd figure out the next phase of my life, that the questions I still had weren't stupid ones, and that they had answers.

For a moment, nothing happened, and then someone grabbed my outstretched hand. I opened my eyes.

"Damn, man!" Skee said, sitting down on the edge of the cot. I hadn't seen him in eight months. "What's your definition of 'perseverance'?"

On Sunday night, the expats gathered on the sloping Mala Strana side of Charles Bridge, at a small hangout called Jo's Bar that sometimes got less of a crowd than the clubs of the Old Town or Václavské Náměstí. Skee had a flock of Czech girls in tow, and we sat on the sidewalk patio drinking small beers and *Becherovka* and eating nachos with green beans. Fast Dave was already gone, but Cameron and Lindsey and Shannon and the two French architectural students were there, and my classmates Melissa and Jay stopped by with Beata, the jaw-dropping Pole. Shannon laughed at Cameron's new mustache. Skee told us about a plan he'd had to sell Soviet night-vision goggles to his uncles back in Texas, about how he'd been wearing them around his darkened flat in the *panelacs*, and about how the plan had hit a snag when he learned that the goggles gave off radiation. The evening sun shone off of doorway coats-of-arms, and the shadows of castle spires reached toward us like fingers.

An old man limped down the sidewalk toward our outdoor table. He gestured to us and moved our plate of nachos aside before turning a small cloth bag upside down onto our table. Small parcels fluttered out of it, like dying birds. We looked through them. They were bills, money, old currencies from vanished places—extinct republics, overthrown governments, severed unions.

Back at Cameron's basement apartment, my own bags were already packed. My treasures were tucked away—a thimble of *Becherovka*, Dejda's heart pendant, my uniform, my diploma. Amber from Krakow and garnet earrings for my sister. Despite them, I didn't feel like I was leaving with much more than I'd had when I arrived. I didn't have a job or a career and hadn't developed any real skills; I'd lost the girl; I'd been something of an inconsistent contributor on a team that had lost most of its games; and my teammates had vanished without formal goodbyes. All of the friends I'd made and classmates I'd met were dispersing. None of us would ever really be back. A year calling myself a semipro basketball player, and I never even got paid.

But … Košíře and Chvalkovicka, and the long road to Maurienne. Slapy and the chalky hills of Mikulov. I thought about Skee and Krakow's wide Sukiennice, and the winter shadows on Auschwitz. The lefty finger-roll against Meteor. The bullet holes in the church walls on Resslova where the Nazis cornered the doomed paratroopers of the Czech resistance. Great Slava and Honsa and graceful Tomas and Vykli, whose objections had just been a call for order, a call for team cohesion. The villains: Eight and Mullet and Bug-Eye and the Goat. Big Bob dunking in his green Reeboks and Kratcha taking the ball to the hole. The invisible Gypsies and Otto Pick, talking to the microphones in the walls. The spot on Václavské Náměstí where you could look down the long square and imagine it full of people rattling keys, as they had done five years earlier. Vaclav Havel and the other members of Charta 77 moving through hidden passageways among the buildings; the small memorial near the statue of Prince Wenceslas, overlooked by most tourists, where mad, brokenhearted Palach lit himself on fire. St. John Nepomuk, taking his confessions over the side of the bridge, and Jan Masaryk, taking his country's future over the window ledge. Lovely Dejda, who'd been as much an enigma as a girlfriend, who seemed to embody so many of the things I both did and didn't want. And Vinohrady, the hidden neighborhood behind the Museum, where St. Ludmila kept watch, lit up against the sky, looking out for Bohemians and converts.

What could we reasonably ask of the things we loved? That they take us somewhere—in my case, somewhere beyond the asphalt courts of my hometown's community center where the tourists and the sixth graders played. And it had, finally and not easily. It had taken me as far as I'd ever been. I could live with the terrible tyranny of basketball. And there was something to be said for risk taking and soft kisses and contusions and adventure. They made you grow. They made the world both real and imaginary at the same time. In 1981, at a postchampionship rally in Boston's Government Center, Larry Bird saw a fan holding up a sign that said MOSES MALONE EATS SHIT and responded, from the podium, "Moses Malone *does* eat shit." In one game during Chris Jackson's sophomore season at LSU, just after he'd drilled a three for points thirty through thirty-two, commentator Dick Enberg asked Clark Kellogg, "But will he be able to do it at the next level?" and Kellogg just laughed and laughed.

Skee began to talk about Latvia. Lindsey sat next to Cameron, leaning back into him and gazing off into the golden evening. *Finish with a kick*, my dad had said before he left. Shannon and I looked through the old man's old money, mapping out a history of resilient Central Europe in faded bills: high-denomination Polish *zloty*, thin tan rubles, a blue-green thousand-crown note issued by the Austro-Hungarian Bank in 1902. One stack of bills, rubber-banded together, came from the treasury of *Bohmen und Mahren*, the Nazis' World War II name for the Czech Republic, the dream-like, patient protectorate that had plotted for centuries against the terrible tyranny of its occupiers, sustaining itself through the plotting, the effort, the next death and rebirth. The notes were wide and threadbare and as purple as a bruise.

Jordan, John Paxson, and World B. Free shared at least one thing in common: No matter how many shots they put up, they were only ever thinking about the next one. One of the French architecture students brushed my arm and said, "The problem with Prague is that it is just *too* romantic." What a wonderful world it was that let you go so far and feel so much, and didn't make you learn a thing.

I gave the old man my last fifty-crown note, slipped a few of his old bills free from their rubber band, and tucked them into my passport for the trip home.

VŠECHNO

Epilogue

I **NEVER SAW MANY** of the Vinohrady Bohemians again. Among the last things I heard were the following, circa 2006:

For a while, Slava became a "businessman," among other things running an office maintenance service. He may now be a schoolteacher.

Honsa stayed in coaching, and became the head coach of the best women's basketball team in the Czech Republic.

Vykli became a lawyer and a *Superliga* referee.

Tomas is a regional manager for Xerox. He is married and has two boys.

Big Bob went back to school.

Mondy became a schoolteacher. He, Poli, and Kratcha still play with Vinohrady.

Cameron and Lindsey are married with two boys and live in Seattle, where Cameron is an investment banker. He was never in the CIA, as far as I know.

Shannon and Joel got married and now live with their children in India, where Joel works for the World Bank.

EPILOGUE

Fast Dave lives in Phoenix, where he coaches track and field. He is married and has a son named Charlie.

Skee, at last account, was working for a company that sold rare coins and trying to sell a movie script about Sasquatch.

Jack Levy still lives in Prague with his wife and sons, and still doesn't speak Czech.

I never saw Dejda again.

The unstoppable Jan Wiener was the subject of a documentary called *Fighter*. He still lives in Lenox, Massachusetts.

My college roommate married his girlfriend, teaches history, and coaches soccer at a high school in Maryland, has three beautiful daughters, and is, as far as I can tell, as happy as a clam.

Acknowledgments

I AM GRATEFUL FOR the support and generosity of each of the following people: Lauren Abramo and Jane Dystel of Dystel & Goderich Literary Management, Mark Weinstein and Erin Kelley of Skyhorse Publishing. Tomas, Daniela, Matyas, and Krystof Krysl. Honsa, Slava, Vykli, Peli, Poli, Mondy, Kratcha, Big Bob, Radek, and all of the members of the 1994–95 Sokol Vinohrady Men's Basketball Club, who were each incredibly kind and generous to a clueless foreigner. Cameron and Lindsey Hewes, Jack Levy and family, Shannon and Joel Turkewitz, David Allison, Barry T. Graf, Deven and Melinda Clemens, Diane Chandler.

Thank you to Pia Z. Ehrhardt, Jim Ruland and Nuvia Guerra, Roy Kesey, John Leary, Ellen Parker, Susan Henderson, Jordan Rosenfeld and the members of the Zoetrope online writing community. Thank you to Todd Zuniga, who published an excerpt of this memoir in the second print issue of his literary magazine, *Opium*.

I am also grateful to David Berry and Alison Hood, Zara and Jamie Berry, Adam Levine, Seth Keller, Aaron Korsh, Tom O'Keefe, Jayme Casey, Katie Keator, Alexander Wolff, and Darcy Frey.

ACKNOWLEDGMENTS

Thanks to George Soros, Jay Lewis, Melissa Bennett, and the staff and students of the Central European University, which has developed into a world-class institution and continues to operate in Budapest and elsewhere.

For early representation and encouragement, thank you to Clyde Taylor and Kate McKean.

Finally, thank you to my parents, Maryjane and Jerry Fromm, to whom this book was originally dedicated, to Katie, Rick, Trey, and Kai Shinholster and, most especially, to my wife, Jenny, and son, Leo.

About the Author

DAVE FROMM RECEIVED an MA in international relations from
Central European University in 1995 and a JD from the
Georgetown University Law Center in 1998. He grew up in western Massachusetts, and was a two-year starter at point guard for the
Lenox Memorial High School Millionaires. He lives with his wife
and son in Los Angeles, California, where he works as an attorney,
and believes that he once scored forty-three points in an officiated
college intramural game, although it was in England and against predominantly English opponents. *Expatriate Games* is his first book.